THE PASTORAL EPISTLES

THE PASTORAL EPISTLES

THE GREEK TEXT
WITH INTRODUCTION AND
COMMENTARY

BY

E. K. SIMPSON, M.A.
Trinity College, Oxford

WM. B. EERDMANS PUBLISHING COMPANY
GRAND RAPIDS, MICHIGAN

First Edition September 1954

Printed in Great Britain at the University Press, Cambridge
(Brooke Crutchley, University Printer)

CONTENTS

v

PREFACE

THERE is extant a drawing by Michelangelo representing a wrinkled greybeard who displays as his chosen device the motto *ancora imparo*, 'I am still a learner'. No more appropriate watchword could be adopted by the most indefatigable student of ancient Greek; for its prolonged history and dialectical ramifications present an inexhaustible field of research. New Testament Greek itself, though conformable in general to its Hellenistic model, exhibits sufficient distinctive features of its own to attest its Hebrew parentage, and sufficient approximations to popular usage to receive illustration from the dust-heaps of Egyptian papyri.

The diction of the apostle Paul displays a wide range of literary acquisition, derived from a variety of sources by an intellect pre-eminently flexible and assimilative. He can wield all the stock resources of ancient rhetoric, when called for; yet he manifestly cares nothing for mere embellishments as such. His earlier Epistles, monumental as they are in build and weight, have their familiar unbendings; and the looser texture of the Pastoral Epistles, which is made a ground of suspicion regarding their authorship by negative critics, accords well with outpourings of heart to two trusty lieutenants, largely occupied with practical instructions for the institution of a gospel ministry. Undue stress has been laid upon divergences from previous usages discernible in their vocabulary; but the fresh subject-matter accounts for the greater part of them. Nor must we forget that Paul was a chosen vessel in God's hands. In Bishop Moule's words, the Lord 'can take a human personality...and throw it freely upon its task of thinking and expression—and behold, the product will be His'.[1]

Another factor deserves notice. The Pastorals form a group by themselves, obviously detached from their predecessors by an interval measured in years. Now, first-class verbal critics like Cicero[2] and Quintilian[3] affirm that a subdued style befits an elderly speaker or writer; and Cicero observes elsewhere[4] of his own later style that it

[1] H. C. G. Moule, *The Epistle of St Paul to the Romans* (Expositor's Bible), p. 8.
[2] *De Senectute*, ix.
[3] *Inst. (Orat.)*, xi, 1.
[4] *Brutus* ii, 8.

vii

showed signs of ageing (*coepit canescere*). The plainness of manner disparaged is in fact a token of their genuineness, in view of the writer's time of life. Superhuman labours such as Paul had gone through in any case entail a measure of lassitude as their sequel.

Our knowledge of the final stadia of his marvellous career depends chiefly on the testimony borne by these Letters to the period of recovered liberty granted him, subsequent to that appeal to Caesar which brought him at length to Rome. We know that he cherished the hope of visiting Spain;[1] and Clement of Rome's testimony[2] presumes its notorious accomplishment. Moreover, without some such epilogue to the apostle's history, his life is reduced to an inexplicable torso; whereas by accepting the hypothesis of a second Roman imprisonment culminating in martyrdom, we scrutinize a coherent record of a life-work fraught with world-wide issues.

I am greatly indebted to Mr F. F. Bruce for assistance in correcting the proofs and for furnishing the bibliography.   E. K. S.

[1] Rom. xv. 24, 28.
[2] Clement's *Epistle to the Corinthians*, i. 5; see p. 4 below. That Clement's expression τὸ τέρμα τῆς δύσεως refers to Spain can scarcely be doubted. Compare Dionysius of Halicarnassus, who specifies τὰ μέχρι δυσμῶν ἡλίου πάντα in connection with Iberia (*History*, i, 34), while Livy repeatedly dubs the Peninsula *ultimae terrarum orae*.

INTRODUCTION

I. THE AUTHOR

THE spell cast by Saul of Tarsus over minds of any moral earnestness admits of no question. Unlike his namesake, the first king of Israel, he was shortish of stature. Chrysostom styles him ὁ τρίπηχυς ἄνθρωπος, and Augustine, playing on his Roman cognomen, *paullum modicum quid*; but the extent of the shadow he has spread over posterity bears witness to the bulk of his spiritual build. Indeed, his most ardent admirers do not pay him more signal homage in this respect than those detractors from his just fame who ascribe to his influence an age-long perversion of primitive Christianity so entire as to set him at cross-purposes with his Master. Such a man's career throbs with interest to all serious thinkers.

That career, as we all know, bisects itself into two wholly discrepant halves. To explain how the hunting leopard of Pharisaism came to be transformed into one of the Good Shepherd's most docile lambs has always baffled sceptical ingenuity. The change of front is so utter, and pregnant with such far-reaching issues, that it positively demands the supernatural cause which he himself assigns for it to render the phenomenon intelligible.

But our theme restricts us to those closing days of this marvellous biography about which, strange to say, we know less than about the rest. Whatever be the verdict we pass on the Pastoral Epistles, it cannot be denied that they form a group by themselves, detached from the residue of Paul's writings and attached to one another by links of their own. Some of the older commentators, in common with Wieseler, a German theologian of the last century, have sought to isolate Titus and the first Epistle to Timothy from its twin brother, and affix on them a date prior to what are known as the 'Prison Epistles'. They seem to have thought that on any other supposition the apparent references to a revisit of Paul to Ephesus clashed with his declaration in Acts xx to the elders at Miletus that they should 'see his face no more'. But there are two or three ways of parrying this over-hasty conclusion. The expression *I know* which he there uses does not seem to imply prophetic foresight, inasmuch as Paul employs the selfsame phrase in Philippians (i. 25) in regard to the presentiment he had that he would regain his liberty. And in view of the unusual order of the words ὑμεῖς πάντες in Acts xx. 25, placed last in the sentence, it would be possible to argue that the apostle is preparing them for the long duration of his absence by the statement, '*ye shall see my face no more*, that is to say, *all of you* will not, because of the manifold changes that will inevitably intervene'. Nor is it quite certain that I Timothy predicates a later sojourn in Ephesus; for the two passages (i. 3, iii. 14) concerned can be otherwise explained. Miletus is the only spot thereabouts where we are sure that he had again set foot (II Tim. iv. 20).

It is the common diction and outlook of these Epistles that militate fatally against any hypothesis that parts them asunder. They cleave together inextricably. Nor can any dexterity fit their contents into the framework of the narrative in Acts. The Church catholic has ranked them among her sacred writings, thus ratifying their apostolical origin; and that act involves a tacit persuasion that the Gentile apostle enjoyed a period of missionary activity posterior to the date at which Luke's narrative closes. *His* trustworthiness has been abundantly vindicated in recent years, and it is the loss of his invaluable aid in tracing the story of the early Church that leaves the final stage of Paul's labours under a veil of obscurity. Are the Pastoral Epistles not meant to fill the gap? Do they not yield us first-hand evidence on the point? Does he not himself here enter the witness-box to supplement the else unfinished tale? We think he does.

We grant, however, that the negative school of critics can make out a considerably more plausible case for their assault on these Letters than when they impugn the genuineness, for example, of the Fourth Gospel. For the vocabulary varies a good deal from the earlier Pauline models, and the style, notably in I Timothy, is of a looser texture. Not that we meet with anything incompatible with Paul's authorship. All we are conscious of is less intensity of current and volume of flow, and a more circumscribed orbit of expatiation than before. In short, these documents exhibit a less majestic and commanding phase of the apostle's genius than that which storms our hearts in his sublimer and more towering flights.

But that is not the whole of the story. To correct our first impression, we need only note the unabated fervour they occasionally breathe, and the positive evidence forthcoming on their behalf. For they are not newly discovered papyri, without historical pedigree. Before a structure is condemned as unsound, the edifice ought to be inspected both without and within. Let us then first of all test the Pastoral fabric externally. We find it buttressed by a body of patristic testimony more substantial than we could have anticipated.[1]

II. EXTERNAL EVIDENCE

1. The second-century witness to *the presence and familiarity* of the Pastorals possesses a cumulative force, even if one or two of its items should be called in question. We encounter an apparent acquaintance with them, before the close of the first century, in Clement of Rome; for he employs the striking phrase 'King of the Ages', and an expression, 'ready unto every good work', which is thrice repeated in these Epistles and nowhere beside; also the expressions 'serving with a pure conscience' and 'lifting to Him holy hands'. Both Polycarp and Ignatius stigmatize love of money as the root of all ills. Possibly the saying was proverbial, but it is likelier to be a reminiscence of Timothy. For Polycarp also calls Christ our Hope, and admonishes deacons not to be slanderers or double-tongued. Justin Martyr is quoted by Eusebius, himself, of course, a voucher for the canonicity of the Pastorals, as using the unique locution 'the mystery of godliness', and Hegesippus as speaking of 'knowledge falsely so called'; and Clement of Alexandria cites from Heracleon, gnostic though he was, the dictum 'He cannot deny Himself'. Justin furthermore borrows from Timothy the expression $\tau\hat{\eta}s$ $\pi\lambda\acute{a}\nu\eta s$ $\pi\nu\epsilon\acute{u}\mu\alpha\tau\alpha$ (I Tim. iv. 1) and from Titus $\acute{\eta}$ $\chi\rho\eta\sigma\tau\acute{o}\tau\eta s$ $\kappa\alpha\grave{\iota}$ $\acute{\eta}$ $\phi\iota\lambda\alpha\nu\theta\rho\omega\pi\acute{\iota}\alpha$ $\theta\epsilon o\hat{u}$ (Tit. iii. 4). Theophilus of Antioch inculcates prayers for rulers, 'that we may lead a quiet life', and Irenaeus excerpts several Pastoral phrases and explicitly alludes to Paul's *letters* (in the plural) to Timothy. Moreover, the Muratorian Canon recognizes them as Pauline and canonical. Their validity underlies the common ascription of thirteen Epistles to the apostle; nor do we hear of any dispute concerning them such as gathered round

[1] See the evidence marshalled by J. D. James, *Genuineness and Authorship of the Pastoral Epistles* (1906).

Hebrews. If Marcion is reported to have rejected them, and Tatian to have followed suit, with a reservation in favour of Titus, the reason is not far to seek. The matter of importance is that these awards were deemed subjective eccentricities by the Church catholic.

2. There is a second line of testification to them of a more indirect kind. The supposition of a *second Roman imprisonment* of St Paul entwines itself with the question of their authenticity; and that supposition gains definite support from patristic sources, whilst of evidence to the contrary they supply none. *Something* must have happened to the apostle after the close of Luke's narrative, which leaves him awaiting trial for his life; and it is hard to imagine, had the crown of martyrdom hovered over his head at that juncture, that he who tells the tale of Stephen's investment with that coronet of glory so feelingly would have broken off where he does, leaving his bosom-friend's good confession a sheer blank. For few care to endorse Sir William Ramsay's very precarious inference from the superlative πρῶτος in Acts i. 1, that Luke meditated a third treatise, in completion of the story left untold.

Now all authorities are agreed that Paul suffered in Rome; yet Clement of Rome, writing on the spot only thirty years later, treats it as an accepted fact that he had sealed his testimony with his blood after preaching the gospel in both east and west, ἐπὶ τὸ τέρμα τῆς δύσεως ἐλθών. Moffatt and others have sought to identify this limit of the west with the imperial city itself. But that notion flies in the face of current usage. Clement's phrase can bear only one construction. Rome was not a point on the circumference of her own empire, but its proud centre, *Roma domina rerum*. The phrase τὸ τέρμα τῆς δύσεως denotes either the whole or a specific portion of the Spanish Peninsula, entitled by Strabo τέρμονες τῆς οἰκουμένης and by Philostratus τὸ τέρμα τῆς Εὐρώπης. That distinguished classical scholar, J. E. B. Mayor, cites Clement's phrase in his notes on Juvenal as clear proof of Paul's visit to Spain, pointing out how Gades, the modern Cadiz, was reckoned the frontier-line of western civilization; in the words of Velleius Paterculus, *extremus nostri orbis terminus*. Both Seneca and Pliny call Spain *terrarum fines*; and this conception reaches back as far as Pindar, and becomes a commonplace with the latter-day Roman poets. So Ramsay and Mayor and Zahn confidently, and Harnack with more

4

hesitation, infer from Clement's phraseology a personal visit of the apostle paid to Spain. That presumes his acquittal, a result not improbable at a moment before A.D. 64, when Christianity had not yet been branded a *religio illicita*.

However, a missionary journey to Spain is not essential to the authenticity of the Pastorals; for it obtains no mention in their pages. The total absence of any tradition associating Paul's memory with any specific locality thereabouts may render it a trifle dubious. On the other hand, the fact that he had actually mapped out an expedition to Spain as his goal beyond Rome tells in its favour; for the apostle's programmes were not purposed 'after the flesh' or casually, as he reminded the Corinthians, so as to remain a dead letter. If his detention in Rome be urged as having laid an arrest on this project, we reply that both Philippians and Philemon betoken such a change in his prospects as made him no longer view recovered freedom as an event beyond hope. Besides, the Muratorian Canon, our best informant regarding Roman tradition, accredits the Spanish campaign; and so do Chrysostom, Cyril of Jerusalem and Jerome; while Eusebius, if he passes it over, postulates his release and re-entry into Rome for the final scene.

3. Many a superficial reader of the Epistles has carried away, no doubt, the impression of a single Roman imprisonment. For that mistake we can adduce an instructive modern parallel. The rank and file of John Bunyan's admirers credit him with one long term of confinement in Bedford Gaol. But this conclusion is erroneous. Dr John Brown has shown that he underwent two distinct incarcerations in two distinct Bedford prisons, with a lengthy interspace of liberty between them, and that, contrary to general opinion, the *Pilgrim's Progress* was penned during his second and shorter spell of prison life. Let us stretch the comparison for a moment, and suppose that a score of centuries had rolled between Bunyan's day and our own, and that time had cast a haze over the minor details of the immortal tinker's biography, so that an assumption that he had died in prison was widely current. How could it be best combated? By producing booklets of his—and such do exist—bearing dates subsequent to the known era of his imprisonment, and evidence of journeys which imply that he was once more at large and busy preaching the Word.

Now that is what the Pastoral Letters profess to furnish in Paul's own case. They purport to be his parting instructions to two of his trustiest deputies, and their whole validity depends on the truth of that claim. Of course rationalistic critics are never tired of harping on the classical historian's habit of putting speeches suitable to the occasion into the mouths of military leaders on the eve of decisive affrays, a device fostered by the current passion for rhetorical declamation, but based on the actual custom of haranguing troops on such occasions from the *suggestus*. But that usage bears a very remote resemblance to, and affords no precedent for, the cheat of palming off a bogus rule of faith and practice on the Church in the name of St Paul, aggravated by the impiety of taking God's name in vain in the process. If the solemn avowal of these Epistles that they are the apostle's authoritative missives be not instinct with the most sterling honour and integrity, but an equivocation, or if they are a patchwork of truth and falsehood, they form no part of the Church's treasures, but sink to the level of pious frauds—the worst of all cajoleries—as disreputable in their line as the romance of *Paul and Thekla* in its, which cost its concoctor degradation from the presbytership, notwithstanding his protestations that he meant no harm. Viewed as the production of a charlatan personating the apostle, and parroting Paul's voice in order to facilitate their reception, these documents incur the taint of moral obliquity and deserve to be held in contempt.

Dr Harrison, in his book impeaching their genuineness, tries to varnish the matter by asserting his factotum's 'loyal devotion to Paul's name'; but how a fraudulent abuse of that name breathes the spirit of loyalty is hard to perceive. He opines that this same intriguer in making Paul his stalking-horse was 'unconscious of deceiving any-body'; and that his hocus-pocus may have been known to be such by his friends without lowering the shammer's character. We cherish a loftier estimate of the ethical standard of primitive Christianity than that. How could those who had plighted troth for evermore to Him who is Faithful and True act otherwise? Can anyone deny that the New Testament demands absolute transparency of aim and uncompromising straightforwardness of practice, and recoils absolutely from all false pretences and stage effects? Treacherous breaches of faith in the supposed interests of faith have, alas! since then been often applauded by churchmen of supple consciences, and forged decretals done Satan yeoman service in ages of crass superstition. But such sanctimonious knaveries are the antipole of the code of veracity taught by Christ and His apostles, with its drastic disavowal of all disingenuous artifices. Has not Paul himself in no measured terms reprobated doing evil that good may come? He was a sorry specimen of a Paulinist, this pseudo-Paul, conjured up from a nameless grave by the magic hand of criticism to vend smuggled wares under sacred auspices with such cool effrontery.

These Epistles *may* have been elicited in response to queries addressed to their commanding officer by his two lieutenants, but their significance extends to all generations. The prospect of Paul's speedy removal (he is now *lampada traditurus*) rendered them timely and the uprising of a visible Church made them indispensable. The exact fulfilment of the predictions of future apostasy they contain attests their author's prophetic afflatus, and their canonical status tallies with the seal of unction and authority impressed upon them, so different from the secondary tone and lifeless tenor of the products of the age of the apostolic fathers. Moffatt owns their 'astonishing superiority'.

III. INTERNAL EVIDENCE

Let us take a bird's-eye view of the testimony in support of their genuineness that may be culled from the Letters themselves, before canvassing the objections urged against them. It has to be borne in mind that we are scanning the veteran apostle, wearied by titanic labours and shattering trials, and that he is handling a severely practical topic, not adapted to call forth all his latent powers. He writes in a subdued vein, by this time looking wistfully backwards rather than forging ahead at full speed; yet gleams of the old fire flash forth ever and anon to certify us of the writer's identity.

1. The first Epistle to Timothy, penned confidentially and at liberty, moves at a leisurely pace which permits of sundry side-glances, yet discloses not a few mint-marks of Paul's composition. The position of a home-bird assigned to woman may surely be reckoned as one of these. And who save the apostle himself would have stigmatized his former self an ὑβριστής, a hectoring bully? Nor can we conceive of a Paulinist camp-follower entitling his chief of men the 'chief of sinners', a trophy

of mercy displayed to the uttermost. And who but Paul could have preserved that exquisite blend of authority and affection that pervades the Timothean Letters? Note too how precisely in keeping with all we know of Timothy are the exhortations given him, with their recognition of his gentle-spirited temper, weakly physique, and motley environ- ment. And how appropriately do admonitions to the rich find place in a letter addressed to opulent Ephesus!

A cavil has been raised touching the application of the term νέος to Timothy. Holtzmann derisively remarks that he 'seems to have pos- sessed the secret of perpetual youth'. But this is mere empty splutter. For there were only two recognized standards of age to the Greek or Roman, νέος and γέρων, juvenis and senex, and the former of these con- veyed no such juvenile implication as our term youngster, with which μειράκιον or ἔφηβος would correspond. It was employed of adults in the full vigour of life and of soldiers of military age to the verge of forty. There is no more incongruity here than in the use of the word τέκνον (cf. 'my lad') four times over as an endearing address to his son in the faith.

2. Titus was obviously of a sturdier make than his colleague, and the directory sent to him takes a more compendious shape. It is written with a special eye to the local conditions of the less developed Cretan mission, known to Paul through a recent visit. That explains why all mention of the diaconate is omitted. Need we remark how much in Paul's manner is the caustic hexameter cited from Epimenides, and still more the appositional clause, 'a prophet of their own', with its subtly ironical flavour? κρητισμός is used by Plutarch as a graphic synonym for lying. Yet more characteristic of the Tarsian is the sixfold repetition of the title Saviour, thrice applied to God and thrice to the Lord Jesus Him- self, and the inculcation of civil obedience on the obstreperous Cretans. Some surmise that Titus was Luke's brother, and find in that a reason for the suppression of his name in Acts. At all events he was the apostle's trusted envoy. Paul is at freedom thus far, and proposes to winter at Nicopolis, probably in Epirus, near the Egnatian route westward.

3. The second Epistle to Timothy presents a changed aspect of affairs. Here we find Paul once more in duress, rated as a malefactor and under stricter custody than before; for Onesiphorus discovers his whereabouts in Rome only after painful search. Everything now fore-

bodes his offering up, and in this touching *finale* we have what Bengel styles his swan-song. He who does not catch Paul's accents in this letter must be remarkably hard of hearing. His strongly individualizing propensity comes out in the twenty-three personal allusions, starting with the tender eulogy passed on Timothy's mother and grandmother. Some sixteen of these are unknown from other sources. Holtzmann tries to minimize this pledge of actuality with the gibe that the author was 'bound to render his fiction as plausible as he could'. Yes! but the taunt recoils on the taunter, for false witnesses are careful not to compromise themselves by too many specific particulars, and even more so not to reproduce old figures, like Demas, in a completely altered guise. And why should this wily dissembler be at the pains to triplicate his web of deceit? But we lose patience at the notion that we can attribute to a source like that such soul-stirring strains, once heard never forgotten, as 'I know whom I have believed and am persuaded that He is able to keep my deposit with Him (Paul's ancient image) against that day'; or his *certavi, cucurri, custodivi*, 'I have fought a good fight'— ἀγών often refers to military operations—'I have finished my course, I have kept the faith', with its triumphant sequel. In these lofty chords we hear the intrepid old warrior chant his own solemn yet serene requiem.

The *prima actio* of his trial is over (for surely Zahn errs in making the passage refer to his examination years before; what need to inform Timothy of that?); yet though all had forsaken him at need, the lone witness had been enabled to bear effectual testimony to his beloved Lord before a representative auditory. Now he awaits his exit through the gateway of martyrdom with unshaken resolution, pining only to clasp Timothy's hand once more before the end. Who can ascribe the clarion blast of that parting charge to any composer but him whom Donne aptly names the *fusile* apostle, of potency when fully roused to sound a bugle call fitted to 'create a soul under the ribs of death'?

IV. ARGUMENTS AGAINST AUTHENTICITY

What then are the leading objections to their authenticity?

1. It is alleged that they disclose *too advanced a stage of Church organization* for Paul's day. Yet surely some structural form was imperative for the consolidation of the building of God which the apostles

were commissioned to rear. For the New Testament ideal of the Church is not what many today desiderate, a 'syncretism of religious good feeling' and flabby sentiment cemented by the glue of compromise, but a symmetrical fabric, the arsenal of revealed truth and citadel of disciplined liberty. Even Forsyth has said: 'a mere brotherhood has no theology, but then it has no influence. It is nothing but a sympathetic group.' If a visible Church were to exist to any purpose, the 'law of the house' required distinct enunciation. That is furnished to us here in a most unostentatious pattern, void of all show and officialism, given that men may 'know how to behave themselves in the house of God', pillar and stay as it is of the truth (I Tim. iii. 15).

Baur's allegation that Paul cared not a straw for Church government begs the question of the genuineness of the Letters at the outset, and is palpably false as well. Already we find him in Acts xiv ordaining presbyters together with Barnabas, whom Hort regards as the predecessor of Titus, in every city he revisited; and these presbyters play a prominent part in the Council of Jerusalem. The diaconate had taken shape yet earlier; and in Philippians the local 'bishops and deacons' are greeted as an established institution. Even in Thessalonians we hear of those who 'bear rule'. The Ephesian tabulation of Church officers, ordinary and extraordinary, concludes with the mention of 'pastors and teachers'. Some of these ordinations were doubtless provisional, others permanent. Timothy and Titus may be classed, in Dr Moberly's words, as 'instruments of an absent rather than wielders of an inherent authority', vicars apostolic discharging temporary functions here and there. Observe that they are in no wise exalted into grandees, as a second century *falsarius* might have been expected to glorify them, but admonished to watch heedfully over their own souls. The main emphasis is laid on the functions of the under-shepherds, with the specific flocks consigned to their charge. For the Church is now settling down to her task, and probationers for the ministry are forthcoming in proportion to the call for them.

It is not our province to touch on denominational 'differences of administration' concerning which we might not see eye to eye. But we cannot fail to perceive the unpretentious type of Church rule that is here sketched, a *sodalitas* incapable in fact of coming into collision with civil authority without wanton aggression on the part of the latter.

Does not this picture reflect primal conditions in contrast with later developments? Westcott holds that it is plainly anterior to Clement's *Letter to the Corinthians*. Indeed, the early date of the Pastoral Epistles can be warrantably inferred from the equivalence of the terms *bishop* and *presbyter*, which is peculiarly manifest in Titus i, and finds its counterpart in Clement and the *Didache*. (See Bishop Lightfoot's well-known dissertation on the Christian Ministry.) ἐπίσκοπος was the ordinary Greek term for a *supervisor* of any kind, whereas the noun πρεσβύτερος, with its Hebrew associations, denotes the office rather than the function it subserves. Long after the entrenchment of the prelatical bishop, the memory of the ancient meaning of ἐπίσκοπος still lingered. Chrysostom, for example, acknowledges it in his comment on the opening verse of Philippians, and Augustine in a letter to Jerome writes: *secundum honorum vocabula quae iam ecclesiae usus obtinuit episcopatus maior presbyterio est.* Jerome himself likewise remarks in his Commentary on Titus: *idem est presbyter qui et episcopus*; and concludes his discussion of the matter: 'Let the bishops lay it to heart that their superiority to presbyters arises rather from custom than from the verity of an ordination of the Lord.'

Now in reality that constitution of things strongly argues in favour of the genuineness of these Epistles. 'If the Pastoral Epistles contained a clear defence of the episcopal system of the second century', writes Dean Farrar, 'that alone would be enough to prove their spuriousness.' As it is, the ministerial portrait here drawn lays stress almost entirely on moral and spiritual qualifications. Mark, too, how the apostle passes without a break from the bishop or presbyter to the deacon and deaconess and then to the church-widows. Not a vestige of sacerdotalism can be descried here. In what full canonicals that spirit would have tricked out the leading figure may be guessed from the fact that some of its devotees have been insensate enough to elevate the cloak Paul left at Troas into a priestly chasuble or dalmatic.

2. A second exception taken on similar grounds affirms that *Gnostic doctrines of a later date* incur censure in these Epistles. Baur hailed the occurrence of the word *antithesis* at the close of I Timothy as supplying proof of a covert polemic against Marcion's treatise bearing this title. But that Aristotelian term was no novelty; and whereas Gnosticism

proper is radically anti-Jewish, the parties here rebuked appertain to a semi-Rabbinical school. So nebulous a creed scarce allows of definition; but we shall not be far out if we designate Gnosticism an intellectual caste, professing an esoteric philosophy of religion, one of whose main tenets was the evil of matter. Oriental theosophies of this cast sprang up rankly in the soil of a putrid paganism. And foreshadowings of coming cults usually precede them, even as Oken's speculations and Robert Chambers's *Vestiges of Creation* betokened Darwin's *Origin of Species*. These vaguer pretensions to superfine illumination had ascetic elements in common with the schools of Marcion and Valentinus. The term γνῶσις may have been pillaged from Paul's own use of it; but we have no right to infuse the second-century meaning, much akin to the German *Aufklärung*, into such a clause as 'knowledge falsely so called'. Nor ought we to wrest prophecies of prospective heresies into descriptions of phenomena actually then present. The parties immediately chastised here are a coterie of legalists, tenacious of wire-drawn subtleties, dubbed 'Jewish fables' in one passage and 'old wives' tales' in another. It is only in the predictive contexts that they acquire a malignity that engenders moral contamination and is totally subversive of the faith. An incipient stage of declension has already been reached; but the inclined plane has not yet carried those launched upon it to its goal of necrosis. Only the αἱρετικὸς ἄνθρωπος (Tit. iii. 10), the obstinate factionist, is to be entirely abjured, as things stand.

3. A third demur (strange on the lips of its propounders) discovers in these Epistles a *lowered theology*, shorn of the watchwords of the apostle's previous teaching. Moffatt insists much on this point, and an American critic contends that, 'if they are indeed Paul's composition, he has descended from the lofty plane on which he had moved to the level of mere piety and morality'. Mere piety indeed! These criticisms are altogether wide of the mark. For doctrinal edification lies outside the immediate scope of the Pastorals; they comprise executive counsels blended with ethical. Moreover, no chasm yawns between Christian doctrine and Christian practice. 'Immortal principles forbid the sons of God to sin' (Watts). Justification and sanctification are twin-born children of grace. Are not Paul's most systematic arguments rounded off with pressing admonishments to godliness of life? 'As ye have

received Christ Jesus the Lord, so walk in Him.' Works wrought to procure salvation Paul rates as worthless, yet makes them indispensable evidences of a gracious state. Here he is battling with barren speculations, and their inevitable aftermath, unholy living masked under the vizor of religious profession.

Besides, the allegation contravenes the facts. Occupied as he is with practicalities rather than principles, he does not wholly drop his old battle-cries. Do they not ring in our ears when we read in Titus: 'not by works done in righteousness by us, but according to His mercy He saved us, by washing of regeneration and renewing of the Holy Ghost, that being justified by His grace we might be made heirs according to the promise of eternal life' (iii. 5, 6); or of Christ Himself as having given 'Himself for us, to redeem us from all iniquity' (ii. 14; doctrine and practice welded together)? And what can bear Paul's autograph more plainly than the unique expression ἀντίλυτρον ὑπὲρ πάντων, of I Tim. ii. 6, so lamely rendered by all our translators, 'a ransom for all'? For it is not λύτρον, but ἀντίλυτρον, one of Paul's own coinages. The verb ἀντιλυτροῦν occurs but once in all Greek literature with a slightly different sense, in Aristotle's *Nicomachaean Ethics*, ix. 2. Here the noun must signify '*counterprice*', *pretium ex adverso respondens*, as the Puritan divine Flavel well paraphrases it, setting forth the intrinsically infinite virtue of the atoning sacrifice, its equipollence when set over against human guilt. If these passing reaffirmations of his gospel fail to satisfy critical censors, we would remind them that a tract on Church government differs from a body of divinity, and that one mark of a disciplined intellect consists in ability to keep to the subject in hand. St Paul digresses now and then; he never rambles from pillar to post!

4. But the capital objection urged against the Pastorals bears reference to their *vocabulary and style*. Dr Harrison's assault on them relies almost entirely on this consideration, which he illustrates by an elaborate series of diagrams. It is said that anything can be proved by an array of statistics adroitly manipulated, and perhaps this may be a case in point. We are bidden to remark that we encounter here twice or even thrice as many fresh words as Paul's other writings would lead us to expect. The proportion of vocables previously unused amounts to some 168 in sum, against a total of 627 for all the rest of his Epistles.

That sounds impressive, if we make the law of averages our touch-stone, but in a case of this kind computations of numerical ratios are apt to be illusive. We might rejoin that a plagiarist would not deviate from his model so extensively; but, accepting the data for what they are worth, we observe that change of vocabulary does not always imply transference of authorship. Mahaffy has noted how singularly diverse is Xenophon's vocabulary in different treatises of his; and he attributes it to his vagrancy of life and sociable propensities, an explanation that applies also to the apostle Paul. Besides, wider reasons for modifications of a writer's diction present themselves.

Both style and diction are functions of the topic handled. When Xenophon treats of horsemanship he employs a novel set of terms to match a novel subject. Now Paul is here dealing with the circum-stantials of church organization, and with certain local heretical tendencies, rife or yet to be rife; and he uses new terms, and an unusual proportion of negative adjectives, naturally of rare occurrence, because they suit his subject-matter. Thus the sheaf of fresh epithets descriptive of the model pastor or deacon, and the disparaging terms applied to false teachers, are accounted for by their contexts. Meanwhile the staple of the vocabulary and syntax abides intact. Harrison forages assiduously in quest of grammatical innovations, but with the most insignificant results.

Having had a sum in addition, we are next favoured with one in sub-traction. Stress is laid on the *withdrawal* from active service of *certain Pauline locutions* we should expect to meet. Among the *lacunae* are υἱοθεσία, πείθειν, περισσεύειν, χαρίζεσθαι and certain particles of transition or inference. But were not these latter quite uncalled for in directions largely couched in the imperative mood? As to the absence of some favourite usages, as Dr White notes in the *Expositor's Greek Testament*, 'it is folly to expect a practised writer to distribute his vocabulary in the mechanical fashion of spots on a wall-paper'. In another writer's words, to content our critics an author 'must never break out in a new direction; having had his vision and his dream, he must henceforth be like a star and dwell apart. To be stereotyped is his only salvation.' Yet the very fact that he is addressing members of his inner circle here colours the apostle's phraseology. Are Cicero's Letters to Atticus replicas of his philosophical tracts? By no means; in

point of vocabulary least of all. Our opponents have insisted on making
the matter a literary question; then as a literary question let it be argued.
The fact of the matter is that what the critical magnates sorely need is
enlargement of vision.

Critics concerned with words only are not very competent appraisers
of men of genius; and Paul has a right to be judged by his peers. To
content these gentlemen, an author must adopt a recitative, and re-
duplicate himself monotonously. Now we are too broad-minded to
demand that. Believing as we do in Paul's special inspiration, we never-
theless hold that that fact does not supersede, but sublimates his natural
gifts. And in all true genius there lurks an incalculable element, refractory to strait-waistcoats of all sorts. Applied to your third-rate author
who takes his ply early in life and repeats himself ever afterwards like a
hurdy-gurdy, syllabic tests may answer. But intellectual powers of a
higher cast pursue their own path unshackled, and exhibit plasticities
and aptitudes not to be gauged by the word-fancier's ell-wand. Moreover, if ever the personal equation should count, it is in a case so
anomalous as St Paul's. For this Roman Empire ranger (aye, and
besieger too!) was anything but a recluse cramped within his shell or a
pedant hidebound by a quickset hedge of verbiage. He does not revolve
painfully in a closed circle of dictionary-terms; his language is attempered
to his surroundings and immediate design. Saul of Tarsus ranks as a
Christian cosmopolite of the keenest sensibilities, fertile in resources,
a rapid yet profound thinker, to whom words are not satraps but
subalterns, not tyrants but thralls. Averages befit average cases; but
here is a most exceptional case, that of an adept in assimilation, pledged
to become all things to all men, a brother-in-arms to bond and free, a
connecting-link between Jew and Gentile, one imbued with Greek as
a living speech from boyhood, and whose prolonged experience of
preaching indoors and out must have given to his vigilant intellect and
glowing heart a command of Hellenistic as expansive and flexible as the
man himself.

Great souls are not their own mimes. How wide the interval betwixt
Horace's roughest-hewn Satires and his stateliest Odes, or between the
sepulchral pomp of Tennyson's *In Memoriam* and the money-grubbing
jingle of his *Northern Farmer*! What a contrast between the ornate
luxuriance of the more sonorous cadences of *Paradise Lost* and the

tragic austerity and loin-girt athleticism of Milton's latest work, the *Samson Agonistes*! In minds of the finest texture strands of likeness and unlikeness intertwine.

It is well to reflect that St Paul's whole extant writings occupy only some 150 octavo pages of letterpress and comprise in all about 3000 main vocables. Surely that scanty total does not represent the entire Greek exchequer of this student by predestination and speaker by vocation. Think of the compass of his instrument at its full *crescendo*, and you will have to own the ample linguistic reserves at his command, instinctively adjusted to his immediate theme. In this connection our myopic critics would do well to ponder the sentence of a great Continental classical scholar, Wilamowitz-Möllendorf, who in his manual of Greek literature styles Saul the Tarsian 'a classic of Hellenism', and remarks that his Greek is indebted to no particular school or model, but is his own, 'not translated Aramaic but real Greek, the utterance of a fresh and living experience'.

V. VOCABULARY

Since such emphasis is laid on verbal dissimilarities, let us come to close quarters with this verbal bogey. Harrison spies in the Pastorals a new literary tone and less 'grip and verve' than in the other Pauline Epistles, and Peake borrows from his German prompters the paltry insinuation of senility. A diminution of momentum we should expect after the tremendous 'Marathon-race' Paul had been running. On the other hand, the immense strain and pressure of those earlier years must have precluded study, whereas the comparative inactivity of the imperial prisoner may have yielded him breathing-space for reading or being read to. There are traces of such an influence at work in his later letters. If an influx of literary Hellenistic be alleged, that tallies with these conditions. What then are the facts about the new ingredients?

1. Among the novel features we note words belonging to the older literary strata, for instance, ἀνδραποδίστης and αἰσχροκερδής. ἀπαίδευτος (II Tim. ii. 23) at once recalls Plato; but that verbal adjective belongs to all stages of literary Greek, as do plenty of the other verbal innovations of these Epistles, such as ἀναζωπυρεῖν, γυμνάζειν, μελετᾶν, ὀρέγεσθαι, πειθαρχεῖν, στεφανοῦν, φροντίζειν, φλύαρος, ὑπόνοια.

2. Of purely vernacular usages, for example αὐθεντεῖν (I Tim. ii. 12) in the sense of *having authority over*, the list is very brief. Hardly another can be found.

3. But of course a much larger percentage of the new terms consist of samples of ordinary literary Hellenistic. Take a few specimens. There is the interesting verb ἀστοχεῖν, thrice used in the sense of *missing the mark, going astray*; a Polybian, Plutarchian and Lucianic expression, which obviously took the place of ἁμαρτάνειν in proportion as that word acquired an ethical significance. ἀνανήφειν (II Tim. ii. 26) was passing through the same process; and so was κακοπαθεῖν (II Tim. ii. 3, 9), *to rough it*, opposed by Plutarch to ἡδυπάθεια, which answers to our *mollycoddling*. Another Polybian phrase twice repeated greets us in ἀποδοχῆς ἄξιος, and in ἀγωγή, *training, upbringing*, first thus used in Aristotle. οἱ ἐν ὑπεροχῇ ὄντες is another Aristotelian phrase for *the authorities*. κατάστημα, *demeanour, carriage* (Tit. ii. 3), occurs in Josephus and Plutarch, the latter employing the adjective καταστη-ματικός for *staid*. καταστολή (I Tim. ii. 9), *decorum*, is a kindred term found in the same authors and in Epictetus. κοινωνικός (I Tim. vi. 18), *sociable*, has much the same provenance. περιίστασθαι, twice meaning *to shun*, appertains to Josephus, Philodemus of Gadara, a first-century B.C. Palestinian text-book writer, and Marcus Aurelius. πορισμός (I Tim. vi. 5), *livelihood*, has also the sanction of Philodemus, Plutarch and Vettius Valens; and so has ῥητῶς (I Tim. iv. 1), *expressly*, used by Polybius and Plutarch to introduce word-for-word quotations. The metaphorical ναυαγεῖν (I Tim. i. 19) and περιπείρειν (I Tim. vi. 10) are figures characteristic of literary Hellenistic; as much may be said for the military image, στρατολογεῖν (II Tim. ii. 4). The new vocables σωφρονίζειν, σωφροσύνη, σωφρονισμός, descriptive of *self-command*, are favourite terms with Plutarch. Ὑποτύπωσις carries two meanings; in Galen that of *conspectus* or *synopsis*, as here apparently in II Tim. i. 13; but in a passage of Quintilian (ix. 2. 40) it clearly signifies a *vivid picture*, and that sense suits best in I Tim. i. 16.

4. We cannot pause longer over these accessions to the apostle's word-lists. Lest we make too much of them, let it be observed that the Pastorals likewise contain plenty of old friends to form connecting links with his other Epistles. We can only specify a batch of Paulinisms taken

almost at random. Paul's favourite verbs, ἐνδυναμοῦν, *to empower*, and its antithesis καταργεῖν, *to nullify, render nugatory*, duly reappear, and his distinctive phrase παραστῆσαι τῷ θεῷ recurs; and so do his favourite adjectives, εὐάρεστος and its counterpole ἀδόκιμος, and his designation κήρυγμα for the gospel message. Grammatical hallmarks, such as the threefold ἠλπικέναι, *to fix one's hope on*, in place of ἐλπίζειν, as in Corinthians (cf. κεκραγέναι for κράζειν), and his well-known πεπίστευμαι and ἐπιστεύθην, recur in like manner. Of Hebraic Greek the tokens are very slight.

We meet the reassertion ἀπόστολος...κατ᾽ ἐπιταγὴν θεοῦ in I Tim. i. 1; also a lowly term for his apostolate, διακονία, as elsewhere, not likely to have been chosen, if only to avoid confusion, except by himself. The noun χάρισμα and the phrase ἀφορμὴν διδόναι (I Tim. v. 14) are highly characteristic, and so is the compound ἐκτὸς εἰ μή (I Tim. v. 19).

VI. STYLISTIC MANNERISMS

To my mind, however, underlying watermarks of the apostle of the Gentiles are discernible more convincing than these verbal correspondences, which are chiefly of value as a set-off against paraded verbal discrepancies. I refer to his stylistic mannerisms. In this respect the Pastoral Epistles conform thoroughly to type.

1. The figures carry his monogram upon them. They are, as a rule, drawn not from the physical but the human realm. Who does not recognize his badge in the image of the martial aspirant to fame, or the competitor at the games, or in the figure of the seal, or the steward, or the outpoured libation, or vessels unto honour? If the similitudes of a gangrene and a cauterized conscience, or of sound and sickly doctrine, wear a novel air, may these medical images not be traceable to Luke's comradeship?

2. Another delicate token of Paul's sign-manual, which he shares with Luke, comes to light in the employment of *meiosis* or understatement. In other contexts we have heard him dub himself a citizen of no mean city, and aver that he was not ashamed of the gospel nor 'disobedient to the heavenly vision'. Paul likes to leave some scope for the exercise of his reader's or hearer's faculties, for he was not one to suffer

fools gladly! This former trait re-emerges here. 'I am suffering thus; yet am I *not ashamed*', we hear him exclaim. Onesiphorus, he tells us, was *not ashamed* of his chain, and Timothy is *not to be ashamed* of the Lord's testimony, nor of me *His prisoner*, the selfsame appellation he had taken in Ephesians. Or again: 'the word of God is *not bound*'. The very phrase ὁ ἀψευδὴς θεός, whencesoever derived—it occurs in Euripides—embodies a *meiosis*.

3. *Apposition* is another figure to which he was partial, not of single words so much as whole clauses. We all remember two classical instances in Romans, 'what the law could not do', and so on, in chapter viii, and the opening sentence of chapter xii, where the entire statement is poised against the concluding clause, 'your reasonable service'. Of this feature we find several examples in the Pastorals. To name only two in I Timothy, τό μαρτύριον καιροῖς ἰδίοις (I Tim. ii. 6), 'the testimony for its own seasons', in reference to Christ's redemptive work just named, and in iii. 15 the famous στῦλος καὶ ἑδραίωμα τῆς ἀληθείας, 'a pillar and stay of the truth', where it is not quite certain whether the appositional clause relates to the church or the ensuing sentence. These specimens of Paul's condensed style may be compared with the elliptical ὁ ἐξ ἐναντίας of Tit. ii. 8, the frequent omission of the copula, not without its bearing on the translation of II Tim. iii. 16, and the zeugma, 'forbidding to marry, bidding (understood) to abstain from meats', in I Tim. iv. 3. We could almost stake the authorship of I Timothy on the wording of iii. 5: 'if one know not how to rule his own house, how shall he care for the church of God?', a compressed form of interrogation exclusively Pauline, of which there are four examples in I Cor. xiv alone.

4. The apostle's fondness for *compendious compounds* is well known to all careful students of his style. We at once recall previous instances of this, such as ἀνεξιχνίαστος, ὀφθαλμοδουλεία, ὑψηλοφρονεῖν (the last found both here and in Romans). Now in the Pastorals we meet with at least a score of such new short-hand verbal formations, some of them ἅπαξ εἰρημένα. For example, αὐτοκατάκριτος, *self-convicted*, found once in Philo; διαπαρατριβαί (unique), *mutual altercations*, ἑτερο-διδασκαλεῖν (twice, unique)—so ἑτεροζυγεῖν in II Corinthians; εὐ-μετάδοτος, *generous*, elsewhere only met with in Vettius Valens and

Marcus Aurelius; καταστρηνιᾶν (unique), *to wax lusty against*; λογομαχεῖν, λογομαχία, the title of a satire of Varro, ὀρθοτομεῖν, a figure probably drawn from cutting a straight furrow (cf. ὁδὸν τέμνειν), which at once recalls ὀρθοποδεῖν in Galatians, πραυπάθεια, the Latin *mansuetudo*, once used by Philo; φρεναπάτης, of which the papyri furnish one instance, reproducing the φρεναπατᾷ of Gal. vi. 3. The very rare, but important epithet, θεόπνευστος, *God-breathed* (II Tim. iii. 16) occurs nowhere beside save once in Plutarch's *Morals*, where it is applied to dreams, once in Vettius Valens, who terms man a θεόπνευστον δημιούργημα, 'a God-breathed piece of workmanship', and as an epithet of wisdom in the probably Jewish hexameters of the pseudo-Phocylides. These conglomerates fully accord with Paul's manner.

5. His proclivity for *enumerations*, especially of moral or immoral qualities, is another marked trait, shared in a minor degree by the apostle Peter. Who can forget the awful catalogue of pagan vices in Romans i, or the counter-lists in Galatians v of the works of the flesh and the fruit of the Spirit? This hallmark of his meets our gaze here likewise. In I Timothy there fronts us the inventory of the delinquents who fall under the lash of the law, and of the graces to be cherished by the man of God. Here and in Titus we have a table of the virtues befitting bishops and matured saints and of the contrary vices that are tabooed. Notice how convincingly Pauline is that touch, 'once *we* were such' (Tit. iii. 3), by which the writer classes himself with his readers and their guilty past. In II Timothy we encounter another list of the corrupt practices of future seducers of unwary souls.

6. Paul cannot refrain from *playing on words*. Herein the Pastorals follow precedent. 'The law is good, provided it be used lawfully', he writes. Another paranomasia meets us in the τοῖς πλουσίοις ... πλουσίως of I Tim. vi. 17. In II Timothy we can count at least three: φιλήδονοι μᾶλλον ἢ φιλόθεοι (iii. 4); ἄρτιος ... πρὸς πᾶν ἔργον ἀγαθὸν ἐξηρτισμένος (iii. 17), and εὐκαίρως ἀκαίρως, like *fanda nefanda* (iv. 2).

7. Further, *latinistic influences* are more legible than heretofore in the apostle's Greek. Holtzmann enlists this circumstance in the cause of

scepticism; but the argument is double-edged; for Paul's susceptibility to his environment was abnormal. Sir William Ramsay holds that the Gentile apostle must have cultivated a knowledge of Latin as part of his equipment for his task, and detects Roman forms *Illyricum* and *Philippenses* in the Greek of Romans and Philippians. Surely when his steps drew nigh to the world's metropolis, if not before, this must have been the case, just as a British missionary in the Belgian Congo or Madagascar has a stimulus to acquaint himself with French. In II Timothy we come across two Latin terms, *paenula* and *membrana*, transliterated; nor could anything be more natural than this phenomenon.

The truth is, Greek and Latin had now reached that stage of interpenetration when mutual loans wax inevitable. At a much earlier date Polybius introduces a sprinkling of Latin vocables into his text, and his Greek occasionally reflects Latin usages, much as we take over French phrases like 'thinking furiously' or 'the defects of his qualities'. The reflex influences of a Roman environment are thus mirrored in the Pastorals. χάριν ἔχειν is twice substituted for the usual εὐχαριστεῖν, echoing *gratiam habere*, and ματαιολογία recalls *vaniloquium*, ἑδραίωμα *firmamentum*, δι᾽ ἣν αἰτίαν *quamobrem*, πρόσκλισις *inclinatio*, πρόκριμα *praeiudicium*, ἀδηλότης *incertitudo* (a Plutarchian usage), and σεμνότης that choicest fetish of the Roman mind *gravitas*. The adoption for the first time of the word εὐσέβεια and its cognates seems due to the vogue of *pietas* in Latin lips, and the replacement of κύριος by δεσπότης to the similar prominence of *dominus*. οἱ ἡμέτεροι for *our folk* (Tit. iii. 14), like the Latin *nostri*, occurs in Philodemus (*Rhet.* iii. 8) and Strabo. The phrase *cumulatae peccatis* corresponds with σεσωρευμένα ἁμαρτίαις (II Tim. iii. 6), and the unique δίλογος, *double-tongued* of I Tim. iii. 8 seems modelled on *bilinguis*, purposely varied because δίγλωσσος already signified 'bilingual'. And a phrase that puzzled Bentley and nonplusses Moulton and Milligan, προσέρχεται ὑγιαίνουσι λόγοις (I Tim. vi. 3) is best elucidated by the Tacitean expression: *Galba suadentibus accessit.*

8. We have seen how St Paul's profile may be clearly discerned in these pages. Here is his practical sagacity, his love for generalizations (e.g. *to the pure all things are pure*); a bold assertion, as in Romans, of his commission against its impugners, chastened by a vivid feeling of

personal unworthiness; his unshaken loyalty to his Lord coupled with an acute sense of the loyalty or disloyalty of fellow-workers. Here are three of his irrepressible doxologies breaking in on the thread of his discourse, and here is that wave of tremulous emotion which invariably comes over him when he recalls the wonder of his conversion. But the figure is that of a scarred campaigner, forced to husband his debilitated strength.

So signally Pauline are some of the touches in II Timothy that many of the negative critics have to hedge a little here, and further complicate their cross-word puzzle by the surmise that sundry genuine utterances of his have been pieced into these Epistles. This concession goes far to compromise their position; for they have to admit that the seams in the patchwork defy demarcation, and that the resultant text must be attributed to a single hand, underhand of course, yet a dovetailer of the finest talent. The second century must have been the golden age of fancy work, barring the incomparable twentieth!

Dr Harrison labours to discover affinities of diction with latent remains of the second century; but no watertight compartment labelled second-century Greek can be isolated from the rest. He also loftily pronounces it 'an impossibility that the apostle should have given these instructions to his evangelists'. But it is a vastly greater one that a Mr By-Ends, craftily personating his patron-saint for interested ends, should have denounced liars and impostors so trenchantly, and stickled so earnestly for a conscience void of offence. 'A genuine Paulinist', says Dr Shaw incisively, 'at once so skilful and obtuse, inventing unreal situations with the utmost *sangfroid*, yet breathing an air of profoundest reverence for truth, is an absolute chimera.' The word *faithful* (πιστός), seventeen times repeated, forms the very keynote of these Letters. The phrase πιστὸς ὁ λόγος may be fresh, though we have had πιστὸς ὁ θεός in Corinthians and πιστὸς ὁ κύριος in Thessalonians; but its fivefold recurrence seems to indicate either snatches of catechetical lore or prophetic canticles current in the Church. Nor is the objective sense of πίστις a novelty. It occurs in Romans and would naturally arise as soon as Christians were called *believers*.

In conclusion we cannot help feeling that it is the rebukes dealt in these Epistles to some of the fondest shibboleths of the modern mind that really chafe that mind. The stress laid on soundness of doctrine built on a fixed deposit of inspiration cannot but give offence, and the sinister portraiture of the last days kindle a spark of resentment. Such an epithet applied to seducers as τετυφωμένος, which is the Greek equivalent of *swollen-headed*, or *consequential*,[1] must rankle in circles where this spirit is not unknown.

[1] The new (ninth) edition of Liddell and Scott inclines to the rendering *crazy, demented*, involving a still stronger condemnation; but we think that evidence could be produced in favour of the older interpretation of arrogant assumption (cf. ἄτυφος, ἀτυφία).

THE FIRST EPISTLE TO TIMOTHY

i. 1, 2. SALUTATION

i. 1. Παῦλος ἀπόστολος Χριστοῦ Ἰησοῦ κατ᾽ ἐπιταγὴν θεοῦ σωτῆρος ἡμῶν καὶ Χριστοῦ Ἰησοῦ τῆς ἐλπίδος ἡμῶν

In the very forefront of this missive to his trusty aide-de-camp, Paul inscribes his official title, in token of the authoritative nature of his message. Though addressed to Timothy in the first instance, it contains not a few intimations of a wider reference; and the writer, by thus assuming, so to speak, his robes of office at the outset, prepares his readers for a document of public rather than private destination. When furthermore he subjoins the clause, *according to God's behest*, a phrase which recurs in Rom. xvi. 26 and Tit. i. 3, he enforces the immediacy of his divine commission in the clearest terms. Inscriptional data show that κατ᾽ ἐπιταγήν was in use as a recognized formula, not unlike our heading on official notices, *by order of* so and so.

An attempt has been made of late to minimize the vocation of apostleship by construing the word etymologically, as nearly equivalent to *missionary*. The fact that in certain New Testament passages such as Phil. ii. 25, II Cor. viii. 23, it bears the sense of *envoy* lends a degree of plausibility to this assumption. But the entire tenor of the New Testament conflicts with any theory that tends to disband 'the glorious company of the apostles', properly so called. Obviously the Twelve ranked apart from the rest of the disciples. Even Lightfoot allows too much weight to the circumstance that Luke bestows the title of apostle on Barnabas and Paul alike (Acts xiv. 14). But is not that because at the moment he is regarding them as delegates from the church of Antioch, sent forth on a specific errand? The more restricted meaning of the term cannot be gainsaid. It was because of its implicit speciality that St Paul asserts his right to the title so vehemently. His apostolate was in fact challenged because it constituted him a supreme dignitary in the Church, invested with a special mandate and accredited by special qualifications. An apostle in this acceptation was of necessity an eyewitness to his risen Lord (I Cor. ix. 1), one ordained by Him to be an umpire and upbuilder of the infant Church, and in his official capacity an unerring exponent of the mind of Christ (Gal. i. 11, 12; I Cor. ii. 16; Jn. iv. 6), among whose credentials miraculous signs must have a place (II Cor. xii. 12). Nor was his province confined to anything like a diocesan sphere (Rom. i. 5; II Cor. x. 13). The apostles were oecumenical foundation-layers, unique 'master-builders', and as such left no lineal successors.[1]

Note that the Father is here styled *God our Saviour*, as in the Magnificat and in Jude's doxology. Assailants of the genuineness of the Pastoral Epistles discover in that appellation an un-Pauline usage. But the 'God of our salvation' is an Old Testament title and the very expression excepted to occurs in the LXX text (e.g. Dt. xxxii. 15). Moreover, a ground for its adoption nearer at hand suggests itself in the cult of Nero as σωτὴρ τῆς οἰκουμένης to which Deissmann has drawn pointed attention (*Light from the Ancient East*, p. 364). How suitable the transference of the function falsely ascribed to the Roman Emperor to Him in whom 'we live and move and have our being'! In any case the glory of salvation in a far profounder sense belongs to the Father who sends as well as to the Son who is sent. In Titus we find the ascriptions interchanged.

Accordingly the apostle proceeds to conjoin the Father and Son indissolubly as co-ordinate sources of his own deputed authority: no slender proof of his conviction of the deity of Christ, especially when we reflect that the statement comes from a monotheist to his finger-tips like this Hebrew of the Hebrews. The designation *Christ our hope* enhances the impression; for not only had the Psalmist in the LXX version of Ps. lxv. 5 apostrophized Jehovah as both σωτὴρ ἡμῶν and ἐλπὶς τῶν περάτων τῆς γῆς, but Jeremiah had invoked Him twice (xiv. 8, xvii. 13) as the 'Hope of Israel'. Paul himself elsewhere applies that phrase to the Messiah (Acts xxviii. 20) and names Him the 'Hope of glory' (Col. i. 27). Rome itself contained many temples dedicated to *Spes*, and that fact would give additional point to the title, which Ignatius borrows (*ad Trall.* 2) from this passage. The argument is developed in Warfield's *Biblical Doctrines*, p. 213.

---

[1] We have in them interpreters of God's revelation, who 'had a special vocation to display the central genius of the gospel by a new departure germinal for all Christian time' (Forsyth).

i. 2a. Τιμοθέῳ γνησίῳ τέκνῳ ἐν πίστει·

χαίρειν may be supplied; but its omission tallies with common usage. γνήσιος=*genuine, true-born.* M. & M. incline to a vaguer meaning; but both Philo and Longinus contrast the epithet with νόθος and Appian (*B.C.* iii *sub fin.*) with a case of adoption. τέκνον strikes a caressing note, peculiarly fitting from an elder to a younger man whom he loves dearly. So both the papyri and Marcus Aurelius (xi. 18) use it. ἐν πίστει seems to be attached to τέκνῳ. The thought of concord in faith may colour the phraseology; but we agree with Alford in the rendering 'child in the faith'. The suppression of the article after a preposition need cause no difficulty; indeed, in this whole superscription every article save one, as not uncommonly, is omitted; and we shall meet with other examples of πίστις employed in an objective sense. Faith, the watchword of Christianity, may well become one of its synonyms.

i. 2b. χάρις ἔλεος εἰρήνη ἀπὸ θεοῦ πατρὸς καὶ Χριστοῦ Ἰησοῦ τοῦ κυρίου ἡμῶν.

The greeting itself requires little comment. Again the Father and the Son are united in the invocation as co-equal Agents, and the only peculiarity consists in the insertion of the noun *mercy* between the customary *grace and peace*, as in II John 3. That sounds a tender chord, suggested possibly by Timothy's fragile health. A copyist would have surely avoided such a deviation from precedent, which does not occur in the preface to Titus.

i. 3–7. EPITOME OF TIMOTHY'S INSTRUCTIONS

i. 3a. καθὼς παρεκάλεσά σε προσμεῖναι ἐν Ἐφέσῳ πορευόμενος εἰς Μακεδονίαν,

This sentence presents us with a characteristic specimen of Paul's *anacolutha*, in which the thought, through its rapid development, loses touch with its initial clause. The R.V., like the A.V., supplies the missing correlative by a *so I do now*, or *so do*. Others would insert, *so I write*. The verb παρακαλεῖν, a favourite with St Paul, may signify 'to exhort', as it does in ii. 1, but is more probably used here in the sense of *request*. προσμεῖναι=*to stay on* (Plut. *Ant.* 53). There are hints in these Epistles that Timothy was loth to be parted from him, or to serve as his deputy at Ephesus. πορευόμενος needs careful translation. *As I was en route for Macedonia* would be our version (cf. Lk. xiv. 31), for it is important to note that Paul does not specify his starting-point. At first sight one is disposed to conclude, with the majority of expositors, that it was Ephesus; and on that supposition other suppositions have been reared. Entire theories of the pre-Roman date of this letter have been based on these grounds. But even if we interpret Paul's statement to the Ephesian elders (Acts xx. 25) that he 'should see their face no more' with the strictest literality, we possess no conclusive evidence that Paul had re-entered the city when the Pastorals were written. A passage in II Timothy (iv. 20) suggests that Miletus formed his definitive terminus in that region. It is conceivable that he was suffered to depart unmolested after the famous uproar, on the stipulation that he would not again set foot in the city of Artemis. Be that as it may, the journey here alluded to cannot coincide with any recorded in Acts; for the condition of affairs has altogether changed since then and the details differ materially.

i. 3 b, 4 a. *ἵνα παραγγείλῃς τισὶ μὴ ἑτεροδιδασκαλεῖν μηδὲ προσέχειν μύθοις καὶ γενεαλογίαις ἀπεράντοις,*

Timothy himself is now past his novitiate and invested with responsible authority. παραγγέλλειν is a word of command, and such a tone Timothy is commissioned to assume. Decisive action on his part was imperative, for an insubordinate faction was manifestly encroaching on recognized standards of the Church's doctrine. Paul here charges it with the offence he calls ἑτεροδιδασκαλεῖν, an ἅπαξ εἰρημένον, *teaching amiss*. The compound is quite in his manner, parallel with ἑτεροζυγεῖν in II Cor. vi. 14 and well illustrated by the ἑτεροσεβεῖν of Vettius Valens (184, 5). ἀπεραντολογία is a Ciceronian phrase (*Att.* xii. 9) for endless jabber. A pattern of sound teaching already subsists and must not be displaced by idle vapourings. Obviously, these 'troublers of Israel' ranked as accredited διδάσκαλοι who were slighting the gospel and addicting themselves to puerilities devoid of edification. They toyed by preference with legendary lore and interminable pedigrees, wherein their allegorizing bias detected all manner of mysteries. Readers of Philo will be at no loss to gauge the methods of these puzzle-brains.

Many have understood the genealogies referred to as pertaining to semi-Gnostical theories of aeons and emanations. That view is espoused by Bengel and Alford among others and was held by Irenaeus and Tertullian. But it must be borne in mind that these Fathers stood face to face with current fabulizings of that stamp. Indeed the late date of the Epistle has been inferred from this very passage, thus interpreted. But a comparison with Tit. i. 14, iii. 9 warrants the opinion that the apostle's strictures concern a Judaizing circle whose affinities lay with the Rabbinical *haggadoth* and their anile fables (iv. 7), which are censured rather as trivial than traitorous.[1] So he adds,

i. 4b. αἵτινες ἐκζητήσεις παρέχουσιν μᾶλλον ἢ οἰκονομίαν θεοῦ τὴν ἐν πίστει.

αἵτινες (*quippe quae*) gives a reason for the rebuke incurred. They promote cavillings, not God's ordinance of intelligent faith. The unique ἐκζήτησις (T.R. ζήτησις) found only in the verbal form in the rhetorician Aristides and the papyri outside the LXX and the New Testament, recalls the archaic English vocable *quiddities*. The other variant reading in this verse, οἰκοδομίαν, has a captivating air, but somewhat slender uncial confirmation. The critical reading is more difficult. The sense may be *stewardship* as in the tractates of Xenophon and Philodemus περὶ οἰκονομίας (cf. I Cor. ix. 17). But the term can cover administration in general (Plut. *Mor.* 1050) like its English derivative. The divine dispensation of truth does not beget fable-spinning but faith. True religion is not a 'notional' pastime, intent on antiquarian lore, but a mighty moral and spiritual dynamic, instinct with affiance in God our Saviour (verse 1). By faith we stand, not by weaving webs of whimsical fancies.

i. 5. τὸ δὲ τέλος τῆς παραγγελίας ἐστὶν ἀγάπη ἐκ καθαρᾶς καρδίας καὶ συνειδήσεως ἀγαθῆς καὶ πίστεως ἀνυποκρίτου,

παραγγελία, *injunction*, echoes the verb in verse 3. We have already been told that the gospel is God's commandment; and Paul now adds that its design is to set the graces of love and faith, so conspicuously

---

[1] Wetstein suggests that Timothy's own genealogy was one cause of wrangling. A Jewish mother's son might be argued to lie within the pale of Jewish obligations (cf. Acts xvi. 3).

lacking in these wordmongers, in the front rank. Without them no Christian teaching can be valid. It was not so much the mentality of these sophisters as their spirit that was at fault. The soil in which love flourishes is a renewed nature, indwelt by the Holy Ghost, with sterling faith for its root and devout affection for its fruitage. *Fundamentum fides, finis amor* (Bengel).

Another line of exegesis takes the passage to refer to the Law, which these sticklers for its value misconstrued entirely. Its purpose was not to lend itself to their wire-drawn subtleties, but to promote that love to God and man which constitutes its real fulfilment and is the highest employment of human nature. Rightly viewed, the Law subserves higher ends than itself; for as the Italian proverb runs, *amor regge senza legge*. But παραγγελία (cf. *infra* verse 18), is not the proper term for the legal statute-book. Notice how the phrase *a good conscience* embraces the broader contents that the term acquires in Christian terminology.

i. 6, 7. ὧν τινες ἀστοχήσαντες ἐξετράπησαν εἰς ματαιολογίαν, θέλοντες εἶναι νομοδιδάσκαλοι, μὴ νοοῦντες μήτε ἃ λέγουσιν μήτε περὶ τίνων διαβεβαιοῦνται.

It is clear that these vapourers affected the repute of specialists in regard to the Mosaic code. Luke invests the word νομοδιδάσκαλος with honourable associations when he applies it to Gamaliel. Accordingly Paul hastens to deny the justness of their pretensions to the title. These whipper-snappers have an exchequer of words, but no fund of insight. They are what Philo styles 'syllable-squabblers', whose most confident dogmatisms are mere wills-of-the-wisp. Experts in name, they are sciolists in reality.

ὧν refers to the factors of spiritual love previously specified. τίς interrogative, as often in later Greek, ousts the relative in the final clause, where the characteristic Hellenistic verb διαβεβαιοῦσθαι, *to dogmatize*, makes its appearance. ἀστοχεῖν is another similar formation, replacing ἁμαρτάνειν (='missing the mark'), in proportion as the latter verb acquired an ethical significance. Thus Plutarch uses ἀστοχεῖν τοῦ πρέποντος (*Mor.* 414, *Galb.* 16). ἐκτροπή=*bypath* in Diodorus Siculus and ἐκτράπελος=*perverse*; so that ἐκτρέπεσθαι (Plut., Polyb., Epict.) pictures a swerving from the track of faithful discipleship to ματαιολογία, *babblement*, another post-classical formation cognate with the Latin *vaniloquentia*, extant in Plutarch and Vettius Valens. These fumblers were on a false trail. The quest of recondite subtleties and tortuous rigmaroles had greater charms in their eyes than the sublime themes of vital Christianity. Their lenses were out of focus, their perspective false and erratic.

i. 8–11. THE USE AND ABUSE OF THE LAW

i. 8.   οἴδαμεν δὲ ὅτι καλὸς ὁ νόμος ἐάν τις αὐτῷ νομίμως χρῆται,

The apostle grants the Law its due function. 'We know'—a Paulinism again—'that the Law is excellent, if one use it *lawfully*'. This play on words is eminently characteristic. νομίμως, as in Plut. *Alex.* 59, plainly means *in a legitimate way*, and the context shows that the reference is to the Hebrew *Torah*. Paul always distinguished its proper use from its abuse. By the Law comes consciousness of sin (Rom. vii. 7). Its sentence upon transgressors cleaves a chasm between the righteous and the unrighteous which abides, as far as it is concerned, unbridged. 'Law can discover sin, but not remove' (Milton).

i. 9a.   εἰδὼς τοῦτο, ὅτι δικαίῳ νόμος οὐ κεῖται,

The apostle proceeds to elucidate his own proposition. He begins by laying down the principle that the Law is not *instituted* or *enacted* for the righteous man (cf. Ps. cxix. 3). κεῖμαι furnishes a passive for τίθημι (cf. Phil. i. 16). The *dativus commodi* is very Pauline (Blass). Despite the absence of articles we do not take this statement for a generalization as in the iambic ὁ μηδὲν ἀδικῶν οὐδένος δεῖται νόμου quoted from Menander. The attempt made by many to differentiate between νόμος and ὁ νόμος in the Epistles breaks down upon examination. νόμος belongs to the class of anarthrous nouns represented by one signal example (cf. Winer xix. 1). For though the Law may doubtless be viewed as the guardian of innocence, its main business lies with the criminal class in the community. It curbs their vicious propensities and visits their trespasses with penal sanctions. Uprightness can dispense with its precautionary barricades. 'The law of love is a higher form of the law of obedience.' Unfallen Adam required no decalogue of prohibitions; he was the custodian of his own virtue, trusted to obey of his own accord, without coercion, moral or physical. The golden age of paganism was drawn in similar colours by Ovid and Tacitus. Not the saint as such, but the sinner, is the Law's target; its aim to bring the wrongdoer to book. This good citizen is not daunted by its danger-signals; for he fulfils its requisitions spontaneously, as Plutarch has remarked (*Mor.* 745). Calvin quotes the scholastic aphorism: *e malis moribus nascuntur bonae leges*, and points out that Paul is not (as some have supposed) formally discussing the Law's office, but noticing one aspect of it in passing. The noblest law is the law of the spirit of life (Rom. viii. 2), the perfect law that of liberty.

i. 9b, 10. ἀνόμοις δὲ καὶ ἀνυποτάκτοις, ἀσεβέσιν καὶ ἁμαρτωλοῖς, ἀνοσίοις καὶ βεβήλοις, πατρολῴαις καὶ μητρολῴαις, ἀνδροφόνοις πόρνοις ἀρσενοκοίταις ἀνδραποδισταῖς ψεύσταις ἐπιόρκοις καὶ εἴ τι ἕτερον τῇ ὑγιαινούσῃ διδασκαλίᾳ ἀντίκειται,

Enumerations are among Paul's literary hallmarks. We have here a typical sample, and have noted several others in our Introduction. No student of his can forget the tremendous list of pagan vices rehearsed in Rom. i. The negative prefixes of many of these offences themselves confirm the argument in hand. We see the Law's eagle eye fastening on the law-contemners, on the refractory, on the impious, and the profane. Probably πατρολῷαι and μητρολῷαι signify not parricides, but smiters of fathers and mothers, adjudged a capital crime in Ex. xxi. 15; for the root ἀλοᾶν means 'to cudgel' (cf. Plato, *Laws*, 881, Aristoph., *Clouds*, 911, and cf. the ambiguity of the Latin *caedere*). ἀνδροφόνος means *homicide*.

ἀντίκειται may be rendered *contravenes*. Bengel deems that the word echoes κεῖται above; but the assonance seems undesigned. As Lock notes, the list is based on the Decalogue itself.

Those who dispute the Pauline original of the Pastoral Epistles regard the repeated occurrence of ὑγιής, ὑγιαίνειν in a metaphorical sense—an innovation in the apostle's diction—as a suspicious feature. But their ethical employment was quite familiar to Greek thought. Not only Thucydides and Plato, but Plutarch and Philo and Palestinian writers like Josephus and Philodemus exemplify it. Paul's own recourse to the figure may moreover be a vestige of Lucan fellowship or traceable to recent absorption of Roman influences, in view of the analogous use of *sanus* and *sanitas*. Having met with a serviceable phrase, it is the apostle's manner to impress it on his readers by reiteration. διδασκαλία recurs naturally in the Pastorals, which are filled with *instructions*.

i. 11. κατὰ τὸ εὐαγγέλιον τῆς δόξης τοῦ μακαρίου θεοῦ, ὃ ἐπιστεύθην ἐγώ.

A note of apostolic authority sounds in this extension of the sentence. Paul's explanation of the office of the Law is no conclusion of his own, but the testimony of its divine Ordainer, whose gospel sheds light on the elder dispensation and unriddles its enigmas. Romans has already taught how the Law works as an unmasker of sin, and how the Christian is not under its suzerainty, but wedded to Christ. The children of the freewoman do not slave in the house of bondage; they are the Lord's freedmen. A 'glory that excelleth' such as could never light up the dusky sphere of condemnation illumines that sunlit economy with which Paul has been put in trust. The Authorized Version, 'the glorious gospel', traceable to Luther's *herrliches Evangelium*, rests on the baseless assumption that the phrase τὸ εὐαγγέλιον τῆς δόξης reproduces an Hebraism. But what the writer celebrates here is τὰ μεγαλεῖα τοῦ θεοῦ (Acts ii. 11), the glory of God everblessed, so radiantly reflected in the gospel. Philo likewise entitled God μακάριος. ἐγώ is emphatic. Paul thrills with joy at the thought of his high commission of proclaiming a gospel so ablaze with the divine perfections. The idiomatic use of πιστεύεσθαι with accusative case is peculiarly Pauline, and can be paralleled from Josephus and Galen (Deissmann, *Light from the Ancient East*, p. 374). It may also be found in Vettius Valens (pp. 65, 168, 333). The last-named example, βασιλέως πράγματα πιστεύονται, would serve as no inapt description of the mandate of the apostolical college.

i. 12–16. THE GRANDER MINISTRY OF THE GOSPEL, MIRRORED IN HIS OWN BIOGRAPHY

Saul of Tarsus never fails to catch fire at the mention of the gospel of the grace of God. The personal digression that follows gives vent to an involuntary outburst of gratitude and wonderment at the privilege bestowed on such an arch-rebel as himself of preaching the unsearchable riches of Christ.

i. 12. χάριν ἔχω τῷ ἐνδυναμώσαντί με Χριστῷ Ἰησοῦ τῷ κυρίῳ ἡμῶν, ὅτι πιστόν με ἡγήσατο θέμενος εἰς διακονίαν,

χάριν ἔχω replaces the more usual εὐχαριστῶ, possibly adopted elsewhere to avoid confusion with the Christian glorification of χάρις. ἐνδυναμοῦν (LXX) may be termed one of Paul's favourite expressions, found (for example) in the corresponding but abbreviated utterance in Phil. iv. 13, where the true sense ought to be preserved by translating the verb 'my Enabler (Christ)'. Mark how the apostle here gives His full imperial title to his Master. Some construe the complement πιστός believing, but it is more naturally rendered trustworthy. Paul's was an eminently sincere character, as he is about to remind us. In his Pharisaical role he had firmly believed that he was doing God service in harrying the Church; and when he became a Christian, he put his hand to the gospel plough with staunch resolution, girding up his loins to drive a rectilinear furrow through the stubbornest of soils. Notice too with what humility he picks out the most unpretentious word, διακονία, to designate his ministry; no slight token this of his authorship, for he alone of the apostles terms his life-work by preference a *ministry*, as in II Cor. iv. 1, and the ambiguity arising from the other current meaning of *deaconship* would have deterred any fabricator from adopting it. No fervent admirer would have chosen such a word as descriptive of Paul's lofty vocation. Still less likely would a personator have been to subjoin

i. 13a. τὸ πρότερον ὄντα βλάσφημον καὶ διώκτην καὶ ὑβριστήν·

This is the language of self-accusation and self-upbraiding. The term *blasphemer* must be understood in its gravest acceptation; for he had heaped reproach on the name of Jesus (Acts xxvi. 11) in those benighted days, over which he now groans. διώκτης, meaning *persecutor*, appears to be a coinage of his own, kept in countenance by the LXX ἐργοδιώκτης for 'taskmaster' (Ex. iii. 7); and the fondness of Paul for the verb διώκειν in his Epistles renders the formation strictly in character. To complete the forbidding portraiture he adds the substantive ὑβριστής as of one arrogant, overbearing, blustering, applied to Philip by Demosthenes (*Olynth.* i. 23), descriptive of an Old Testament 'scorner'. So mighty had been the change wrought in him that we scarcely recognize this self-drawn sketch of one who went to the utmost lengths in antagonism to Jesus.

i. 13 b. ἀλλὰ ἠλεήθην ὅτι ἀγνοῶν ἐποίησα ἐν ἀπιστίᾳ,

'Yet mercy was shown me (I was *bemercied*—Thomas Goodwin) because I acted ignorantly.' The sentiment bespeaks one who could never forget the arresting arm laid upon his frenzy of blind zeal. And he singles out that blindness as a ground of the forbearance he had experienced. For, though all alike are guilty before God, men's deeds are weighed, and degrees of guilt gauged, in scales of unerring equity by the Most High. The record teaches us that sins of ignorance are more capable of pardon than sins against knowledge, committed by one conscious of his wrongdoing, yet resolved to have his way at all costs (cf. Lk. xxiii. 34). At least he had not been a trickster or hypocrite. Paul is not pleading unbelief in bar of sentence, but in order to acclaim the signal clemency accorded him in spite of his fond zealotry for Judaism. Palliations do not exculpate culprits, nor sheathe the sword of justice, nor does the plea of sincerity wipe out a multitude of sins.

i. 14. ὑπερεπλεόνασεν δὲ ἡ χάρις τοῦ κυρίου ἡμῶν μετὰ πίστεως καὶ ἀγάπης τῆς ἐν Χριστῷ Ἰησοῦ.

A reign of grace alone can account for his non-exception from amnesty. Compounds with ὑπέρ are one of the apostle's specialities, albeit this rare word occurs in Vettius Valens (85). Like Bunyan, 'grace abounding' had stopped him in his mad career, and a new spirit of faith and love (Eph. vi. 23) replaced scornful malevolence. Here was a crucial instance not of law-work, but of what a vision of Christ as Saviour and Lord could accomplish, *Paulinizing* Saul once for all.

i. 15. πιστὸς ὁ λόγος καὶ πάσης ἀποδοχῆς ἄξιος ὅτι Χριστὸς Ἰησοῦς ἦλθεν εἰς τὸν κόσμον ἁμαρτωλοὺς σῶσαι· ὧν πρῶτός εἰμι ἐγώ·

The novel formula, *a faithful saying*, recurs five times in the Pastorals to lend emphasis to salient statements. Wetstein finds it also in Arrian and Dion. Halicarnassus. Opponents of the genuineness of these documents set this among their non-Pauline features. We see no good reason for that assumption. What hinders us from postulating a cluster of λόγοι πνευματικοί as by this time in circulation, on certain of which Paul places his imprimatur? The prefatory πιστός meets us in his earlier Epistles. Thrice in Corinthians (I Cor. i. 9, x. 13; II Cor. i. 18) we find the phrase πιστὸς ὁ θεός repeated, and πιστὸς ὁ κύριος in II Thes. iii. 3. In fact, this adjective, occurring no less than seventeen times in the Pastorals, may be reckoned as their veritable keyword. A call to fidelity is their chief burden. ἀποδοχῆς ἄξιος, a Polybian expression, common in papyri, became a regular formulary in the Koiné, and we come across the noun ἀξιοπιστία in Philodemus. Field traces its use also in Diodorus Siculus.

This passage breathes the very soul of the gospel. It presumes a message not merely of salvability, but of achieved salvation; and the mention of the Lord's 'coming into the world' not only witnesses to His pre-existence, but has a Johannine ring which may intimate the source of this saying, cited by the writer rather than his own. Both extremes of sinnership and saintship met in his single person, and we gain a glimpse into Paul's inmost soul when we hear him exclaim (notice the order), *chiefest of whom am I*; for he still ranks as a sinner, 'not already perfect'.[1] Tenacious of his rightful claims, he yet feels himself the least of all saints, with the stain of an inquisitor discolouring his chequered past. Rabbi Duncan observes: 'If there is any word of Christ I should be inclined to deprecate, it would be if I heard Him say, Well done, good and faithful servant!' Yet there is another side to this matter, as we have seen in verse 12 and shall see in II Tim. iv. 8.

i. 16. ἀλλὰ διὰ τοῦτο ἠλεήθην, ἵνα ἐν ἐμοὶ πρώτῳ ἐνδείξηται Ἰησοῦς Χριστὸς τὴν ἅπασαν μακροθυμίαν πρὸς ὑποτύπωσιν τῶν μελλόντων πιστεύειν ἐπ' αὐτῷ εἰς ζωὴν αἰώνιον.

Here we have the humanity of Jesus marked by the reversed order of His name. Why had such superlative loving-kindness been shown him? His reply is, to encourage the deepest dyed sinners to put their trust in Immanuel. He was sensible that his own provocations had been on the greatest scale, so that he might well have been left to work out his perdition unchecked. But the Lord had Himself laid hold of this ring-leader in revolt against Him to display the utmost riches of His grace. A precedent for the pardon of arch-offenders was set when such a

[1] So Luther: 'Christ saves to the uttermost, which uttermost Martin Luther is.'

prototype was saved. πρώτῳ may mean *signally* or *to begin with*. The latter seems to be the correct exegesis, because Paul dwells on the influence of his transformation on future centuries. If a persecutor like Saul of Tarsus could be freely forgiven and favoured, so might other flagrant culprits be. In view of longsuffering at its acme (τὴν ἅπασαν) shown in his own case, none need despair. μακροθυμία is a sample of literary Hellenistic. It occurs first in Menander (*Fr.* 549) and has a place in Plutarch's vocabulary. According to Parry, who quotes Galen as his voucher, ὑποτύπωσις signifies an 'outline sketch', cf. Aristotle's use of the verb ὑποτυποῦν, and the locution ὡς ἐν ὑποτυπώσει, recurrent in Sextus Empiricus. This sense accords well with its employment in II Tim. i. 13. Only one ground of demur presents itself. Quintilian (*Inst.* iv. 2. 3, ix. 2. 40) assigns a different meaning to the expression, that of a *word-picture*, which suits best of all in this context, to our thinking.[1] Observe how the possession of eternal life hinges on faith in the Redeemer. πιστεύειν ἐπί (with the dative) is a phrase of somewhat rare occurrence in the New Testament, used twice, however, in Romans (ix. 33, x. 11). It sets Christ forth as the bedrock of saving faith, its essential *fundus*, or base-line.

i. 17. DOXOLOGY

The apostle's soul is thrilled at the remembrance of such grace abounding, and an irresistible impulse prompts him to break forth into a thanksgiving to the Father of mercies. Who cannot trace Paul's hand here? Peter twice inserts doxologies midway in his discourse; but the practice belongs distinctively to the apostle of the Gentiles, and well does it tally with his spirit of fervent adoration.

i. 17. τῷ δὲ βασιλεῖ τῶν αἰώνων, ἀφθάρτῳ, ἀοράτῳ, μόνῳ θεῷ, τιμὴ καὶ δόξα εἰς τοὺς αἰῶνας τῶν αἰώνων· ἀμήν.

The striking phrase *King of the Ages*, founded on Ps. cxlv. 13, was already current in Jewish circles for it may be seen in Tobit xiii. 6, 10. But for solemnity of effect the stately Authorized Version procession

---

[1] His words are: *proposita quaedam forma rerum ita expressa verbis ut cerni potius videatur quam videri.* He is dealing, of course, with terms of rhetoric in particular. Cf. German *Schilderung.*

of epithets, *eternal, immortal, invisible,* cannot be bettered. ἄφθαρτος, in its highest application, is one of these privative compounds in which the positive element swallows up the negative. To the Tarsian philosopher Antipatros it connotes imperishability (Plut. *Mor.* 1052). μόνῳ θεῷ, *God alone,* fitly closes the diapason of praise. σοφῷ (T.R.) lacks uncial support, and seems interpolated from Rom. xvi. 27, where the critical text retains it. The *ages of the ages* expresses eternity in Hebraistic terms, blended with Paul's earliest religious associations.

i. 18–20. A PERSONAL CHARGE

i. 18. ταύτην τὴν παραγγελίαν παρατίθεμαί σοι, τέκνον Τιμόθεε, κατὰ τὰς προαγούσας ἐπὶ σὲ προφητείας, ἵνα στρατεύῃ ἐν αὐταῖς τὴν καλὴν στρατείαν,

The apostle reverts to the main purpose of his letter after a most characteristic digression, casting a glance backward to verses 3 and 5. παρατίθεμαι represents the verbal form of παραθήκη, which we shall meet later on, and may be translated *consign,* whilst προάγων in an intransitive sense recalls Latin *praecedens.* Timothy's mission has received the ratification of the Spirit no less than did that of Barnabas and Paul, for explicit predictions concerning him seem to have been affixed as seals on his ordination to the ministry. In fact, Hort translates 'predictions leading up to thee'. These tokens not only served to place his election to a divinely planned career beyond dispute, but also to incite a somewhat diffident nature to steadfast perseverance. ἐν αὐταῖς is a trifle obscure. Perhaps we may construe it *therewith,* leaving the reader to fix its reference; for to find in it, as some do, an image of the armour in which Timothy was to be accoutred seems finical.

The military note, at any rate, furnishes one more indication of Paul's hand. As Calvin puts it, his *alumnus* is to count himself an *antesignanus, sub Dei auspiciis militans,* a swordsman in the best of causes, in which the only reason for solicitude is lest he should fail to play the man of God. Let him not sink beneath the grandeur of the holy warfare he is called to wage. The thought that the Lord had drawn the outline of his career beforehand should inspire him to fill it in. στρατείαν στρατεύειν or στρατεύεσθαι was a technical phrase.

i. 19. ἔχων πίστιν καὶ ἀγαθὴν συνείδησιν, ἥν τινες ἀπωσάμενοι περὶ τὴν πίστιν ἐναυάγησαν·

In contrast with ἀπωσάμενοι, which implies *discarding*, ἔχων must be used in the sense of *holding fast*, in fact equivalent to the archaic ἴσχων, not extant in the New Testament. *Faith and a good conscience* embrace both doctrine and practice, and the surrender of the one may be either cause or effect of the cession of the other. 'Be sure of thy panoply, Timothy', we hear the veteran cry; 'thou art not out of the enemy's range, nor proof in thyself against his strategy. Others have made shipwreck in thy neighbourhood; therefore, look to thy tackling.' Faith is the overcoming grace, and a sensitive conscience will tamper with nothing lax or doubtful. Paul had witnessed many a downfall traceable to heedless walking. So he warns his *protégé* lovingly, not as one in hazard of relapse at the moment, but because soldiership demands unslacked vigilance.

The metaphor of shipwreck pertains to literary Hellenistic (cf. Latin *naufragus*). Polybius and Arrian employ it, and so do Lucian (*Paras.* 8), Philo, Cebes and Philodemus (*de Vita*, 33). περί with accusative here = Latin *circa*.

i. 20. ὧν ἐστιν Ὑμέναιος καὶ Ἀλέξανδρος, οὓς παρέδωκα τῷ Σατανᾷ, ἵνα παιδευθῶσιν μὴ βλασφημεῖν.

To point the admonition two recent instances of backsliding are adduced. Hymenaeus is stigmatized in II Tim. ii. 17 as holding false views of the resurrection; and some German critics, like De Wette, have insisted that the charge there made must have preceded the excommunication of this passage; but that heresy may have been a fresh lapse on his part. Alexander was so common a name that it would be rash to identify him with the coppersmith of II Tim. iv. 14, and still more with the Alexander of Acts xix. 33. Like other *sodalitates*, the Church possesses an inherent right of exercising discipline on scandalous offenders in her ranks, and of expelling them, on sufficient grounds, from her communion. For the sake of her own purity and peace and of her Lord's honour, that authority has been lodged in her custody, and her definitive sentence—*clave non errante*—receives divine endorsement (Mt. xviii. 18). Whether the 'delivery to Satan' here

alluded to covers more than a solemn suspension from Christian fellowship remains uncertain. The case of the Corinthian offender favours a
negative conclusion. Yet we know from the histories of Ananias and
Bar-Jesus in Acts that physical debilities were sometimes incurred by
flouters of apostolical authority. Even that measure, however, except
in final judgments, might be not a sentence of reprobation, but a
sifting process. The gates of mercy were not shut against such delinquents, nor place of repentance denied them, as among the Novatians
of later days. παιδεύεσθαι implies an element of castigation, cf.
II Cor. vi. 9 (*gezüchtiget* is Luther's translation); but the discipline was
meant to heal the distemper, and where possible, promote convales-
cence. 'Excommunication', says John Milton, 'is a kind of saving by
undoing.' Hierarchical bannings, enforced by civil penalties, as
practised by the Romish Church and her congeners, constitute one of
the vilest perversions of a Scriptural institution conceivable.

ii. 1–8. PRAYER FOR THE PUBLIC WELFARE AND ITS GOSPEL GROUND

The writer now advances from his general charge to specific regulations, first of all, those that concern divine worship. There may have
been some suspense of judgment among the Ephesian church-members
concerning the range of their public prayers; and the apostle selects for
notice the topic of supplication for the outside world. There have
always been Christians so preoccupied with their own circumscribed
sphere of interests that their intercessions have tended to confine themselves within a narrow radius. But Paul was a great spiritual statesman,
whose full-orbed vision extended far and wide. His primary injunction
enforces catholicity of outlook. Enumerating, after his manner, all
varieties of prayer, he prescribes that they should be offered for 'all
sorts and conditions of men'.

ii. 1. παρακαλῶ οὖν πρῶτον πάντων ποιεῖσθαι δεήσεις, προσευχάς,
ἐντεύξεις, εὐχαριστίας, ὑπὲρ πάντων ἀνθρώπων,

δεήσεις represents the species (*rogationes*) and προσευχαί the genus
(*precationes*), according to Calvin. ἐντεύξεις in Polybius represents
audiences of a more familiar kind (cf. Trench); but the evidence of the

papyri links the word rather with specific *petitions* or *intercedings*[1] whilst εὐχαριστίαι of course denotes *thanksgivings*. The visible Church sustains relations to the visible order, and must not isolate herself from the terrestrial nexus with which she is entwined, nor from her duty of interceding for the manifold members of the one human family.

ii. 2. ὑπὲρ βασιλέων καὶ πάντων τῶν ἐν ὑπεροχῇ ὄντων, ἵνα ἤρεμον καὶ ἡσύχιον βίον διάγωμεν ἐν πάσῃ εὐσεβείᾳ καὶ σεμνότητι.

From the era of Alexander, βασιλεύς had been the favourite title of rule, and both Josephus and the inscriptions apply it to the Roman Emperors. οἱ ἐν ὑπεροχῇ ὄντες reproduces a phrase of Aristotle (1211 a) for the *magistracy* or *authorities*, echoed in οἱ ὑπερέχοντες, 'their Excellencies', the phrase itself being used in Polyb. v. 44, Josephus and Vettius Valens (189, 197), much like the German *Obrigkeit*. ἤρεμος (i.e. *untroubled from without*), the late form of ἠρεμαῖος, can scarcely be paralleled except in Lucian. εὐσέβεια forms one of the novel words peculiar to these Epistles, though perfectly classical in usage and found repeatedly in II Peter. Perhaps St Paul's resort to it in his latest writings may be traced to the Roman circles in which he had been moving, where the Latin *pietas* was so perpetually harped upon. The same remark applies to the fresh vocable σεμνότης, which at once recalls the Latin *gravitas*, of paramount rank in every Roman inventory of virtues. It connotes *propriety* or *self-respect*, for Aristotle (1233) places it midway between self-will and complaisance, and Plutarch conjoins τὸ σεμνόν and πρέπον (*Mor.* 1140).

No Bible-taught Christian can dispute the efficacy of believing prayer in regard to public events and their supervisors. More things are wrought thereby than this world dreams of. The supplication of faithful intercessors for the common weal lays invisible restraint on the powers of darkness and their tools and brings reinforcement to honest rulers from the Governor among the nations (Ps. xxii. 28). Lack of prayer menaces national as well as individual welfare. Civil government may be grievously perverted, but divine sanction ratifies its right to exist. The exiled Jews were bidden to pray for the peace of Babylon as interwoven with their own (Je. xxix. 7); cf. Clem. *Ep. ad Corinth.* 59–61, Justin *Apol.* 31.

[1] See Deissmann, *Bible Studies*, pp. 121 ff.

ii. 3. τοῦτο γὰρ καλὸν καὶ ἀποδεκτὸν ἐνώπιον τοῦ σωτῆρος ἡμῶν θεοῦ,

γάρ, omitted in some texts, seems requisite to associate this verse with the preceding. It sets forth one chief reason for prayers of universal compass, their acceptability to heaven. Here we encounter the criterion of all true worship. Is it well pleasing in the Lord's sight, or is it a piece of will-worship of our own devising?

ἀποδεκτός (Latin *acceptus*) is a late formation of the higher *Koiné*, exemplified in Philodemus and Plutarch. The papyri supply instances of the prepositional ἐνώπιον which used to be classed as a Hebraism.

ii. 4. ὃς πάντας ἀνθρώπους θέλει σωθῆναι καὶ εἰς ἐπίγνωσιν ἀληθείας ἐλθεῖν.

This sentence marks an old battlefield between the followers of Calvin and Arminius, often hotly contested in the seventeenth century. Arminian exegetes have argued that the word *all* must be construed with the utmost latitude, and Calvinist expositors, in accord with Aug. *Enchir.* 203, have urged its undoubted use in an indefinite rather than universal sense, either inclusive of all classes of the concept in question, or certifying the catholicity of a dispensation freed from the trammels of Judaism. Others, jealous of universalistic inferences, have stressed the distinction between βούλεσθαι and θέλειν, between the 'love of benevolence' of the schools, the Lord's goodwill towards men (Ezk. xviii. 23), His unwillingness that any should perish, and His 'love of complacency', which belongs to the hidden secrets of Omniscience. It is not for us to reconcile the antinomy between divine sovereignty and human free agency. That abyss mocks our sounding-lines. Those, however, who firmly believe in the effectual sovereignty of the Most High will always shrink from the assumption that the issues of His redeeming course are suspended on the contingent pliancy or obstinacy of the rebels to whom salvation is tendered, or withdrawn from His entire control.

But there is another reading of the passage that calls for notice. σώζειν is one of those terms which Christianity has immensely enriched. To the ordinary Greek ear it conveyed the idea of *making safe* or *preserving*. Deissmann has dwelt on the employment of the term σωτήρ in references to the Ptolemies and Roman emperors. No doubt it was a popular form of adulation; yet in itself the title signified little more than 'Lord Protector'. Cicero remarks (*De Amicitia*): *Jovem Salutarem dicimus, quia salus hominum in eius tutela est.* Conservation is a constant meaning of the verb in Plutarch (cf. τὸ σωθῆναι, as here, *Brut.* 31). This weaker meaning receives due recognition in the New Testament. It occurs in Mt. xiv. 30; Jn. xi. 12, xii. 27; Acts xxvii *passim*, and in the LXX usage of *Soter* (Jdg. iii. 9; Ne. ix. 27). Lower down in this very Epistle (iv. 10) Paul styles God the Saviour of all men, specially of those that believe. And it *may* be so used in this verse. The ordination of prayer for rulers accords with the divine willingness that all men should be preserved from lawless misrule. What chiefly recommends this version is that it makes the ensuing clause, 'come to the recognition of the truth', fall into its proper place; for peaceful conditions give scope for the propagation of the gospel. If, on the other hand, spiritual salvation be understood, there is an *hysteron proteron*; for salvation is an intelligent transaction, the sequel of hearing and of the Spirit's enlightenment. Note that ἐπίγνωσις ἀληθείας is a phrase found in Epictetus (ii. 20).

ii. 5. εἷς γὰρ θεός, εἷς καὶ μεσίτης θεοῦ καὶ ἀνθρώπων, ἄνθρωπος Χριστὸς Ἰησοῦς,

The apostle now advances a solid argument for the cosmic scope of the gospel horizon, drawn from monotheistic premisses. The Fountain of mercies is one and the same for all, and Christ the sole medium of their bestowal. Paul will not allow that there is a God of the Jews or Gentiles *per se*, or that the knowledge of God's truth is an Israelitish perquisite, to be communicated with caution to Gentile proselytes. We know how cruelly this Hebrew parochialism had chafed his catholic spirit. As the best antidote to such exclusiveness, nursed sometimes by Judaized Gentiles, he proceeds to lay stress on the inclusive aspect of Christianity. For the Son of Man is the Head of a new race, the Mediator of a new covenant, our Fellow as well as God's Fellow, the unique Daysman who unites in His own Person the dissevered fractions of humanity, and reknits the sundered hemispheres of heaven and earth. Job's pathetic cry for an *internuntius* has been answered in Him who has 'extended a fraternal hand to us' (Calvin). That μεσίτης was a business term for *middleman* we learn from the papyri, but it had long been current to denote an intermediary of any sort. St Paul had already hailed his Lord in Galatians and Ephesians as the supreme Bond of Union, the Mediator *par excellence*. Nor was that all.

ii. 6. ὁ δοὺς ἑαυτὸν ἀντίλυτρον ὑπὲρ πάντων, τὸ μαρτύριον καιροῖς ἰδίοις·

The mediatorial work of the Son was an exhaustless source of grateful wonder to Saul of Tarsus, and he can never pass it by without an act of homage. Scanning the bright vision once more, he pens one of his indelible sentences, once heard, never forgotten; 'who gave Himself an ἀντίλυτρον for all'. He who was Heir of all things, whose was the wealth of all the worlds in space, has given to this strayed planet a treasure far grander than that, given *Himself*, the Gift unspeakable. Paul is looking at the outer, not the inner, circle of this intermediation; so he selects a peculiar expression to describe it, which has been strangely ignored by translators in general. Christ Himself has told us, in a memorable utterance, that He came to give His life λύτρον ἀντὶ πολλῶν (Mt. xx. 28). But ἀντίλυτρον—almost an ἅπαξ εἰρημένον[1]— intimates something more than that declaration. It signifies a *counter-ransom-price*, and fixes our gaze on the infinitude of the Offering. Of priceless jewels we say that they are 'worth a king's ransom'; but Christ crucified presents the ransom of the King of kings, a Sacrifice intrinsically illimitable, outweighing everything that can be placed in the counterscale. 'In Christ's finished work I see an ocean of merit; my plummet finds no bottom, my eye discovers no shore' (Spurgeon). That transcendent satisfaction for sin, as Rabbi Duncan boldly puts it, 'saves all who hear the gospel, except those who reject it'; but it is also the basis of God's longsuffering towards a world laden with iniquity. We may pray for respite and mercy to be shown to sinful men everywhere, because of the glorious propitiation of a divine Person (I Jn. ii. 2), 'not only on behalf of our sins, but on behalf of the whole world'. The divine purpose determines the application of redemption with the Calvinistic thinker; but all intelligent Calvinists readily grant that that persuasion of theirs does not transmute an infinite into a finite

[1] The verb ἀντιλυτροῦν occurs once in Aristotle (*Nic. Eth.* ix. 2) of setting ransom against ransom.

expiation. When Crassus invested Jerusalem on his march eastward, Josephus tells us (*Antiq.* xiv. 7) that the priest Eleazar proffered him a beam of solid gold from the temple to save its other contents from spoliation; his language is, τὴν δόκον λύτρον ἀντὶ πάντων ἔδωκεν. The golden beam was tendered as their adequate redemption-price. In a far nobler sense the Lord Jesus is the golden Ingot of the violated shrine of human nature, its perfect ἀνταλλαγή (*Epistle to Diognetus*), and His obedience unto death an ample indemnity for its forfeited status. 'The person of Christ', says Archbishop Leighton, 'is of more worth than all creatures; therefore His life was a full ransom for the greatest offender.' Thus Athanasius styles the Redeemer ὁ ἀντίψυχος ὑπὲρ πάντων.

The pregnant appositional clause, *the testimony for its appointed seasons*, condenses so much meaning into four brief vocables as to verge on obscurity. The hidden secret of the ages, τὸ μυστήριον τοῦ θεοῦ, concealed from prior generations, is now divulged to all and to be proclaimed from the housetops in this 'fulness of time'. It has a world-wide reference and the Church's prayers must take a corresponding sweep. The crowning message of revelation, redemption by the blood of the Lamb, must be published abroad as the supreme panacea for all the ills that flesh is heir to. 'Now is the day of salvation.' καιροὶ ἴδιοι is a phrase that occurs in Polybius (i. 30) for a chosen occasion. Cf. Is. lx. 22; Acts i. 7.

ii. 7. εἰς ὃ ἐτέθην ἐγὼ κῆρυξ καὶ ἀπόστολος, ἀλήθειαν λέγω, οὐ ψεύδομαι, διδάσκαλος ἐθνῶν ἐν πίστει καὶ ἀληθείᾳ.

At first blush this deposition wears a superfluous aspect. What need to certify Timothy so solemnly of his apostleship? What occasion to asseverate the fact in terms of a witness on oath? Our hypercritical friends allege that a pseudo-Paul is here mimicking Rom. ix. 1, where the same phraseology recurs. But these first impressions admit of revision. It is not for Timothy's sake, but that of his challengers that Paul asserts his vocation so vehemently. The old detraction may have waned by this time, but would always raise its crest anew wherever a knot of malcontents longed to resuscitate the fray. The strength of the affidavit reflects the soul of one who had fought his way to recognition, not without controversy and debate. A 'teacher of the Gentiles' was himself a proof of the universality of the embassage allotted him, and his favourite figure of an herald a fit emblem for a preacher of a gospel 'worthy of all acceptation'. We understand faith and truth here subjectively. He is making a disclaimer of all those sinister motives which his decriers pertinaciously imputed to him. Scornful gibes leave a self-respecting mind sensitive to the claims of vindication, not so much for his own as his Lord's honour, whose spokesman he is.

ii. 8. βούλομαι οὖν προσεύχεσθαι τοὺς ἄνδρας ἐν παντὶ τόπῳ ἐπαίροντας ὁσίους χεῖρας χωρὶς ὀργῆς καὶ διαλογισμοῦ.

βούλομαι, the strong verb for willing, may almost be rendered, *my sentence is*. Two main items in this pronouncement deserve notice. The more public supplication to which the context seems to restrict us is to be offered by *men* (τοὺς ἄνδρας), for reasons about to be detailed, *in every place*. ἐν παντὶ τόπῳ reproduces Mal. i. 11 (LXX), a Gentile prophecy of the latter days, but there may be an allusion to our Lord's statement (Jn. iv. 21) that the era of local sanctuaries was waning, and that any spot where believers meet in Christ's name may become an oratory provided the supplicants draw near with preparation of heart. The gesture here specified, unstudied and familiar to Hebrew worshippers, cannot be deemed obligatory. What does matter is that the hands lifted up should be unsullied (Ps. xxvi. 6) and the act divested of any element of carnal passion. Some render διαλογισμός *doubting*, a sense unrecognized by L. & S.; but that of *controversy* (cf. Phil. ii. 14), adopted by the Vulgate, suits best with *wrath*. However, the primary Platonic meaning of the word, *cogitation, reasoning*, is not excluded. It survives in Epictetus (*Enchir.* 24), and Plutarch (*Otho*, 9). We should have expected ὁσίας χεῖρας; yet even Plato writes (*Laws*, 831) πρᾶξις ὅσιος, and another adjective in -ιος takes only two terminations in the next verse.

ii. 9–15. THE CHRISTIAN WOMAN'S DEPORTMENT AND DEPARTMENT

The apostle now touches on another matter that required careful handling. It may have been submitted to his arbitrament by the Ephesian elders, and concerned feminine proprieties of action or attire, a topic of perennial recrudescence and dissonance of opinion.

ii. 9, 10. ὡσαύτως καὶ γυναῖκας ἐν καταστολῇ κοσμίῳ μετὰ αἰδοῦς καὶ σωφροσύνης κοσμεῖν ἑαυτάς, μὴ ἐν πλέγμασιν καὶ χρυσῷ ἢ μαργαρίταις ἢ ἱματισμῷ πολυτελεῖ, ἀλλ᾿ ὃ πρέπει γυναιξὶν ἐπαγγελλομέναις θεοσέβειαν, δι᾿ ἔργων ἀγαθῶν.

ὡσαύτως replaces the verb βούλομαι. καταστολή can signify *dress*; but usage favours the wider sense of demeanour, so that the entire phrase bespeaks a well-ordered carriage (cf. Epict. ii. 21; Joseph. *B.J.* ii. 8; Aristeas 284). The philosophical virtue σωφροσύνη answers fairly to *self-control*. So Cicero defines *temperantia* as *moderatio cupiditatum rationi oboediens* (*De Fin.* ii). Perhaps *sobriety of mind* represents it still better. πλέγματα here means *braided hair*. ἱματισμός suggests sumptuous array, as Trench has noted. In one passage (*Mor.* 218) Plutarch couples it with this very epithet πολυτελής. The word appears in the papyri of a bride's *trousseau*, which would imply a complete outfit.

ἐπαγγέλλεσθαι is Attic Greek for *making pretension to*. Augustine remarks (*Enchir.* 99) that θεοσέβεια, another classical term, expresses *godliness* more clearly than εὐσέβεια. The emphasis no doubt here rests on the prefix. Cf. I Pet. iii. 1–6.

We must bear in mind that the apostle's admonitions address themselves to church members, from whom even worldly opinion exacts a higher standard of decorum than its own. They are to adorn the doctrine of God their Saviour by unassuming simplicity of garb, modesty of behaviour and benignity of action. Paul has in mind the feminine type of an opulent Asiatic centre of commerce, a class whose mental training was of the flimsiest description, so that the snare of ostentatious finery would offer tempting appeal to the sprightlier members of the sisterhood.

ii. 11, 12. γυνὴ ἐν ἡσυχίᾳ μανθανέτω ἐν πάσῃ ὑποταγῇ· διδάσκειν δὲ γυναικὶ οὐκ ἐπιτρέπω οὐδὲ αὐθεντεῖν ἀνδρός, ἀλλ᾿ εἶναι ἐν ἡσυχίᾳ.

Accordingly he lays a veto on their known tendency to gabble and assume the role of teacher upon themes with which their acquaintance was slender. The apostle was doubtless not unaware of the divergent views upon woman's education entertained by the leading ancient philosophers. Plato had allotted them a virtual equality with men, whilst Aristotle had curtailed their province of expatiation within very narrow bounds, and in practice his theory had prevailed. Paul now repeats the adjudication he had given in his Corinthian Letter (I Cor. xiv. 34) respecting their duty to be under tutelage 'in the church'. His award accorded with Greek sentiment (γυναιξὶ κόσμον ἡ σιγὴ φέρει, Soph. *Aj.* 293) and with the dictates of social use and wont (cf. Plut. *Mor.* 785); but the apostle takes yet higher ground. He declares that its violation would clash with the deference due, in view of the creative order of the sexes, from the physically weaker, and therefore more sheltered, sex to its natural champion and protector.

Teaching in public assemblies appertains to the administrant, not to the impulsive and impressionable sex. αὐθεντεῖν (= *wield sway*) has one parallel in the papyri (L. & S.) and appears as a doubtful reading in Philodemus (*Rhet.* ii. 133), but the Atticists stigmatize it as vernacular like our *lord it.* αὐθέντης, however, carries this sense in Euripides (*Suppl.* 442) and αὐθεντία signifies *sway* to Chrysostom. Its etymology (see M. & M.) differentiates it from the commoner αὐθέντης, 'a murderer'. It reappears in the modern Greek *Effendi* (Mr.).

ii. 13, 14. ᾿Αδὰμ γὰρ πρῶτος ἐπλάσθη, εἶτα Εὖα· καὶ ᾿Αδὰμ οὐκ ἠπατήθη, ἡ δὲ γυνὴ ἐξαπατηθεῖσα ἐν παραβάσει γέγονε·

Paul reinforces his decision by two arguments drawn from the sacred oracles, to him, as to his Master, a final court of appeal. One consists in the priority of Adam's creation, consummated by an help-meet. πλάσσειν exactly describes moulding in clay, and is used in the LXX of our first parents, and by Menander (*Fr.* 525) of Prometheus fashioning human bodies. The independent creation of Adam and the ancillary conformation of Eve typified their prospective offices in the mundane economy, offices not competitive, but concordant and counterpart.

The second reason he adduces founds itself on Eve's lead in transgression, itself an outcome of temerity on her part. The subtle serpent first assailed the weaker vessel and caught 'our credulous mother' with guile; but her husband was not equally duped. His robuster understanding perceived the cheat put upon his spouse, and he sinned with open eyes, to keep her company, ceding his right to rule

> Against his better judgment, not deceived,
> But fondly overcome with female charms.[1]

The record of Gen. iii, *wherein all subsequent human history lies capsuled,*

[1] Milton, *P.L.* x. 998. So Augustine: *City of God,* xiv. 11.

makes woman's ὑποταγή, or subordination, part of the curse resultant from the Fall. Many, to be sure, have argued that because in Christ there is 'neither male nor female', all sexual trammels are forthwith dissolved. But they have in some way to invalidate these injunctions, seemingly not to be set aside as superseded vetos. We cordially agree that Christianity has a mighty work to do in raising unrighteously degraded woman in the line of her true development. That is another matter. Let it be noted that it is primarily with married couples that the apostle here, as in Corinthians, is concerned; and starting from the principle that the husband is 'the head of the wife', he pronounces it most unseemly and a virtual betrayal of his trust, that he should sit publicly at his wife's feet, while she, an ὕπανδρος γυνή (Rom. vii. 2), plays the part of religious directrix, and he dwindles to what Euripides styles ὁ τῆς γυναικός (El. 931).

ii. 15. σωθήσεται δὲ διὰ τῆς τεκνογονίας, ἐὰν μείνωσιν ἐν πίστει καὶ ἀγάπῃ καὶ ἁγιασμῷ μετὰ σωφροσύνης.

Minds of a mystical cast discover in this verse a covert reference to the incarnation, regarded as the well-spring of redemption. They point to the insertion of the article and the strict meaning of διά with genitive, by means of. But διά can also mean throughout and refer to the whole crisis of child-bearing. Moreover τέκνον is a name never applied to Jesus except by His mother in boyhood (Lk. ii. 48). If the doctrinal allusion be there, it is strangely shrouded in mist. Surely St Paul is once more reverting to the primeval story, where we read in the sentence passed on Eve, 'I will greatly multiply thy sorrow and thy conception.' Many a godly woman had dreaded the pangs of travail; so it is not unfitting that, to relieve the pressure of the doom, Paul should assure Christian matrons of the coveted boon of εὐτοκία, safe delivery, provided that they abide in faith and love, amid the throes of parturition. If that be the right interpretation, σώζεσθαι here again carries its natural, rather than its spiritual connotation.

The Scriptures portray the relationship of the sexes as complementary, not competitive. They are designed to blend in a mutual unison. We see diversity of function linked with equality of nature. From this law none depart unpunished (Carlyle). That does not imply that the feminine element is underrated. The Hebrew ideal was not the down-trodden thraldom of paganism, but division of labour, such as Xeno-phon at least hails in the sketch of husband and wife in his *Oeconomicus*. Home life presents an enviable field of influence, woman's *normal* sphere of dominion, where she sits a queen. 'The hand that rocks the cradle rules the world' (Lowell). The pity is that the 'new woman' so often scorns her rightful crown and seems to nurse a standing grudge against heaven that she was not born a man. There are doubtless excep-tions to the rule, Deborahs and Huldahs, Abigails and Priscas, whose career swerves from the common track. But then theirs was an un-wonted phenomenon, like the prophetesses of the primitive Church, and Paul is laying down the law of the kingdom for ordinary cases. Where extraordinary cases arise, they must be accredited by peculiar circumstances, like David's seizure of the shewbread. Many tasks not strictly feminine must fall to the lot of female mission pioneers in solitary posts, or in seasons of emergency elsewhere. But the Head of the Church allots the posts of the members of His body as His wisdom wills; and those who quit that appointed station for one of their own affecting flout His prerogative of choice to their certain harm and loss.

iii. 1–13. PASTORAL AND DIACONAL QUALIFICATIONS

In proportion as the season drew near for the home-call of the apostles, it was the dictate of the Spirit of wisdom and counsel that steps should be taken for the consolidation of the visible Church. The vessel was launching out into the deep; and if the apostolic and prophetic pilotage were to come to an end, a permanent chart of guidance and model of regulation for her voyage must be sketched. For that necessity, by this time every day more clamant, provision had already in sundry cases been made. The Philippian church had its stated 'bishops and deacons' (Phil. i. 1) and the Ephesian its elders (Acts xx. 17); and 'pastors and teachers' occupy a place in the list of church officers in Eph. iv. 11. In the ensuing paragraph Paul details the qualifications requisite in an ἐπίσκοπος; for, having debarred women from the function of public teachers, it is fitting that he should ordain that only men of choice endowments may by right aspire to that honourable office, for theirs is no task to be undertaken lightly. 'The ministry is the best calling and the worst trade on earth', says Matthew Henry.

iii. I. πιστὸς ὁ λόγος· εἴ τις ἐπισκοπῆς ὀρέγεται, καλοῦ ἔργου ἐπιθυμεῖ.

The formula, *Faithful is the saying*, here repeated for the second time, has puzzled the commentators. Parry, copying Chrysostom, tacks it on very incongruously to the previous chapter; yet this *nota bene* looks somewhat superfluous in the connection where it stands. The most plausible explanation to our minds would be that the apostle employs this phraseology to mark his endorsement of propositions tendered for his adjudication by those to whom he writes. There may have been a group at Ephesus who, like some modern sects, disparaged the pastoral office. ἐπισκοπή is a LXX vocable, the sole profane example of which is its use for *oversight* in one passage of Lucian (*Dial. Deor.* xx. 6).

iii. 2. δεῖ οὖν τὸν ἐπίσκοπον ἀνεπίλημπτον εἶναι, μιᾶς γυναικὸς ἄνδρα, νηφάλιον σώφρονα κόσμιον φιλόξενον διδακτικόν,

Fifteen requisitions of the overseer are tabulated, and it may be well to scan their nature before canvassing the application of the term. *Irreproachability* stands at the head of the list. ἀνεπίληπτος (τὸν βίον, Dion. Hal. ii. 63) is classical Greek for *unexceptionable*. *Husband of one wife* has caused much controversy. Does it penalize second marriages? So Tertullian and the Montanists construed it; but they were biased in favour of celibacy. By the Greek Church, on the contrary, it has been supposed to enjoin a married clergy. The obvious sense would lead us to regard it as a prohibition of polygamy, practised not uncommonly among the Jews of later days, and of course, excessively rife in pagan circles. We know that Paul treats the nuptial tie as dissolved by death (Rom. vii. 2) and he was the last man to institute a clerical ban inapplicable to the laity, as some have construed it. To postulate grades of official sanctity among members of the same spiritual body may be orthodox clericalism, but it is heterodox Christianity.[1] *Sobriety*, *self-command* and an *orderly walk* explain themselves. The trait of *hospitality* intimates one who is not a churlish recluse, but willing to spend his spare hours and share his belongings with his fellow-pilgrims. The dearth of respectable houses of entertainment rendered, to use Tyn-

---

[1] For an exhaustive discussion of this point see Dr Patrick Fairbairn's *Commentary on the Pastoral Epistles*, Appendix B.

dale's fine word, a *harborous* disposition an important matter. διδακτικός turns our minds in another direction; for it assesses the probationer's mental gifts. The word, repeated in II Tim. ii. 24, is almost unique, the only example producible being drawn from Philo.

iii. 3. μὴ πάροινον, μὴ πλήκτην, ἀλλ᾽ ἐπιεικῆ ἄμαχον ἀφιλάργυρον,

Four negative and one positive qualification are here tabulated. They surprise us at first sight, conveying an impression that the raw material available for the ministry was such as a fastidious taste would have sniffed at. But the apostle's missionary toils had taught him that God for the most part chooses nonentities to bring entities to naught; and so he reckons with hereditary susceptibilities which we should not anticipate. πάροινος, descriptive of the state of a wine-bibber or the indulgence commonly known as *flustered with wine*, is identified by Aristotle in his *Problemata* with ἀκροθώραξ, *tipsy*, and παροινεῖσθαι usually implies rowdy behaviour. Plutarch joins it with loss of self-control (*Lucull.* 35). πλήκτης again, also a Plutarchian vocable, marks a propensity to violence suggesting the translation *brawler*. However, a cuff on the head was a common spectacle at tables where down-trodden slaves served (cf. I Pet. ii. 20). Carlyle tells us that in the old days on the Borders, a 'good striker' was quite a complimentary epithet. Paul is insisting that the Lord's servant must not be splenetic or passionate. ἐπιεικής defies exact translation. Trench affiliates it with εἴκειν, but probably it is cognate rather with εἰκός. It denotes a suavity and affability of demeanour akin to that of John Henderson when a nettled disputant at dinner threw a glass of wine in his face, and he wiped it off with the amicable remark: 'That was a digression; let us resume the argument'! *Gracious, kindly, forbearing, considerate, magnanimous, genial*, all approximate to its idea. In Attic Greek ἄμαχος signifies *invincible*; here it supplements ἐπιεικής, and may be rendered *placable* or *inoffensive*. Nothing mars the influence of a religious teacher more than snappishness. Nor must he be a money-grubber. Both of these negative terms appear in Greek sepulchral inscriptions as laudatory epithets for the deceased. Manifestly for the purpose in hand, graces outweigh gifts. The stress throughout is placed on moral qualifications, and a pagan community forms their evident background. A pastor's life is vocal either for good or ill.

iii. 4, 5. τοῦ ἰδίου οἴκου καλῶς προϊστάμενον, τέκνα ἔχοντα ἐν ὑποταγῇ μετὰ πάσης σεμνότητος· εἰ δέ τις τοῦ ἰδίου οἴκου προστῆναι οὐκ οἶδε, πῶς ἐκκλησίας θεοῦ ἐπιμελήσεται;

The apostle's inspection of the probationers now casts its searchlight on their home. What sort of a control do they exercise over that? So utterly foreign to the primitive model is the ideal of sacerdotal celibacy, that it is presumed that the candidate is already a married man of mature age. Slipshod paternal discipline disqualifies him at once for rule in the church. προεστάναι indicates the presidency of the household. In parallel wise Plutarch (*Mor.* 875) propounds the question πῶς προΐστασθαι τέκνων προσήκει; as a sample of a practical problem, the exact phrase used of the deacons in verse 12. His family must reflect the seriousness of its head. Somewhat of a Puritan sedateness of tone should pervade the establishment. And a cogent reason clenches this requirement; for fidelity to principle exhibited in a lesser sphere warrants promotion to a larger, as every business firm knows. Children's obedience to a parent witnesses to his power of moral suasion, sense of duty and tact, and these are valuable elements in the equipment of a servant of God.

Observe the Pauline rhetorical conditional followed by πῶς with a future verb. Nothing could more surely disclose his hand than this pungent query suddenly raking a possible hostile party like a volley of grape-shot from a masked battery. We at once recall other instances in his Epistles, such as 'If the trumpet give an uncertain sound, who shall prepare himself for the battle?'—one of a whole cluster in I Cor. xiv— or the triad in Romans x ending 'How shall they preach if they be not sent?' The εἰ followed by οὐ cannot be deemed anomalous where the negative joins itself closely to the verb; οὐκ οἶδε = ἀγνοεῖ. ἐκκλησία θεοῦ means *God's church*, here, in the judgment of most expositors, meaning a particular congregation.

iii. 6. μὴ νεόφυτον, ἵνα μὴ τυφωθεὶς εἰς κρίμα ἐμπέσῃ τοῦ διαβόλου.

A warning is subjoined against the ordination of novices as instructors. Whether this admonition refers to immaturity of age or recent initiation in the doctrines of the faith remains doubtful. At any rate there

exists in many Christian bodies a foolish inclination to install mere
striplings in the chair of office which deserves this reproof. There is a
time to learn and another time to teach. Callow nestlings should not
try to soar. The word νεόφυτος pertains properly to nurseries of plants,
and its metaphorical sense, whence comes our term *neophyte*, unexampled except tentatively in the LXX version of Ps. cxliv. 12, may
have suggested the image to the apostle.

We take the *judgment of the devil* (not, of course, 'the slanderer' as
some would have it, for διάβολος almost invariably denotes a person
in the New Testament; else why the article here?) to be an objective
genitive, and κρίμα, as in other passages, to verge on κατάκριμα,
condemnation. The angels that sinned are 'reserved unto judgment'
(II Pet. ii. 4; Jude 6) and that judgment overtakes an outbreak of
vainglorious presumption on their part. This interpretation meets with
verification in the insertion of the participle τυφωθείς, *infatuated* or
inflated; German *aufgeblasen*: cf. examples furnished by Wetstein and
Bengel. An inexperienced adherent, invested with premature authority,
unless the grace of God prevent, will be likely to be puffed up in consequence of his too rapid advancement, and give himself all manner of
lofty airs. τῦφος, *delusion* or *humbug*, connects itself with τύφειν, to
smoke, smoulder and its cognate τυφοῦν, and comes to signify *swagger*.
Thus ἀτυφία is employed by Plutarch (*Mor.* 82), Cicero and Marcus
Aurelius for 'unpretentiousness', in contrast with self-conceit; and
μισότυφος='anti-humbug' in Lucian (*Pisc.* 20). See further below,
on chapter vi. 4. That pride, chafing against control, was Lucifer's
primal sin, does not need proof, and as Thomas Adams wittily phrases
it: 'Enter pride, exit wisdom.'

iii. 7. δεῖ δὲ καὶ μαρτυρίαν καλὴν ἔχειν ἀπὸ τῶν ἔξωθεν, ἵνα μὴ εἰς
ὀνειδισμὸν ἐμπέσῃ καὶ παγίδα τοῦ διαβόλου.

One more qualification finds mention, a good reputation in the
esteem of the neighbourhood generally. We recognize in οἱ ἔξω one of
Paul's favourite expressions (I Cor. v. 12; Col. iv. 5; I Thes. iv. 12),
slightly varied after a preposition of motion. Josephus (*Antiq.* xv. 9)
and Plutarch (*Mor.* 220) use the same phrase of foreigners. It has been
objected that such commendation must have been difficult to procure
in behalf of members of a new sect 'everywhere spoken against'. But

although its public heralds incurred contumely, it does not follow that an honest citizen, favourably known for blandness of demeanour and probity of dealing, might not obtain a certificate of good manners from heathen witnesses. Did not the γραμματεύς of Ephesus himself bear record in favour of Paul and his staff that they were no disturbers of the city's peace nor fired by sacrilegious zeal? Integrity commands a meed of respect in circles which are far from imitating its example. *Probitas laudatur et alget.*

The minister of the word must be respected and not sink to the level of despicability owing to glaring flaws in his character. That will not only mar his usefulness, but expose him to ensnarement by Satan. Loss of self-respect readily ensues upon the loss of others' regard, and tempts to misguided policies. A career so blighted may end ignobly and bring reproach on the Church of God. Mark the devil's skill in trap-laying. But 'the snare of the devil' may be a subjective genitive, and refer to his outstanding sin of pride.

No one can peruse this catalogue of the qualities requisite for an ἐπίσκοπος worthy of his vocation without noting their elementary nature. They afford *prima facie* evidence that the office concerned was not one of high pretension or wide-reaching surveillance. Taking antecedent conditions into account we can see how they might apply to a body of local pastors; but we do not wonder that Chrysostom felt puzzled to square some of them with the monarchical prelacy of his own day. It is indisputable, especially in view of the evidence supplied by the papyri in recent years, that the term embraced a variety of meanings, circling round that of *supervisor*, such as 'guardian' or 'inspector'. Cf. Plut. *Pericl.* 13, *Mor.* 272, where both terms are joined. Communal officials bore the title not infrequently and the LXX had borrowed it to denote a subordinate state-officer. Its New Testament signification tallies with general Greek usage in conveying the idea of a superintendent or overseer, but falls far short of diocesan episcopacy. Candid inquirers of very diverse schools of thought, both in Germany and Britain, have assented to the proposition that ἐπίσκοπος and πρεσβύτερος are coincident terms, the one expressive of function, the other of office. That the word (in common with *deacon*) had changed its meaning in later ecclesiastical usage was known to some of the chief representatives of that subsequent stage of development.

Chrysostom shirks the topic to some extent in his sermons on the Pastorals; but in commenting on Phil. i. 1, he speaks in plain terms:

οἱ πρεσβύτεροι τὸ παλαιὸν ἐκαλοῦντο ἐπίσκοποι καὶ διάκονοι Χριστοῦ καὶ οἱ ἐπίσκοποι πρεσβύτεροι· ὅθεν καὶ νῦν πολλοὶ συμπρεσβυτέρῳ ἐπίσκοποι γράφουσι καὶ συνδιακόνῳ.

In the Introduction we have cited similar testimonies from Jerome and Augustine. The interchange of the words cannot be denied in Acts xx. 17, 28; Tit. i. 5, or in Clement of Rome's *Letter* (xlii), or in some passages of Irenaeus. On the other hand, the Ignatian Epistles exalt the episcopal order as the very pivot of the Church's rule. But our concern does not properly extend beyond the ascertainment of its status and character in the Letters under our scrutiny; which is clear enough. That could be inferred from the immediate juxtaposition of the deacon's requisites, and the rehearsal in his case of many of the qualities desiderated in the *episcopus*. The interval betwixt the two could not possibly have resembled that between a 'lord bishop' and a humble deacon of later times.

iii. 8, 9.   διακόνους ὡσαύτως σεμνούς, μὴ διλόγους, μὴ οἴνῳ πολλῷ συνέχοντας, μὴ αἰσχροκερδεῖς, ἔχοντας τὸ μυστήριον τῆς πίστεως ἐν καθαρᾷ συνειδήσει.

The occasion of the inauguration of the diaconate is told us in the narrative of Acts. The deacon was the church's almoner in the distribution of gifts to the poor and associated with the 'ways and means' of its outward maintenance. The fact that he was already a familiar figure could be deduced from the manner in which he emerges here without formal introduction, in the capacity of *aide-de-camp* to the presiding presbyter. The elliptical syntax requires the reader to supply from the preceding paragraph δεῖ εἶναι. σεμνός once more lays stress on high-mindedness, dignified but not austere (Plut. *Nic.* 2), and μὴ δίλογος on sincerity of character. This is an ἅπαξ εἰρημένον, presumably of Paul's own mintage. We hold that he coined it in imitation of the Latin *bilinguis*, because the LXX δίγλωσσος was incorrect in this sense. It regularly signifies *bilingual*. Financial transactions of a religious sort demand sterling integrity. Again, addiction to much wine implies a laxity of carriage at variance with responsible stewardship of funds.

Avarice forms another manifest disqualification for such a trust. The downfall of Demas, as of Judas, may have been due to this vice.

The deacon must be conscientious, *holding the mystery of the faith with pure conscience.* In II Tim. i. 3, the apostle claims this precious endowment as his own possession. He has already dwelt on the treasure of a 'pure heart' (i. 5). Nothing can be more fatal to a Christian profession than duplicity of aim. μυστήριον means a *secret.* The gospel of the grace of God was such an *arcanum Dei,* hidden from past ages, but now made known to His saints. We regard *the faith* as plainly objective in this chapter; for notwithstanding the demurs raised against that rendering, it cannot be eliminated from the later books of the New Testament when fairly construed.

iii. 10. *καὶ οὗτοι δὲ δοκιμαζέσθωσαν πρῶτον, εἶτα διακονείτωσαν ἀνέγκλητοι ὄντες.*

A term of probation will give the membership an opportunity of gauging their merits or demerits, and confirming or rescinding their appointment accordingly. δοκιμάζειν has the special meaning of *approving after scrutiny* in Attic law. So the notion is that of 'passing muster' upon due inspection.

iii. 11. *γυναῖκας ὡσαύτως σεμνάς, μὴ διαβόλους, νηφαλίους, πιστὰς ἐν πᾶσιν.*

It is a matter of controversy whether the women now mentioned in passing are deacons' wives, or deaconesses as a separate institution, or even, as some have contended, women-servants, perhaps the *ancillae* noticed in Pliny's *Letter to Trajan,* in which case the deacons preceding must be construed merely as caretakers like the synagogal *chazzan.* But as Chrysostom observes, both the place they occupy in the apostle's pastoral instructions and the qualifications specified refute this notion. Their position is in line with the pastorate; or why the 'likewise'? We learn from inscriptions and from Rom. xvi. 1 that διάκονος is of the common gender; so that there was no need to repeat the appellation in reference to deaconesses. Social conditions probably required that members of the female sex should be visited by one of their own sisterhood. The suitable person for this office might be a deacon's spouse or she might not. At any rate, her duties were serious; for she is to be herself a pattern of decorum, and no talebearer. Only in the Pastorals do we meet with διάβολος in its classical sense of *calumnious*, or *back-biters* (Field, *Ot. Norv.* p. 69). Her sobriety, both physical and moral, must be unimpeachable and her fidelity entire. It may have been this class of feminine helpers who, in a place like Ephesus, lay under temptation to assume the rank of teachers on their own account.

iii. 12, 13. διάκονοι ἔστωσαν μιᾶς γυναικὸς ἄνδρες, τέκνων καλῶς προϊστάμενοι καὶ τῶν ἰδίων οἴκων. οἱ γὰρ καλῶς διακονήσαντες βαθμὸν ἑαυτοῖς καλὸν περιποιοῦνται καὶ πολλὴν παρρησίαν ἐν πίστει τῇ ἐν Χριστῷ Ἰησοῦ.

The parenthetical nature of the preceding verse appears from the way in which Paul reverts in closing to the male diaconate, imposing on them the same obligation of monogamy as he had laid down for the pastoral probationer, and the same evidence of capacity to preside over a family circle.

Anticipating a possible exception to so high a standard for this secondary office, he subjoins a declaration which seems to affirm that no sacred task is mean, even if it partake of drudgery or insignificance. How can a service done unto the Lord, however lowly, fail of reward from the divine Appraiser? A deacon's work well and truly discharged earns a meed of respect and estimation all its own. The expression βαθμός has received various interpretations. We should translate it *an honourable standing.* τολμημάτων βαθμοί (Joseph. *B.J.* iv. 3) signifies *stages of audacity*, and Vettius Valens (p. 263) pictures a mountain-ascent διὰ βαθμῶν by means of steps or stages.[1] After the establishment of the three clerical orders, the opinion gained ground that we have here an allusion to the promotion from deacon's to priest's orders won by meritorious service; but that note of ecclesiasticism belongs to a later date. Others have understood it to denote spiritual growth, a view rendered plausible by the sequel concerning 'boldness in the faith'. But the place obtained in Christian esteem suits the context best. Influence is a by-product of character, and the apostle's mind has been dwelling on the elements that contribute to a staunch manhood with godliness at its base. To refer the phrase to awards made at the day of

---

[1] ἐπαναβαθμός is figuratively used in Plato, *Symp.* 211, and τρίτος βαθμός (Harrison) in Hadrian's *Sententiae* for a military grade. Cf. Latin *gradum facere.*

judgment seems very far-fetched and incongruous with the concluding clause. παρρησία, *outspokenness*, the degree of confidence engendered by practice in giving advice and help. Exhorting others to repose faith in Christ with happy results will assuredly strengthen the faith of the exhorter himself. It must be a faith centring in Christ Himself as its focal point.

iii. 14–16. THE DIGNITY OF THE CHURCH

iii. 14, 15 a. ταῦτά σοι γράφω ἐλπίζων ἐλθεῖν πρός σε τάχιον· ἐὰν δὲ βραδύνω, ἵνα εἰδῆς πῶς δεῖ ἐν οἴκῳ θεοῦ ἀναστρέφεσθαι,

The present tense, instead of the epistolary aorist, marks the fact that the apostle is in the act of writing, though in hopes of meeting Timothy ere long. τάχιον, a late substitute for θᾶσσον, a comparative form like Latin *ocius*, does not differ appreciably from the common ταχύ. Remark that Paul says nothing about visiting Ephesus itself; Miletus may have been the chosen rendezvous.

He is not certain, however, about his next movements; for even apostles had to put to sea occasionally with sealed orders. The discipline of uncertainty or delay was needful in their training as well as ours. Some, with Diodati and Hort, translate indefinitely *how men should comport themselves in God's house*; and, as Timothy's name is suppressed and the reference appears to be general, that rendering may be accepted. The house of God, or household, is now no longer a material structure, but the 'habitation of God in the Spirit' (Eph. ii. 22), the Church fitly framed together with living stones, here regarded in its visible aspect.

iii. 15 b. ἥτις ἐστὶν ἐκκλησία θεοῦ ζῶντος, στῦλος καὶ ἑδραίωμα τῆς ἀληθείας.

Lest it should be thought lightly of, Paul appends a testification of the nobility of the true ἐκκλησία, built on the one foundation. Primarily the word meant a public assembly duly summoned by a herald. ἐκκλησιάζειν is used by Plutarch (*Mor.* 244) even of a boys' meeting to pass resolutions of a serious kind. The apostle styles it an *assembly of the living God Himself, a pillar and stanchion of the truth*. The employment of στῦλος figuratively for a *mainstay* (cf. Latin *columen*) is quite Pauline (Gal. ii. 9), the metaphor being in fact both Hebrew and Greek (Eur. *Iph. in Taur.* 57). ἑδραίωμα ranks with the ἅπαξ εἰρημένα and would seem to reproduce the Latin *firmamentum, a stay* or *stablishment*; cf. Cicero of the province of Gaul, *firmamentum imperii* (*Phil.* iii. 5). By a common attraction ἥτις takes the gender of its consequent, not antecedent, noun.

We have here a characteristic specimen of Paul's shorthand appositional clauses, condensed expressions verging sometimes on the obscure. This phrase has caused trouble to expositors. The Fathers and some writers of later date associate the phraseology with Timothy, linking the image with the preceding part of the sentence. He should demean himself in God's house as a pillar of truth. They urge that the consistency of the similitude is thus preserved. But can that be alleged? ἀναστρέφεσθαι (Latin *versari*) connotes motion rather than station. Besides, the diffident Timothy was not altogether a 'pillar saint'. That emblem endows him with a massiveness of build to which he could make no pretension; nor does it consort with what follows.

Doubtless this symbolism portrays the Church's spiritual distinction and lustre. The ministration of the Spirit has a glory that excelleth, lowly as its vehicles may appear in worldly eyes. Even heavenly principalities learn lessons of divine wisdom from the spectacle. Not only is it the place where God's honour dwelleth, but it upholds His revealed truth among the sons of men. Its presence testifies to things unseen as yet. It is the bearer or platform of tidings of tremendous urgency. Some remark that announcements were frequently affixed to pillars (Horace's *columnae*), and that this idea underlies the former of the two emblems. Calvin points out that, despite all her infirmities and lapses, a Church which is not dead while she liveth, but is a 'Church of the living God', constitutes the nursery of godliness and the standing witness to divine truth among men, an institution whose office no other institution can fill. In proportion as we abhor the false, we should honour the true. Has not our apostle elsewhere (Eph. i. 23) magnified the body of Christ as 'the fulness of Him who filleth all in all'? True, he is here treating of the visible encasement of the jewel rather than of the jewel itself, 'the sacramental host of God's elect'; but the outer casket ought to commend the treasure it enshrines. The organized Church is set for the defence and maintenance of the faith once for all consigned to the saints in trust. It is no lurker in crypts and catacombs, but a city placed on an hill that cannot be hid.

Jealousy of sacerdotal assumptions has led some Protestant exegetes to put a full stop at θεοῦ, and annex the appositional interlude to the ensuing paragraph, thus: 'The pillar and support of the truth, and indisputably great is the mystery of godliness, namely...'. Bengel espouses this construction of the passage with ardour. But it must be pronounced fatally artificial and cumbersome. Alford goes the length of declaring that such a clumsy period would suffice to prove the Epistle spurious. It would certainly strike a very jarring note in a Pauline document. Such a rhetorical inversion must be dismissed alike on grounds of good taste and sound hermeneutics.

iii. 16a. καὶ ὁμολογουμένως μέγα τὸ τῆς εὐσεβείας μυστήριον·

ὁμολογουμένως is an Attic participial adverb, formed like πεφυλαγμένως, φειδομένως (II Cor. ix. 6); cf. ὁμολογουμένως μέγιστος (Isoc. Evag. 68, Plut. Ages. 10). Observe the emphatic position of μέγα, meaning *wondrous*, a Pauline trait exemplified in I Cor. ix. 11; II Cor. xi. 15. εὐσέβεια belongs to the list of new vocables peculiar to the Pastoral Epistles and to the diction of Peter. If, with Holtzmann, we admit Latinistic influences in these Epistles (as why should we not?), the vogue of the Latin *pietas* in Roman mouths may have favoured its employment. Perhaps, however, it represents *true* (εὐ-) *religion*. μυστήριον in the singular means *secret*, from Plato (*Theaet.* 156) downwards to Menander (*Fr.* 695), the Apocrypha and Vettius Valens (pp. 48, 72): in the New Testament *a revealed secret*. The apostle's mind fastens on the grandeur of New Testament revelations, eclipsing all that went before. The marvel of their mighty theme, the incarnate Son, lends surpassing dignity to the proclamation of this 'purpose of the ages', this 'hidden wisdom of God', now at length made manifest. He proceeds to name some of its leading features in rhythmical language, which some suppose to be quoted from a catechetical summary of the faith or ᾠδὴ πνευματική (Col. iii. 16).

iii. 16b. ὃς ἐφανερώθη ἐν σαρκί, ἐδικαιώθη ἐν πνεύματι,

We can scarcely be wrong in discovering in these strongly antithetical propositions, so skilfully arranged in parallel pairs one after another, in articulate shape, a confession of faith which reads like a citation from canticle or catechism. We seem to be listening to a primitive epitome of Christological instruction, half divulged, half concealed. And on that assumption the initial ὅς, now critically adopted instead of θεός,[1] ceases to be strange or unaccountable. We find another such quotation probably in Eph. v. 14. There cannot be a shadow of doubt who is the unique Person spoken of throughout. Immanuel's Name is Wonderful (Is. ix. 6) and Secret (Jdg. xiii. 18) and may well be couched in allusive terms; for it 'cannot be hid'. φανεροῦσθαι we know to be a favourite Johannine expression, descriptive of the historical reality of Christ's abode among us. *He who was manifested in the flesh* applies only to the pre-existent Son of God. No secret in heaven or earth can be more inscrutable than incarnate Deity. Deeper than ever plummet sounded, beyond the gauge of any created intellect, lies that mystery of mysteries, the hypostatical union. In the espousals of the Infinite and the finite, the miraculous attains its acme.

Justified in the spirit may be understood in more than one way. We may take it to signify that the Redeemer's profound claims are vindicated on the basis of His Deity. Those purged eyes which beheld the glory of the only-begotten Son under its veil of clay were not stumbled by His demand for their whole-hearted allegiance. To them His miracles became outflashings of the hidden Godhead and His paradoxes transcendental verities rending the trammels of human speech. Wisdom was justified by her children. Or we may construe the dark saying juridically. His earthly manifestation culminated in a felon's death attended by a ghastly aggregate of horrors. Was it a futile or a finished work—which? Christian faith has its answer ready. In His cross lay the secret of the heavenly Samson's strength. Herein He triumphed and 'death by dying slew'. Was He under attainder for blasphemy in

---

[1] It is not our province to canvass this crux of textual criticism. The battle formerly raged around the *Codex Alexandrinus*, in which careful inspection by palaeographers of earlier days found traces of the abbreviated Θ͞C, regarded by them as the original text. More recent recension tends to negative this conclusion; but the page in question is now so frayed that it yields no certain result. The *Codex Sinaiticus* reads OC, with a later correction; whilst neither the Vatican Codex nor the early Chester-Beatty papyri, recently brought to light, contain the Pastorals. The patristic testimony varies, the versions favour ὅς, and the Latin versions ὅ (*quod*), making μυστήριον the antecedent. Cursives in overwhelming majority support θεός. If Bengel's canon *proclivi scriptioni praestat ardua* carry weight, the reading must be admitted to conform to its tenor. But the case against its adoption is powerfully argued by Field in his *Ot. Norv.* pp. 204–8.

a human court, yet 'made sin for us' before an auguster tribunal? Then His justification was at hand (Is. l. 8). The resurrection ratified His Sonship and because of our justification (Rom. iv. 25), because the bond was fully discharged, our Hostage stands released, and His justification guarantees that of His people. 'They are as much justified as He is' (R. M. McCheyne). Some deem that the Holy Spirit is here regarded as the assertor of the Saviour's honour. His plenitude of unction rested on the Son of Man, and there is a sense in which the day of Pentecost gave attestation to Calvary. But it is the Second Person whose glory this lyrical canto chants.

iii. 16c. ὤφθη ἀγγέλοις, ἐκηρύχθη ἐν ἔθνεσιν,

He was seen of angels. If Sheol was strangely moved at the arrival thither of the once resplendent son of the morning, little wonder that heaven was stirred by the descent to our sphere in voluntary self-abnegation of the only-begotten of the Father. With what tremulous interest must these lieges of His have followed the steps of His humiliation from the throne of awful majesty to the cross of agonizing shame! And how, as the infernal plot against Him thickened, must they have witnessed with amazement the non-intervention of Omnipotence on His behalf! Far more than twelve legions of angels must have waited breathlessly for that signal to flash across the upper skies which should snatch heaven's Darling from the 'power of the dog'. Surely the resurrection daybreak dawned on them as well as on the dazed disciples 'like some sweet summer morning after a night of pain' and the triumph of His reascension, escorted by their bright squadrons homeward, had been to them its meridian glow. But imagination must fold her fluttering wing, lest we incur the Colossians' rebuke (ii. 18) for prying into angelology! Enough to know that these unseen spectators from another world have drunk in the vision of the 'Word made flesh' and can be summoned to bear record to its supreme reality.

Preached among the Gentiles. Mark that the pulpit is a divine ordinance. At this point we are brought back to the visible plane of things with singular abruptness. Was this fact worthy to be chronicled among divine marvels? So thought those who participated in the early seafarings of the migrant gospel. For ages the truth of God had been a fountain sealed, a garden-plot enclosed, so that a proclamation of amnesty navigable on a world-wide scale ranked as a signal innovation. The expansiveness of the new covenant took the Hebrew mind by surprise; to us it is grown a commonplace.

iii. 16d. *ἐπιστεύθη ἐν κόσμῳ, ἀνελήμφθη ἐν δόξῃ.*

Believed on in the world. 'Faith cometh by hearing', not by appeals to the outward senses. Were the preached gospel devoid of converts, it would be shorn of its honourable rank. But the children of the desolate have been more in number than the children of the married wife. If there are barren missionary fields, others have proved fertile tracts for the seed of the kingdom. Gentile testimony has spread north and south and east and west, and its recipients have been wellnigh ubiquitous. The noble army of martyrs alone constitutes a mighty host, and the company of faithful nobodies a much greater one. The sum total of those who have trusted the Saviour baffles computation; nor is the banner of the Crucified ever destitute of fresh recruits wearing the dew of their youth.

Received up in glory. ἀνάλημψις is the standard New Testament term for the ascension. Fitly does this sixfold declaration of the Lord's mediatorial errand close with His re-entrance within the veil. The words suggest the sweet serenity of His exaltation. Yonder we view the Lord of Glory upsoaring to His native sphere, not, however, that the line of communication with Him may be severed. Our High Priest must needs fulfil His ministry of intercession on high and wield the sceptre of universal dominion, His by double right. And when our Forerunner triumphed, 'He bore up with Him into safety the spiritual life of all His people'.

iv. 1–5. PREDICTION OF APOSTASY

Paul has styled his gospel 'worthy of all acceptation'. Yet its story is destined to be chequered by reverses as well as triumphs; for it will rouse into activity all the latent enmity of the unregenerate heart. He had already warned the Thessalonian church (II Thes. ii. 11) of the peril of those who love not the truth and foretold their judicial abandonment to a 'fermentation of error'; and here that warning is reiterated and expanded. 'They that hate truth shall be the dupes of lies' (Cowper).

iv. 1 a. τὸ δὲ πνεῦμα ῥητῶς λέγει ὅτι ἐν ὑστέροις καιροῖς ἀποστή-
σονταί τινες τῆς πίστεως,

ῥητῶς can mean *totidem verbis*; for Plutarch (*Mor.* 1041) and Sextus
Empiricus (*Pyrrh.* 3. 248) use it to introduce a verbal quotation. Yet in
Polybius (xxiii. 5), Philodemus (*Rhet.* p. 105), Josephus (*Ap.* 14) and
Plutarch (*Brut.* 29) it signifies rather *explicitly*. ἐν ὑστέροις καιροῖς, *in
latter days*, seems to intimate a less distant future than the commoner
phrase ἐν ἐσχάταις ἡμέραις, occurring in II Tim. iii. 1. ἀφίστασθαι
implies a standing aloof from the faith, ἡ πίστις being evidently here
fides quae creditur.

It should be borne in mind that the apostle is not depicting contemporary phenomena, but heresies ere long to be hatched. He fore-
shadows a pending declension from the 'simplicity pertaining to
Christ'. Its first stage will consist in a lapse from the faith, a corruption
of sound doctrine; for a fixed standard of truth is presupposed, from
which the parties in question will swerve. Individual shipwrecks of
faith had already taken place; but he predicts heterodox movements
under organized leadership. The sound ministry of chapter iii constitutes the best prophylactic against the epidemics of chapter iv.

iv. 1 b, 2 a. προσέχοντες πνεύμασιν πλάνοις καὶ διδασκαλίαις δαιμονίων ἐν ὑποκρίσει ψευδολόγων,

The noun πλάνος signifies a 'strolling quack' or 'vagabond'. The
adjective forms a poetical epithet for baits or snares, and Vettius Valens
applies it (p. 74) to charlatans and elsewhere (p. 220) to the fickleness
of mortal hopes. It may be rendered *beguiling*. Mark how διδασκαλία
by this time is acquiring an objective sense. The definite mould that
Christian doctrine is taking accounts for the frequency of its use in the
Pastoral Epistles.

The sombre picture here drawn discloses a teacher of lies who is
himself the dupe of evil spirits to whose lore he lends a ready ear; for
δαιμονίων would seem to be a subjective genitive, with which ψευδολόγων stands in agreement. Thus Chrysostom construed it. Followers
of the father of lies may be expected to retail his stock-in-trade. But
the Revised Version and most recent translators render *through the
hypocrisy of men that speak lies*, on account of the clause which follows,
otherwise difficult to construe intelligently. That may be right; if so, it

transfers the crime of hypocrisy and falsehood to the specious instruments of seduction, springing from the ranks of the Church itself (cf. Acts xx. 30). ψευδολόγος is a Hellenistic word, meaning *mendacious*.

iv. 2 b, 3 a. κεκαυτηριασμένων τὴν ἰδίαν συνείδησιν, κωλυόντων γαμεῖν, ἀπέχεσθαι βρωμάτων,

From the emphatic ἰδίαν it would be possible to infer a change of subject, if αὐτῶν were understood, in order to form a genitive absolute. But the construction runs more smoothly in the newer version. At any rate, we are now in the human sphere, not the diabolic. καυτηριάζειν should signify *to brand*, καυτήριον being the technical term for a 'branding-iron'; and Diodorus Siculus (L. & S.) uses this very image of a stigmatic soul. *Per contra*, if spelt with W. & H. κεκαυστηριασμένων, the figure ought to be medical; for καυστήρ in Hippocrates means 'cauterizing apparatus'. In view of Paul's use of ἀπαλγεῖν in Eph. iv. 19, and of Luke's comradeship, we incline to the latter explanation.

κωλυόντων γαμεῖν, ἀπέχεσθαι βρωμάτων is a notable Latinistic zeugma and a good example of the apostle's stenography. Some have fancied that κελευόντων has dropped out of the text; but there are no variants whatever to give colour to that theory. The meaning, however —*forbidding to marry, bidding to abstain from foods*—cannot be gainsaid. Cf. Cicero (*Nat. Deor.* i. 7), *Nolo existimes me adiutorem venisse, sed auditorem.*

Few dispute that the heresiarchs here pointed at were primarily of a Gnostic type, traitors in the Christian camp whose own consciences were shameproof, who set themselves to seduce others of the King's lieges. Bent on entrapping simple souls, these 'handlers of holy things without feeling', in Bacon's phrase, with an air of peculiar strictness, like the Jewish Essenes, frowned on marriage and advocated a spare diet for the subjugation of the body, ascetically viewed as a clog upon the soul. Such wilful self-mortifications had found supporters at Colossae and condemnation had been already passed on them by the apostle. But in imitation of the Encratites, Manichaeans and other perversities of the patristic era, they grew into potent corruptions, eremitical and monastic, and were absorbed into the lifeblood of the Romish system of later days which cannot claim exemption from the denunciation here fulminated.

iv. 3b–5. ἃ ὁ θεὸς ἔκτισεν εἰς μετάληψιν μετὰ εὐχαριστίας τοῖς πιστοῖς καὶ ἐπεγνωκόσι τὴν ἀλήθειαν· ὅτι πᾶν κτίσμα θεοῦ καλὸν καὶ οὐδὲν ἀπόβλητον μετὰ εὐχαριστίας λαμβανόμενον· ἁγιάζεται γὰρ διὰ λόγου θεοῦ καὶ ἐντεύξεως.

Against these fanatical inhibitions Paul enters his inspired protest in advance. He rejects the root principle of the whole system of delusion by denying the evil of matter or the notion that spiritual purity is secured by a celibate life or meagre diet, a favourite doctrine in all ages of the severer schools of philosophy. But even fasting may puff up the flesh, as with those who, 'in a pet of temperance, feed on pulse'. Many of the ancient hermits had to bewail with Jerome the carnal passions that haunted them in their desert cells. God's gifts are suited to man's appetites and should be received with gratitude, not thrust aside in disdain. Believers are especially entitled to them because of their filial relationship to the Giver. We have already met with the phrase ἐπίγνωσις ἀληθείας (ii. 4), which occurs in Epictetus. Dean Armitage Robinson has led the fashion of denying any real distinction between γινώσκειν and ἐπιγινώσκειν, formerly held to convey the idea of *clear* knowledge. To us it appears to have good warrant. The prefix certainly adds to cognizance the concept of full recognition or discernment, as may be gathered from Soph. *El.* 1297; Plut. *Pomp.* 42, *Ages.* 21, *Mor.* 506; Joseph. *Antiq.* viii. 2, 5; or, in the New Testament, from Mt. xi. 27; I Cor. xiii. 12. In fact, Chrysostom somewhere contrasts the two verbs. Cf. Latin *noscere, agnoscere.*

A reason for the statement is furnished, with allusion, as ἀπόβλητον shows, to an adage as old as Homer (*Il.* iii. 65). Every creation of God is good and none to be flung aside. Note the characteristic omission of the copula. St Paul seems to refer to the 'sevenfold refrain' of Gn. i; perhaps also to the lesson taught Peter at Joppa, 'what God hath cleansed call not thou unclean', or to the Lord's own sentence (Mk. vii. 19).

God's permit conjoined with prayer sanctifies all dishes. 'Grace before meat', says Chrysostom, 'disinfects even what has been offered to idols.'

iv. 6–16. PERSONAL ADMONITION TO TIMOTHY

iv. 6. ταῦτα ὑποτιθέμενος τοῖς ἀδελφοῖς καλὸς ἔσῃ διάκονος Χριστοῦ
Ἰησοῦ ἐντρεφόμενος τοῖς λόγοις τῆς πίστεως καὶ τῆς καλῆς διδασκαλίας ᾗ παρηκολούθηκας.

As he would prove himself a faithful minister of Christ, Timothy is
here exhorted to bring the points touched on before his brethren.
ὑποτίθεσθαι, *to propound*, a mild expression, according to Chrysostom,
though it could signify *prescribe*, conveys the idea of suggestion rather
than injunction, just as the simple term διάκονος eschews the display of
ecclesiastical governance. ἐντρεφέσθαι, like Seneca's *liberalibus dis-
ciplinis innutriri*, is a classical verb repeatedly used by Josephus for
indoctrination in a subject (cf. Plut. *Alex.* 47, *Arat.* 1) and coupled by
Philo (ii. 575) with τοῖς ἱεροῖς γράμμασιν. οἱ λόγοι τῆς πίστεως
appears to imply a compendium of Christian doctrine already drafted,
like the τύπος διδαχῆς of Rom. vi. 17, and the same presupposition
underlies 'the good teaching with which thou hast familiarized thyself'.
Such is the meaning of παρακολουθεῖν in the preface to Luke's Gospel
(M. & M.); but it may indicate an intelligent grasp of a topic. Cf.
εὐπαρακολούθητος (Aristot., Polyb.).

iv. 7, 8. τοὺς δὲ βεβήλους καὶ γρᾳώδεις μύθους παραιτοῦ, γύμναζε
δὲ σεαυτὸν πρὸς εὐσέβειαν. ἡ γὰρ σωματικὴ γυμνασία πρὸς ὀλίγον
ἐστὶν ὠφέλιμος· ἡ δὲ εὐσέβεια πρὸς πάντα ὠφέλιμός ἐστιν, ἐπαγγελίαν
ἔχουσα ζωῆς τῆς νῦν καὶ τῆς μελλούσης.

βέβηλος, an archaic classical term for *profane*, is here linked with
γρᾳώδης, an epithet which Strabo (i. 32) couples with μυθολογία, in
reference to the Jewish legendary trash which the apostle had already
disparaged. We find Cicero writing of *fabellae aniles*, and Plato, Lucian
(*Philops.* 9) and Galen all use the phrase γραῶν μῦθοι. παραιτεῖσθαι,
in its later usage, here exemplified, is the verb employed by Greek
scholiasts for rejecting a reading. Bengel fancies that the athletic
simile, so intensely Pauline, conveys a needed hint to Timothy not to
overindulge in that sort of thing! The rejoinder might be made that
bodily exercise was peculiarly requisite for one of his weakly build.
But the comparison takes a wider range. Timothy is to knit his sinews
for the race of godliness. That is to be the arena of his feats of prowess.

Paul concedes the utility of physical culture within certain limits or for a certain while, if we take πρὸς ὀλίγον as James uses it (iv. 14);[1] but he contrasts its modicum of utility with the lasting profit of true religion, of happy augury as regards the present life of its possessor, but fraught with everlasting benedictions as well. Vicious indulgences shorten men's lives. We all know how Shakespeare moralizes on a kindred theme in his portrait of old Adam, who

> Did not with unbashful forehead woo
> The means of weakness and debility;
> Therefore his age is as a lusty winter,
> Frosty but kindly.

The Christian virtues tend intrinsically to lengthening of days. And whilst worldly pleasures wear 'mutable faces', the believer's joys will stand the keenest scrutiny.

Some interpreters take σωματικὴ γυμνασία for ascetic discipline, and it is true that there is a ground common to both; for athletes in training have often to submit to severe restrictions of diet. But if Paul had meant ἀφειδία σώματος, he could have said so, as in Col. ii. 23. Doubtless he was familiar with the term σωμασκία in its gymnastic connotation. Besides, how should even a qualified commendation of such a regimen follow on the declaration that every creation of God is good and as such to be received without demur?

iv. 9, 10. πιστὸς ὁ λόγος καὶ πάσης ἀποδοχῆς ἄξιος. εἰς τοῦτο γὰρ κοπιῶμεν καὶ ἀγωνιζόμεθα, ὅτι ἠλπίκαμεν ἐπὶ θεῷ ζῶντι, ὅς ἐστιν σωτὴρ πάντων ἀνθρώπων, μάλιστα πιστῶν.

For the second time the new formula of ratification sounds in our ears. Does it endorse the foregoing or the following sentence? The majority of modern expositors accept the former alternative and treat the insertion of the conjunction γάρ as conclusive evidence that they are right. Does it settle the point however? The Greek language is so addicted to particles that they can be intercalated half-redundantly. Here we may regard the faithful saying as clenching the foregoing exhortation or laying a basis for anticipating the gain of godliness.

κοπιᾶν implies *arduous toil*. Between the reading ὀνειδιζόμεθα and

---

[1] *utile a poca cosa; utile ad ogni cosa* (Diodati). But cf. examples in Wetstein, and cf. Seneca's reference (*Ep.* xii) to *exercitatio corporis*.

ἀγωνιζόμεθα (W. & H.), the balance of uncial evidence wavers; but the latter reading reproduces one of St Paul's favourite terms and accords best with the gymnastic imagery of the context. The apostle's hallmark is also stamped on the perfect ἠλπικέναι, repeated later on, which figures in I Cor. xv. 19 and II Cor. i. 10, and stresses the fixity of the Psalmist's expectation, and the construction with ἐπί emphasizes the firm basis of the trust exercised. Σωτήρ here plainly bears its usual Greek meaning of *Preserver* (cf. Ps. xxxvi. 6); but Paul pointedly employs it with a double significance; for Christianity raises the word to a higher plane.

Is the reward of the believer's living and labour commensurate with the outlay? Assuredly, replies the quickened soul, its gaze focused on the Lifegiver and on the infinite riches of His storehouse. The proximate mercy of preservation is in its case eclipsed by the glorious vista of everlasting salvation lying ahead.

iv. 11–13. παράγγελλε ταῦτα καὶ δίδασκε. μηδείς σοι τῆς νεότητος καταφρονείτω, ἀλλὰ τύπος γένου τῶν πιστῶν ἐν λόγῳ, ἐν ἀναστροφῇ, ἐν ἀγάπῃ, ἐν πίστει, ἐν ἁγνείᾳ. ἕως ἔρχομαι πρόσεχε τῇ ἀναγνώσει, τῇ παρακλήσει, τῇ διδασκαλίᾳ.

More directly personal injunctions now ensue. παραγγέλλειν suggests command or proclamation. Timothy is to enjoin what he has himself been taught; and, as many of those admonished would be his seniors in age, Paul bids him so demean himself as to win their involuntary esteem.

νεότης, as Plato remarks (οἱ πρὸς ἡμᾶς νέοι, *Laws* 770), is a relative term. Rationalistic critics have scented an anachronism in its use at the date which these Epistles presume; but like the Latin *juvenis*, it extended considerably farther on than our word *youthful* reaches. In Aulus Gellius (x. 28) soldiers are reckoned *iuniores* up to forty-six, and Josephus applies the epithet to Agrippa (*Antiq.* xviii. 6) when near forty. M. & M. also cite from Irenaeus a passage affirming its application till the age of forty. Plutarch again (*Pomp.* 13) qualifies νέος with the adverb κομιδῇ to denote *early* manhood, not more than thirty (Polyb. xviii. 2), and Philostratus (*Apoll.* 4. 22) trisects human ages into οἱ γέροντες, οἱ νέοι, τὸ ἐφηβικόν. On any fair computation Timothy would at this period have been from thirty-five to forty.

Despise is the emphatic word; for no Greek maxim was more familiar than the subordination of youth to age. πρεσβυτέρους τοὺς ἄρχοντας δεῖ, νεωτέρους δὲ τοὺς ἀρχομένους, says Plato (*Rep.* 412) and re-echoes the sentiment in his *Timaeus* (34) and *Laws* (690, 876, 917). To Xenophon (*Mem.* ii. 3. 16) and Plutarch (*Mor.* 487) the rule is beyond gainsaying. No wonder Paul is concerned to impress on Timothy, himself a Hellene on his father's side, that *he* is not to be ruled by οἱ πρεσβύτεροι in his legation among those who associated authority closely with age. Cf. Peter's ruling, I Pet. v. 5. τύπος means *print* or *impress*, as of a body (Plut. *Mor.* 602); hence, as here, a *pattern* or *model* (cf. our use of 'typical'). Thus Plutarch, copying the Latin *exempli gratia*, writes τύπου ἕνεκεν (*Mor.* 11). Let his walk supply no mark for the enemy to fire at, but be irreproachably watchful. ἀναστροφή covers the whole demeanour and ἁγνεία the entire concept of purity.

ἡ ἀνάγνωσις joined with hortatory and doctrinal labours must appertain to his public services, and is rightly understood of the reading of the Scriptures in the congregation. The phrase occurs in Lk. iv. 16; Acts xiii. 15, of the synagogue lessons. Even in Plato (*Laws* 810; *Parm.* 127) it is used of rehearsals given by authors, and in Plutarch (*Mor.* 514) ὁ ἀναγνωστικός probably means 'public reader'; at any rate, there are reasons for thinking that by this time portions of the New Testament and the Old Testament (cf. Joseph. *Antiq.* x. 6) were read aloud in Christian assemblies (cf. I Tim. v. 18; Col. iv. 16; I Thes. v. 27). The older commentators applied it to study of books in general; but the connection, the article, and Cicero's *anagnostes* (*Att.* i. 12, *Fam.* v. 9) all favour the other meaning. προσέχειν with the dative is, of course, a recognized abridgment of προσέχειν τὸν νοῦν, *to fix one's attention on.*

iv. 14. μὴ ἀμέλει τοῦ ἐν σοὶ χαρίσματος, ὃ ἐδόθη σοι διὰ προφητείας μετὰ ἐπιθέσεως τῶν χειρῶν τοῦ πρεσβυτερίου.

The classical verb ἀμελεῖν takes a genitive construction. χάρισμα forms one of Paul's pet words, once used by Peter. One instance of its occurrence elsewhere can be named, in Philo's *Alleg. Interp.* iii. 78. The apostle employs the term to denote the supernatural gifts of the Spirit accorded to the primitive Church, and in this passage applies it to the special equipment of Timothy for his special ministry. The announcement of his predestined mission appears to have accompanied his ordination and to have taken the shape of a prophecy of his future career, and the conferment of the gift to have attended the imposition of hands that formed part of his official setting-apart for his work. διά should express 'through the medium of' prophecy, itself a manifestation of the Holy Spirit's illumination. τὸ πρεσβυτέριον, found elsewhere in the New Testament only in Luke's writings, where it signifies the Jewish elders, here plainly indicates the collected body of presbyters who bore part in the ceremony. We learn from passages in Acts (viii. 17, ix. 17, xix. 6) that the laying on of hands was frequently coupled with an effusion of the Spirit. Cf. Nu. xxvii. 18, Dt. xxxiv. 9. Paul's treasured 'son in the faith' is here reminded that if he is called to preach and bear rule, that is because he has been divinely sent on these errands, and furnished for their discharge. A final charge concludes the chapter.

iv. 15, 16. ταῦτα μελέτα, ἐν τούτοις ἴσθι, ἵνα σου ἡ προκοπὴ φανερὰ ᾖ πᾶσιν. ἔπεχε σεαυτῷ καὶ τῇ διδασκαλίᾳ, ἐπίμενε αὐτοῖς· τοῦτο γὰρ ποιῶν καὶ σεαυτὸν σώσεις καὶ τοὺς ἀκούοντάς σου.

μελετᾶν can signify either to *study* or *practise*, and which to choose in this context is a puzzle. In favour of the former, there pleads New Testament usage in Mark and Acts; for the latter, the fact that it is the predominant meaning in Greek literature. The phrase occurs in Arrian and Galen. ἐν τούτοις ἴσθι, *be intent on these things*, has a severely practical ring, like the *insumus usque* of Lucretius, and Horace's *totus in hoc sum*; cf. Plut. *Pomp.* 69, *Mor.* 342. προκοπή belongs to Hellenistic writers, like Polybius and Plutarch; it occurs sixteen times in Vettius Valens, so it grew popular in later days.

ἔπεχε σεαυτῷ, *keep an eye on thyself*, another Polybian phrase, has affinity with προσέχειν supra, and may be viewed, like it, as a syncopation. ἐπίμενε αὐτοῖς, *persist therein*, closes a list of almost military orders, redolent of the apostle to the Gentiles, a martinet for spiritual efficiency, if ever there were one! σῴζειν, addressed to a company of believers and their captain in charge, should bear its spiritual sense. It may comprise safeguarding; but we take it here to relate to the salvation of the gospel. That is wholly of grace; yet the fullest assurance of God's power to keep the fire burning on the 'mean altar of our hearts' does not release us from the duty of tending the languishing flame; for the purposes of sovereign grace are accomplished through the instrumentality of second causes. The saving of Timothy's hearers was, as far as he was concerned, dependent on his exemplary carriage.

Mark the triple watch which it is incumbent on every Christian teacher to keep, first over his inner life, secondly over the instruction he gives, and thirdly over his hearers. If any of these be erratic, his influence, instead of being salutary to his auditors, will become mischievous or nugatory.

v. 1–16. TIMOTHY'S RELATIONS WITH CHURCH MEMBERS

v. 1, 2. πρεσβυτέρῳ μὴ ἐπιπλήξῃς ἀλλὰ παρακάλει ὡς πατέρα, νεωτέρους ὡς ἀδελφούς, πρεσβυτέρας ὡς μητέρας, νεωτέρας ὡς ἀδελφὰς ἐν πάσῃ ἁγνείᾳ.

From the evangelist's personal standard of conduct, the apostle turns to his intercourse with, or regulation of, various sections of the flock. Obviously πρεσβύτερος does not in this passage refer to any official character, but simply to a person's age. Still comparatively young in years, Timothy seems to have felt his responsibilities keenly; and the counsel here given may have been drawn forth by a plea of insufficiency for his onerous task. ἐπιπλήσσειν is a classical verb for reprimanding. Paul's lieutenant is not to employ that tone to his seniors, but to honour grey hairs with a due measure of deference (Lv. xix. 32), and the elderly women with similar respect. Plato and Cicero (*De Off.* i. 34) inculcate the same lesson. Brethren and sisters of his own age he should treat as such, a caution being added regarding the careful attention to decorum demanded in the latter case.

v. 3, 4. χήρας τίμα τὰς ὄντως χήρας. εἰ δέ τις χήρα τέκνα ἢ ἔκγονα ἔχει, μανθανέτωσαν πρῶτον τὸν ἴδιον οἶκον εὐσεβεῖν καὶ ἀμοιβὰς ἀποδιδόναι τοῖς προγόνοις· τοῦτο γάρ ἐστιν ἀπόδεκτον ἐνώπιον τοῦ θεοῦ.

ἡ ὄντως χήρα forms an idiomatic adverbial phrase quite common in Plato. *Genuine widows* are to be prized and helped, those, namely, who are truly destitute.

But cases arise where children or children's children (ἔκγονα) are available sources of support, and it is their clear duty to take the charge upon themselves. The Greek states enforced this obligation by law (θρεπτήρια). So Aristotle *Nic. Eth.* ix. 2; cf. Eur. *Iph. in Aul.* 1230, Plat. *Laws* 717. Members of relieving committees are familiar with the tendency often displayed by relatives of slender means, to devolve the task of providing for an aged member of the family on benevolent institutions. Such selfishness must be discountenanced; for it is a palpable breach of the fifth commandment. εὐσεβεῖν with the accusative may be rare, but it governs θεόν in Acts xvii. 23, Joseph. *Ap.* ii. 10 and a decree of Nero quoted in M. & M. ἀμοιβὰς ἀποδιδόναι is a classical and inscriptional formula for *making requital*. πρόγονοι, the Scottish *forbears*, may be used of living progenitors, as by Plato (*Laws* xi. 931). ἐνώπιον with the genitive ranks as a vernacular usage with the literary purists; but the LXX, by adopting it to translate a common Hebrew idiom, had familiarized its readers with the expression.

v. 5–8. ἡ δὲ ὄντως χήρα καὶ μεμονωμένη ἤλπικεν ἐπὶ τὸν θεὸν καὶ προσμένει ταῖς δεήσεσιν καὶ ταῖς προσευχαῖς νυκτὸς καὶ ἡμέρας. ἡ δὲ σπαταλῶσα ζῶσα τέθνηκεν. καὶ ταῦτα παράγγελλε, ἵνα ἀνεπίλημπτοι ὦσιν. εἰ δέ τις τῶν ἰδίων καὶ μάλιστα οἰκείων οὐ προνοεῖ, τὴν πίστιν ἤρνηται καὶ ἔστιν ἀπίστου χείρων.

We have already encountered Paul's peculiar use of ἐλπίζειν in the perfect (iv. 10), though the preposition here governs a different case; the meaning is *has fixed her hope Godwards*, like Anna in the temple. It is difficult to distinguish between the two vocables for *prayer*. Notice the order νυκτὸς καὶ ἡμέρας. John reverses it; but *night and day* is Paul's invariable sequence. σπαταλᾶν (Polyb., LXX, Lucian *Ep.* 50), *to live sumptuously*, or *in self-indulgent style*, breathes the atmosphere of luxurious Ephesus. προνοεῖν with the genitive, meaning *provide for*, has both literary and popular support. οἱ οἰκεῖοι in distinction from οἱ ἴδιοι must express consanguinity, as opposed to connections of a less intimate sort. τὴν πίστιν ἀρνεῖσθαι, *to deny the faith* one professes, is a purely Christian locution which indicates a settled rule of faith and an organized church. The common New Testament usage of the verb is with a personal object, herein deviating from general Greek usage. Cf. Mt. x. 33; Tit. i. 16, etc.

73

Two notable declarations here meet the eye. She that lives petulantly or voluptuously (κατασπαταλᾶν, LXX) ranks as a religious corpse; hers is a living death. It is the callous-hearted, flaunting woman of fashion who gets a rebuke; and the trenchant condemnation passed on the light-minded disowner of his kith and kin reminds us that a religious profession which falls below the standard of duty recognized by the world is a wretched fraud. Philo employs the phrase metonymically in this manner.

v. 9, 10. χήρα καταλεγέσθω μὴ ἔλαττον ἐτῶν ἑξήκοντα γεγονυῖα, ἑνὸς ἀνδρὸς γυνή, ἐν ἔργοις καλοῖς μαρτυρουμένη· εἰ ἐτεκνοτρόφησεν, εἰ ἐξενοδόχησεν, εἰ ἁγίων πόδας ἔνιψεν, εἰ θλιβομένοις ἐπήρκεσεν, εἰ παντὶ ἔργῳ ἀγαθῷ ἐπηκολούθησεν.

The Lord has a special regard for the widow, and so His servant lingers on this topic. But we find it hard to be certain concerning the details of his instructions. Who are these enrolled widows? A separate class? Apparently. It has been ingeniously suggested that they represent what is often a problem in mission fields today, the divorced wives of polygamists who have become Christians, and therefore monogamists. That notion agrees with the etymology of the word, if lacking in evidential support. But compare χηραίνειν, meaning 'to divorce', in Herodas i. 21 and Strabo vi. 3. This passage has also been identified with the official Church-widows or *presbyterae* of later date and made a ground of suspecting the authenticity of the Epistle; but nothing here specified involves official position. They are to be seniors in age, wives of one husband—which must be interpreted in the light of iii. 2, 12— and of approved character. καταλέγειν, *to register, enrol* (e.g. a soldier) is good classical Greek, and is used by Dion. Hal. ii. 68 of Vestals; but L. & S. suggest another sense, *be reckoned* a widow, for which Plato appears as sponsor. Still, we seem to be dealing now with widows of a peculiar type, such as the above-named theory postulates.

μαρτυρεῖσθαι, *to be in good repute*, an expression met with in Acts and Hebrews, can be paralleled from the papyri, Josephus and Marcus Aurelius (vii. 63). τεκνοτροφεῖν, a compound after Paul's manner, dates from Aristotle and may be illustrated by Epictetus (i. 23), Plutarch, *Mor.* 1096, or Polybius's variation τέτροφε τέκνα (xii. 25); and its counterpart ξενοδοκεῖν from much older sources. νίπτειν, used of partial washing, in literary Hellenistic (Menander, Plut.) replaces the earlier νίζειν. θλίβεσθαι, one of Paul's favourite vocables, meaning *to be oppressed*, may be met with in Epictetus, Polybius (ii. 48), and the papyri. ἐπαρκεῖν, meaning *to assist*, can produce excellent vouchers of classicality (Wetstein). However classified, these elder Church-widows are to be marked by the moral qualifications, some of which are singled out for notice. They are to be true 'mothers in Israel', zealous of good works, like the modern deaconesses so-called in certain churches, whose duties vary in accordance with current social conditions. A needy and deserving section of the Christian community is here provided for in a capacity of service for which they have given proof of fitness.

v. 11–13. νεωτέρας δὲ χήρας παραιτοῦ· ὅταν γὰρ καταστρηνιάσωσιν τοῦ Χριστοῦ γαμεῖν θέλουσιν, ἔχουσαι κρίμα ὅτι τὴν πρώτην πίστιν ἠθέτησαν. ἅμα δὲ καὶ ἀργαὶ μανθάνουσιν περιερχόμεναι τὰς οἰκίας, οὐ μόνον δὲ ἀργαὶ ἀλλὰ καὶ φλύαροι καὶ περίεργοι, λαλοῦσαι τὰ μὴ δέοντα.

καταστρηνιᾶν is an ἅπαξ εἰρημένον, but the simple verb, like Latin *lascivire*, occurs in the New Comedy and Rev. xviii. 7, 9 for perversity bred of lustihood. ἀθετεῖν of things = *to cancel, invalidate*; Lucian (*V.H.* ii. 20) employs the term of Homeric passages obelized as spurious by the grammarians. Similarly in Heb. ix. 26 it denotes a cancellation of sin. The expression πίστιν ἀθετεῖν, strictly taken, is used by Polybius (xi. 27) and Diodorus for a breach of engagement. It may be so construed here, or *their first faith* may mean their original confession. ἀργαὶ μανθάνουσιν seems to be an elliptical way of saying *they learn to be idle*, not unexampled with this verb. Cf. καλὸς ἀκούειν, 'to be regarded as fair'. Plato (*Euthyd.* 276) has σοφοὶ μανθάνουσι, and Field supplies other examples. Chrysostom also interprets it thus. περίεργος conveys the idea of meddlesomeness. γαμεῖν of the woman is confined to New Testament usage.

The apostle now casts his searchlight upon an opposite group of widows, whose propensities justify the age-limit he has assigned. Manifestly, in a voluptuous centre like Ephesus there were to be found unworthy parasites of the Christian fellowship, and among them widows of inferior grade to those previously noticed. We are reminded of the criterion, 'He that endureth to the end shall be saved.' Those whom Paul here censures succumb under that touchstone. Their vows are fickle; they betray wanton tendencies which are treasonable against their Lord, however successfully masked for a time. A graphic sketch of these empty chatterboxes (φλύαροι) is thrown on the canvas, and we immediately recognize the portrait. Such praters, whatever may have been their early promise, sink to the level of busybodies, who make their visiting calls opportunities for unseemly (τὰ μὴ δέοντα) tittle-tattle.

v. 14–16. βούλομαι οὖν νεωτέρας γαμεῖν, τεκνογονεῖν, οἰκοδεσ-ποτεῖν, μηδεμίαν ἀφορμὴν διδόναι τῷ ἀντικειμένῳ λοιδορίας χάριν· ἤδη γάρ τινες ἐξετράπησαν ὀπίσω τοῦ Σατανᾶ. εἴ τις πιστὴ ἔχει χήρας ἐπαρκείτω αὐταῖς καὶ μὴ βαρείσθω ἡ ἐκκλησία, ἵνα ταῖς ὄντως χήραις ἐπαρκέσῃ.

Here we remark some more compound verbs of a Pauline stamp of abbreviation. We have already met the noun τεκνογονία (ii. 15). Else-where οἰκοδεσποτεῖν has an astronomical application; but οἰκοδεσ-πότης (Mt. x. 25) occurs in Plutarch (*Mor.* 271), in conjunction with οἰκοδέσποινα, for the *pater* and *mater familias*. ἀφορμὴν διδόναι and λαμβάνειν are peculiar to Paul's vocabulary. λοιδορίας χάριν, *in regard to railing*, places χάριν last, according to the literary, but not vernacular, rule. ὀπίσω with the genitive still belongs to the category of Hebraic Greek.

The authoritative tone of this decision would scarcely have been adopted by a simulator, nor would it have comported with the ascetic exaltation of celibacy and deprecation of marriage so quickly foisted into the patristic *milieu*. Indeed it might seem to conflict with Paul's attitude to marriage in Corinthians, till we remark the exceptional occasion of the advice there given. The medicine prescribed for feminine levity consists in the responsible duties of motherhood and domestic economy, with their sobering effects on the tittle-tattlers. No handle must be afforded to the enemy to point the finger of scorn at members of the Church. From Paul's employment of the term else-where it is plain that ὁ ἀντικείμενος does not signify the devil, as some have fancied, but any traducer of the saints.

The faithful party—πιστὸς ἢ πιστή has considerable MSS. support—*who has widows* appears to be their relative, male or female, who, if he or she exist, ought to relieve the widows here spoken of (discriminated from 'widows indeed'), rather than let the church bear the burden. Again we are tempted to conclude that these widows may be divorced wives, though the alternative presents itself that the ὄντως χῆραι are not relicts merely, but relicts in destitute circumstances.

v. 17–25. TIMOTHY'S RELATIONS WITH CHURCH OFFICERS

v. 17, 18. οἱ καλῶς προεστῶτες πρεσβύτεροι διπλῆς τιμῆς ἀξιούσ-θωσαν, μάλιστα οἱ κοπιῶντες ἐν λόγῳ καὶ διδασκαλίᾳ· λέγει γὰρ ἡ γραφή Βοῦν ἀλοῶντα οὐ φιμώσεις· καὶ ῎Αξιος ὁ ἐργάτης τοῦ μισθοῦ αὐτοῦ.

οἱ προεστῶτες is not a technical term of office, but a general phrase expressive of superintendence. We have seen it applied above (iii. 5) to the father of a family; here it is transferred to the presbyterate in its quality of administration. The ruling as distinct from the preaching elder of certain Reformed Churches finds its authorization in this verse, since it seems to imply that the rule of a church should lie in the hands of a company of elders, a section only of whom are actual pastors. We cannot imagine the apostle Paul discouraging church discipline, after the modern fashion. Another view seems, however, defensible, that two classes of presbyters are not predicated but that presbyters pre-eminently painstaking 'in word and teaching' are singled out (διπλα-σίας τιμῆς ἄξιοι is a phrase of Plato, *Laws* 230) as worthy of generous treatment; for τιμή *may* signify pecuniary reward. Certainly the ensuing Scriptural ratification looks that way.

The Mosaic precept (Dt. xxv. 4) forbidding the muzzling of the ox while treading out the corn, previously used in I Cor. ix. 9, clenches the injunction, for if in its primary design that precept, like the adjacent one forbidding the robbing of bird's nests without compunction, breathes the spirit of Him whose tender mercies are over all His works, it was likewise designed to awaken thoughtfulness and kind dealing towards those by whose labours we benefit. A second corroboration of his judgment follows; *the labourer is worthy of his hire.* It is usual to regard this as the echo of a current proverb, also found on our Lord's lips in Lk. x. 7. But Christ does not appear to be borrowing an adage like 'Physician, heal thyself' in that passage, but uttering a dictum of His own. We think therefore that there is much to be said for the contention of Dr Warfield that we have here a citation verbally exact from Luke's Gospel, treated as an integral portion of Holy Writ. It cannot be denied that the conjunction *and* places the second reference on the same level of authority as the first and under the same category of Biblical proof; and if Paul's own Epistles (of which there is evidence) acquired inspired rank during his lifetime, surely Luke's Gospel may have received the same *imprimatur* as a textual authority within the same period. If apostolicity be the canon of canonicity, early recognition of such a document was naturally consequent. Baur has turned this supposition to sceptical account, and discovered therein a proof of the second-century origin of the Pastorals. But the more warrantable inference is that a New Testament canon was emerging side by side with the Old and the ἀνάγνωσις of iv. 13 points to a public reading of the Scriptures in divine worship inclusive of the newer fount of illumination along with the Hebrew oracles. Assuredly the most wayside of the utterances of Jesus ranks as God's word; for He is our *Ipse dixit*, the Word incarnate; but the Gospels are their sole authentic register.

v. 19, 20. κατὰ πρεσβυτέρου κατηγορίαν μὴ παραδέχου ἐκτὸς εἰ μὴ ἐπὶ δύο ἢ τριῶν μαρτύρων· τοὺς ἁμαρτάνοντας ἐνώπιον πάντων ἔλεγχε, ἵνα καὶ οἱ λοιποὶ φόβον ἔχωσιν.

Further rules for his deputy's regulation are now appended. The presbyter meant is obviously ministerial. Against such a pastor he is to entertain no charge not borne out by abundant evidence. So Plato and Aristotle use παραδέχεσθαι of 'accepting' a definition. ἐκτὸς εἰ μή, *except*, is an exclusively Pauline idiom in the New Testament, met with in inscriptions (Deissmann), but also in Vettius Valens and rarely in Lucian. ἐπί with the genitive, meaning *in presence of*, has classical authority. Observe indeclinable δύο, as often.

Offenders are to receive public reprehension for a warning to others. Once more we gain the impression that the ministerial body fell short of its ideal and required ever and anon explicit censure, though the general terms used may extend to other culprits.

V. 21. διαμαρτύρομαι ἐνώπιον τοῦ θεοῦ καὶ Χριστοῦ Ἰησοῦ καὶ τῶν ἐκλεκτῶν ἀγγέλων ἵνα ταῦτα φυλάξῃς χωρὶς προκρίματος, μηδὲν ποιῶν κατὰ πρόσκλισιν.

The solemn adjuration to Timothy comes rather unexpectedly after previous monitions. Obviously his physical debility tended to colour his treatment of others' misdemeanours, and he was one of those Melanchthonic characters whose judgment is apt to be warped by their native plasticity. He is therefore charged in weightiest terms to deal impartially and to show no favouritism whatsoever. As a word of grave protest διαμαρτύρεσθαι hails from the Attic law-courts, and appears several times in the Acts. Observe again how Paul speaking on oath, as it were, joins the Father and the Son together as his highest attestation. The *elect angels* are added, because 'in this theatre of human life only God and the angels are lookers-on' (Bacon). The spirits who kept their first estate have definite relationships with the Church of God and are attendants on His economy of grace and on those who worship Him in spirit and in truth. πρόκριμα and πρόσκλισις are new Pauline substantives, elicited by a new context. The former answers to the Latin *praeiudicium*, from which it plainly takes its rise. It is unknown to Greek literature in general; but the identical phrase *absque praeiudicio* occurs in Aulus Gellius and χωρὶς προκρίματος may be met with in second-century papyri. πρόσκλισις is less rare; Polybius and Sextus Empiricus employ it in the sense of predilection. κατὰ πρόσκλισιν, *with partiality*, depends on the use of the verb προσκλίνειν by Polybius and the LXX similar in meaning to Latin *acclinare*, or on the Roman term for bias, *inclinatio*. Clement of Rome adopts the expression.

V. 22, 23. χεῖρας ταχέως μηδενὶ ἐπιτίθει μηδὲ κοινώνει ἁμαρτίαις ἀλλοτρίαις· σεαυτὸν ἁγνὸν τήρει. μηκέτι ὑδροπότει ἀλλὰ οἴνῳ ὀλίγῳ χρῶ διὰ τὸν στόμαχον καὶ τὰς πυκνάς σου ἀσθενείας.

He warns his legate not to be overhasty in ordaining aspirants to the ministry, but to be sedulous in keeping himself from connivance with the transgressions of others. Unworthy motives might warp a probationer for office, and it behoves him to exercise spiritual discernment in canvassing motives. The notion that the reference is to the restoration of penitents to membership seems exceedingly far-fetched, nor has it Chrysostom's support.

To trace the connection of verse 23 with its predecessor and successor has fairly nonplussed the commentators. Is it not an *obiter dictum?* The ancients had no footnotes, and so the apostle John inserts in the main text of his gospel observations we should consign to the foot of the page. It may be that having exhorted Timothy to 'keep himself pure' (ἁγνός) Paul's mind reverts to the consecration of the Nazirite in Nu. vi where both ἁγνεία and ἁγνισμός occur in the LXX, with its solemn abjuration of wine. Now Timothy, conversant from childhood with the Old Testament Scriptures, may have regarded this vow of abstinence as a precedent binding on himself, and so it may have been meet to remind him that wine was one of the Lord's good gifts to man, at least medicinally beneficial, and that he lay under no embargo to taboo it. ὑδροποτεῖν (another compound) has classical authority and is found in Arrian's *Epictetus* (iii. 13) close at hand. στόμαχος in our sense of the term may be classed among Latinisms; in earlier Greek it signifies 'throat'. Plutarch first uses it for stomach, the common meaning of *stomachus*, and prescribes wine especially for stomach ailments to those needing a tonic (*Sympos*. iii. 5. 2). Cf. Strabo xiv. 1, 15.

v. 24, 25. τινῶν ἀνθρώπων αἱ ἁμαρτίαι πρόδηλοί εἰσιν προάγουσαι εἰς κρίσιν, τισὶν δὲ καὶ ἐπακολουθοῦσιν· ὡσαύτως καὶ τὰ ἔργα τὰ καλὰ πρόδηλα καὶ τὰ ἄλλως ἔχοντα κρυβῆναι οὐ δύνανται.

We fail to discern the relevance of this verse, unless it reverts to the theme of verse 22. Then it becomes quite clear. Timothy has been called on to diagnose character, and Paul supplies him with a clue for the task, and the verdicts he has to pass. Let him hold the scales in equipoise. There are cases in which a man's defaults stare one in the face and clamour for animadversion. These must needs be dealt with summarily. There are other cases not so patent, round which there hangs a veil of uncertainty. Concerning these suspense of judgment may be discreet. But sooner or later the truth will out, and a religious professor's real character be revealed. The day of judgment will try every man's work and influence, whether personal or posthumous, of what sort it is; but even here and now conscientious estimates of godliness and godlessness respectively find their attestation in the event. Let him not, in his character of assessor, be rash, either in point of condemnation or clemency. πρόδηλος does not mean 'clear beforehand', but *obvious, manifest* (cf. Heb. vii. 14). The late aorist κρυβῆναι, frequent in the New Testament and the LXX, seldom occurs elsewhere.

The indefinite τινῶν should, according to rule, be enclitic; but where, as here, it stands opposed to another τις, even writers like Aristotle place it first in the sentence (cf. Plut. *Mor.* 472). προάγειν εἰς κρίσιν appears to mean *lead the way to judgment*, whether by enabling the human censor to come to a decision, or by rendering a man ripe for the award of the last day.

Most present-day expositors understand τὰ ἄλλως ἔχοντα of good works, not yet brought to light; but to us it seems paradoxical to describe them as incapable of being hidden. Besides, in usage (cf. Plut. *Mor.* 187) ἄλλος and ἄλλως are used of things which are not as they should be. Such a phrase would be an odd negation of πρόδηλος, when τὰ καλά has been placed in the foreground. Cf. Virgil's *dis aliter visum*, 'not unmixed with reproach' (Conington).

vi. 1, 2. MASTERS AND SERVANTS

From church discipline Paul turns to that of the household. A query on that score may have been addressed to him; but we find parallel passages in several of his Epistles. There is one, for example, in Tit. ii. 9 f. (see p. 106).

vi. 1, 2. ὅσοι εἰσὶν ὑπὸ ζυγὸν δοῦλοι τοὺς ἰδίους δεσπότας πάσης τιμῆς ἀξίους ἡγείσθωσαν, ἵνα μὴ τὸ ὄνομα τοῦ θεοῦ καὶ ἡ διδασκαλία βλασφημῆται. οἱ δὲ πιστοὺς ἔχοντες δεσπότας μὴ καταφρονείτωσαν ὅτι ἀδελφοί εἰσιν, ἀλλὰ μᾶλλον δουλευέτωσαν ὅτι πιστοί εἰσιν καὶ ἀγαπητοὶ οἱ τῆς εὐεργεσίας ἀντιλαμβανόμενοι.

ὑπὸ ζυγόν in Polybius often expresses political subjugation; here we take it to signify *under subjection* more or less rigorous; for the first case treated of relates to an unbelieving master, as in I Pet. ii. 18. How is the slave to demean himself where he is *sub iugo*, made constantly sensible of his thraldom? For Christ's sake let a believer in such a plight pay all due honour to his master, that God's name and His doctrine may not incur blame. The exchange of δεσπότης for κύριος, Paul's earlier term in this connection, has been deemed suspicious, though found in Peter's first Epistle. The most natural explanation is that the Latin *dominus* has influenced the apostle's terminology, the more readily perhaps because of the sacred associations of κύριος; or he may have thought fit to borrow the technical phrase for the master of a servile family, exercising δεσποτεία over them. ἡγεῖσθαι ἑαυτόν with adjective is a peculiarly Pauline expression (Acts xxvi. 2; cf. I Tim. i. 12 *supra*).

He then proceeds to deal with the case of a believing master like Philemon, where the risk lay in the direction of a disrespectful tone on the part of the servant towards a brother in Christ. We should not have expected a Christian slave to look down on his master as from a superior platform; but doubtless among Greek δοῦλοι, such as we come across in Menander's Comedies, the apostle had seen evidences of such an inversion of roles. It must be understood, he feels, that 'spiritual equality does not efface civil distinctions' (Fairbairn). Inscriptions show that εὐεργεσία means *service done*, and the somewhat ambiguous verb ἀντιλαμβάνεσθαι must be construed accordingly. The Authorized Version goes wrong in this passage through neglect to mark the subject of the sentence, i.e. the masters, denominated *those partaking of the service rendered*, or possibly *laying claim to* that service. Because their masters are believers and beloved, it is the more incumbent on their believing domestics to render services with the utmost goodwill. Here the slave is raised from a chattel to a spiritual equal in grace.

The abstract question of slavery it was not the apostles' task to handle. Bound up with the social fabric of the ancient world, it had already occasioned sanguinary servile wars, and had to be sorrowfully recognized as one of the elements of judgment in a sin-stricken globe. But Christianity's spiritual campaign would have been fatally compromised by stirring the smouldering embers of class-hatred into a devouring flame, or opening an asylum for runaway slaves in its bosom. Will any one allege that it was John Wyclif's duty, though constitutionally a bit of a leveller, to cast in his lot with Wat Tyler, in a furious attempt to put an end to the evils of the feudal system? Had not Paul's conjunction of slave-dealers with whoremongers (i.10) already branded the institution?

vi. 3-6. FINAL CENSURE OF HETERODOX TEACHERS

vi. 3-5. ταῦτα δίδασκε καὶ παρακάλει. εἴ τις ἑτεροδιδασκαλεῖ καὶ μὴ προσέρχεται ὑγιαίνουσιν λόγοις τοῖς τοῦ κυρίου ἡμῶν Ἰησοῦ Χριστοῦ καὶ τῇ κατ' εὐσέβειαν διδασκαλίᾳ, τετύφωται μηδὲν ἐπιστάμενος ἀλλὰ νοσῶν περὶ ζητήσεις καὶ λογομαχίας, ἐξ ὧν γίνεται φθόνος, ἔρις, βλασφημίαι, ὑπόνοιαι πονηραί, διαπαρατριβαὶ διεφθαρμένων ἀνθρώπων τὸν νοῦν καὶ ἀπεστερημένων τῆς ἀληθείας, νομιζόντων πορισμὸν εἶναι τὴν εὐσέβειαν.

This is one of the apostle's characteristic outbursts, which he always finds it hard to bring to a period as thought mantles into almost impassionate utterance. ἑτεροδιδασκαλεῖν looks back to the opening of the Epistle, to the subject of which Paul here reverts. προσέρχεσθαι with the dative, signifying plainly *to accede to*, has puzzled hermeneutical skill. It led Bentley to suggest his sole New Testament emendation προσέχεται, which actually appears in the Sinaitic uncial. That might signify *cleave to* (cf. Theophrastus, *History of Plants*, iii. 15, 4); but M. & M. are incorrect in affirming that no adequate parallel has been found for this idiom, as it stands in the text. The very term *proselyte* suggests the suitable sense, or the use in Silver Latin of the verb *accedere* or in German of *beitreten*. It occurs more than once in Philo, who writes προσέρχεσθαι γνώμῃ of agreement with an opinion and προσέρχεσθαι ἀρετῇ of addiction to virtue. The notion is that of *attaching oneself to*.

We have already noted the 'vapouring' sense of τυφοῦσθαι (iii. 6), not unlike the German *eingebildet sein*. The notion of bumptious importance, or self-inflation, certainly underlies the employment of this expression, a special favourite with Plutarch and Lucian and well known to Philo and Josephus. One of Plutarch's interlocutors exclaims, πέπαυμαι τετυφωμένος (*Mor.* 80), 'I have left off swaggering'. νοσῶν, of course, contrasts with ὑγιαίνων, but in English the metaphor can scarcely be reproduced; for *ailing* is too weak and *doting* too strong. Yet cf. Soph. *Trach.* 435. λογομαχίαι, in conjunction with its verbal form (II Tim. ii. 14), presents an ἅπαξ εἰρημένον, the only replica of which, until the era of Porphyry, appears to be its occurrence as the title of one of Varro's satires. ὑπόνοιαι πονηραί may be taken to signify *innuendoes*, and διαπαρατριβαί, which is unique, to designate *mutual*

6-2

altercations. Polybius conjoins παρατριβαί with suspicions (ii. 36) in the sense of feuds and διά in composition not uncommonly indicates rivalry. The noun πορισμός, *livelihood*, pertains to literary Hellenistic. Thus Philodemus (*Oecon.* 44) writes ὁ ἐφήμερος πορισμός for 'means of subsistence'.

The mercenary spirit of the false teachers foreshadowed is here set in relief. Their ruling tendency consists in a perversity of outlook which disrelishes the characteristic features of Christian truth and practice and has a morbid craving for speculations, original or borrowed, such as puff up their propagators with fumes of self-conceit and gender suspicion, slander or strife. In the issue these vapourings breed a vitiated moral sense (so Plato, *Laws* 888, uses the phrase διάνοιαν διεφθαρμένοι), inimical to the verities of the faith. Eventually the mask of godliness is worn to promote sordid ends. A sad indictment this, copiously exemplified (alas!) in the annals of the visible Church, and recalling the caustic saying that 'the apostolical succession of Judases has never failed'. *Counting religion a living* is of course the correct version of the final clause. It may be paralleled from Dionysius of Halicarnassus who expresses *profiteering* somewhere by the phrase χρηματισμὸν ἡγούμενοι τὸν πόλεμον. One embodiment of this corruption looms in view in the Romish merchandise of souls, in her commutation of penances for money and the diabolical device of Papal indulgences, by which millions have been, and are being, cheated of their souls.

vi. 6. ἔστιν δὲ πορισμὸς μέγας ἡ εὐσέβεια μετὰ αὐταρκείας·

Godliness is no legitimate source of worldly or priestly gain; but having touched on this topic it is characteristic of Paul not to dismiss it without closer scrutiny. These dissemblers made piety a 'cloak of covetousness'. True religion, however, has far higher assets than sordid lucre, assets computed in a grander coinage. 'Grace is the godly man's treasure, godliness the gain which he covets' (J. Edwards). The chief difficulty is to fix the precise sense of αὐτάρκεια. In a Stoic philosopher we should construe it *self-sufficiency*, independence of extraneous aids; but that sense does not fit this passage. The lexicons scarcely recognize any other; but the LXX expresses a supply of necessaries by the verb αὐταρκεῖν (Dt. xxxii. 10) and Clement of Alexandria interprets the word subjectively: ἕξις ἀρκουμένη οἷς δεῖ. Cf. Vettius Valens 289, Xen. *Mem.* i. 2, 14, and the line in the *Anthology* (i. 21), αὐτάρκης ὁ πρέσβυς ἔχων ἅλα καὶ δύο κρίμνα. Tennyson's 'ranging with humble livers in content' may help to illustrate the proposition.

vi. 7–10. THE DECEITFULNESS OF WEALTH

vi. 7, 8. οὐδὲν γὰρ εἰσηνέγκαμεν εἰς τὸν κόσμον, [δῆλον] ὅτι οὐδὲ ἐξενεγκεῖν τι δυνάμεθα· ἔχοντες δὲ διατροφὰς καὶ σκεπάσματα, τούτοις ἀρκεσθησόμεθα.

ἐκφέρειν is regularly used of funeral cortèges. W. & H. omit δῆλον, but it is tempting to retain it; for δηλονότι (Gal. iii. 11), like the Latin *scilicet*, punctuates a semi-proverbial sentence of this sort admirably. γῆς ἐπέβην γυμνός, γυμνὸς δ' ὑπὸ γαῖαν ἄπειμι is a hexameter from the *Anthology*. The sentiment appears both in Philo and Seneca,[1] and is echoed by Ovid; *Irus adest subito qui modo Croesus erat.* διατροφή for comestibles is common in the papyri, and occurs in the plural in Epictetus (*Enchir.* 12). σκεπάσματα means *clothing materials*, home-made garments for the most part. So in Josephus (*Antiq.* xv. 770). Aristotle (*Pol.* 1336) designates the Celts' scanty dress as σκέπασμα μικρόν. ἀρκεῖσθαι (with the dative), *to be content with*, is a Greek idiom dating from Plato downwards.

The fact that we all arrived in this world naked may be viewed as an augury that our departure from it will conform to that inglorious precedent. Solomon has expressed the sentiment in Ec. v. 15, from the Hebrew text of which we may take this to be a quotation. Whatever a man amasses by the way is in the nature of luggage, no part of his truest personality, but something he leaves behind at the toll-bar of death. Favoured with the necessaries of life we can dispense with its superfluities.

[1] His dictum *non licet plus efferre quam intuleris* (*Ep.* cii) approximates so closely to that of the apostle that it has been urged in proof that Seneca was acquainted with some portions of the New Testament. But Job i. 21 shows how widespread was the sentiment in question. Does not Hesiod echo it?

vi. 9. οἱ δὲ βουλόμενοι πλουτεῖν ἐμπίπτουσιν εἰς πειρασμὸν καὶ παγίδα καὶ ἐπιθυμίας πολλὰς ἀνοήτους καὶ βλαβερὰς αἵτινες βυθίζουσιν τοὺς ἀνθρώπους εἰς ὄλεθρον καὶ ἀπώλειαν.

βυθίζειν, to plunge, sink, often applied to vessels on the deep, has an extended metaphorical sense, approximating to our verb *swamp*. So Alciphron writes: τὸ νῆφον ὑπὸ τοῦ πάθους βυθίζεται, and Philodemus has it of being swamped by greed, much as it is here used. The two strong nouns which close the sentence express destructive ruin. The process of deterioration which the pursuit of gain engenders presents a sad spectacle, as here depicted. It lands a man in temptation, in some doubtful resolution which becomes an entanglement, and in all manner of foolish and hurtful cravings and passions, such as finally plunge him in remediless perdition.

vi. 10. ῥίζα γὰρ πάντων τῶν κακῶν ἐστιν ἡ φιλαργυρία, ἧς τινες ὀρεγόμενοι ἀπεπλανήθησαν ἀπὸ τῆς πίστεως καὶ ἑαυτοὺς περιέπειραν ὀδύναις πολλαῖς.

Some find an anomaly in 'money-loving which some, while they sought after it...', as if the apostle had predicated a desire for a desire of gain; but a compound like φιλαργυρία can be analysed into its component elements, and Paul's mind merely fastens on the ἀργύριον embedded in the word. ἀποπλανᾶσθαι seems to be a philosophic term (L. & S.) for deviation from truth to error. The figurative use of πείρειν dates from Homer (*Il.* v. 399) and is frequent in literary Hellenistic. Philo's ἀνηκέστοις περιπείρειν κακοῖς merely varies the phrase here employed (cf. Vettius Valens 250). 'A root' rather than *the root* seems a dubious translation (cf. Field). Paul is repeating in another form his Master's declaration: 'ye cannot serve God and mammon'. Of devotion to that idol Ephesus was full; and it would inevitably warp its votary from allegiance to Christ, and transfix him with a sheaf of death-dealing javelins. Many a millionaire, after choking his soul with gold-dust, has died from melancholia! The Hebrew (?) author of the pseudo-Phocylides poem enforces this lesson, and so does Bion's apophthegm, echoed by Sallust and Horace: φιλαργυρία μητρόπολις πάντων τῶν κακῶν.

vi. 11–16. FINAL EXHORTATION TO TIMOTHY

vi. 11, 12. σὺ δέ, ὦ ἄνθρωπε τοῦ θεοῦ, ταῦτα φεῦγε· δίωκε δὲ δικαιοσύνην, εὐσέβειαν, πίστιν, ἀγάπην, ὑπομονήν, πραϋπάθειαν. ἀγωνίζου τὸν καλὸν ἀγῶνα τῆς πίστεως, ἐπιλαβοῦ τῆς αἰωνίου ζωῆς, εἰς ἣν ἐκλήθης καὶ ὡμολόγησας τὴν καλὴν ὁμολογίαν ἐνώπιον πολλῶν μαρτύρων.

We detect the old rhetorical note in these characteristically Pauline sentences. The Hebrew title, man of God ('ish 'Elohim), reminds Timothy of his high vocation and lineage, and incites him to bear himself accordingly. What he is bidden to shun cannot be love of money, as some have fancied. He was in small need of that counsel! The apostle's admonition relates to the catalogue of vices detailed in verses 4 and 5, springing from laxity of doctrine and consequently practice. Over against that black list he here tabulates another of virtues to be cultivated, headed by his favourite verb δίωκε, which recurs a dozen times in earlier Epistles. The rare noun πραϋπάθεια and its cognates are found nowhere beside except in Philo and in some of the Fathers. By general consent the imagery employed is transcribed from the Olympic Games. That seems indisputable in view of the prize held up before the combatants. But ἀγωνίζεσθαι, as we shall see when we examine II Tim. iv. 7, is not quite so decisive on that score as many presume. For the verb has a military as well as athletic connotation, which is conspicuous, for example, in Josephus. Every reader of Thucydides is well acquainted with its martial ring, not unexampled even in the Gospels (Jn. xviii. 36). And none can deny that the soldierly metaphor comes as readily to Paul's mind as the Olympic. The fact is, the word ἀγών, like the Latin certamen, embraces the senses both of contest and conflict; so that the Authorized Version and Revised Version Fight the good fight of faith with its clarion call and stirring stimulus, so painfully absent from tamer constructions of the figure, cannot be ruled out of court, more especially as it re-echoes the sentiment of i. 18. Moreover, the guerdon set before the valiant contender matches best with the ensuing ἐπιλαμβάνεσθαι, to grasp hold of, or in Wyclif's picturesque wording 'catch everlasting life', which is rather too substantial a cast of phraseology in the other case. The injunction, as

Calvin says, runs: *primis ultima respondeant.* Timothy's *good profession* before many witnesses evidently signalizes an outstanding landmark in the evangelist's career, such as his solemn ordination to his life-work.

As the man of God must eschew the works of the flesh, visible in the triflers with holy things of whom we have heard, so he must evince the fruit of the Spirit in earnest pursuance of rectitude of aim, godliness of life, faith, love, patience, clemency. Thus let him wage the best of warfares and clasp life eternal with a sure hold, verifying the name he wears. To this enterprise he stands committed by a solemn profession made with his own lips before a concourse of witnesses. To flinch from that would be at once a breach of promise and an àct of treason.

Paul's ardent spirit now kindles into a blaze. His language grows more impassioned, and the fiery glow can only blaze out in a magnificent doxology.

vi. 13–16. παραγγέλλω σοι ἐνώπιον τοῦ θεοῦ τοῦ ζωογονοῦντος τὰ πάντα καὶ Χριστοῦ Ἰησοῦ τοῦ μαρτυρήσαντος ἐπὶ Ποντίου Πιλάτου τὴν καλὴν ὁμολογίαν τηρῆσαί σε τὴν ἐντολὴν ἄσπιλον ἀνεπίλημπτον μέχρι τῆς ἐπιφανείας τοῦ κυρίου ἡμῶν Ἰησοῦ Χριστοῦ, ἣν καιροῖς ἰδίοις δείξει ὁ μακάριος καὶ μόνος δυνάστης, ὁ βασιλεὺς τῶν βασιλευόντων καὶ κύριος τῶν κυριευόντων, ὁ μόνος ἔχων ἀθανασίαν, φῶς οἰκῶν ἀπρόσιτον, ὃν εἶδεν οὐδεὶς ἀνθρώπων οὐδὲ ἰδεῖν δύναται, ᾧ τιμὴ καὶ κράτος αἰώνιον. ἀμήν.

We are disposed to think ζωοποιοῦντος, which appears in the Sinaitic and one or two other uncials, the right reading here. It is the apostle's compound in his other Epistles and ascribes *quickening* to divine agency more fully than the verb adopted in W. & H.'s text. 'Preserving alive' gives a feebler sense, and Paul is plainly alluding to the eternal life he has just mentioned. However, ζωογονεῖν can itself carry the deeper meaning. Hobart has shown that Galen so uses it, and Vettius Valens (162) employs it for *generate*, and so does Plutarch thrice over (*Mor.* 494, 637, 880), as Aristotle and Theophrastus had done before him. A distinction is drawn between the ὁμολογία of the disciple and the Master; for Christ's own testimony to the truth (ἐπί with the genitive is technical for a judicial appearance) is primary and authoritative, that of His followers secondary and subordinate. Jesus Himself stands forth as the faithful and true Witness, to be hearkened to before all others.

Timothy ranks as a man under authority. He is to keep the commandment *unstained* (ἄσπιλον, a rare adjective attested by inscriptions) with an eye to the *appearing of our Lord Jesus Christ*. Note the full honorific title. Much has been made by Deissmann and his school of the application of the term ἐπιφάνεια by flatterers to the Roman emperors. ὁ κυριεύων is another of their adulatory appellations (Plut. *Mor.* 133). But the same writer uses it of theophanies in general (*Marcell.* 20). δυνάστης and ἀθανασία have a lofty ring well suited to this passage, the latter recurring in I Cor. xv. ἀπρόσιτος, *inapproachable*, a Ciceronian vocable (*Att.* v. 20), used by Josephus of flaming Sinai, conforms to the like literary type. Its converse προσιτός occurs in Strabo (vi. 2, 8) in reference to the accessible cone of Etna. The Shekinah glory in Israel is glanced at in this ascription.

Such a display of St Paul's soaring pinions at their full stretch authenticates the source of this passage. He selects the title *Quickener of all things* to remind his protégé of the fecundating energy of the Holy Spirit accompanying the word. He instances the Saviour's unflinching courage, when, 'found in fashion as a man' and confronted by the powers that be and by foes of hellish rancour, He bore witness to the truth, in order to animate his disciple to copy his Master's holy example. The commandment specified may be either God's revealed will or the injunction of this Epistle. Let Timothy not forget that he is posted where he is by the Commander-in-Chief for sterling service, to be reviewed at the day of scrutiny and vindication lying ahead, when the Lord shall reappear in His glory. That blessed consummation has its appointed season, seemingly tardy to impatient watchers for its dawn. But the triumphant issue of the long-drawn campaign rests in the hands of the sole real Potentate, *the King of kings and Lord of lords* of apocalyptic vision, who alone *hath immortality*, the great I AM, whose prerogative it is *to be. Quid est nisi quia Tu es?* asks Augustine. He is the Self-existent One; we only 'borrow leave to be'. Our immortality constitutes an endowment, not an innate property. Thus Justin Martyr interprets the phrase.

It is the Father *whom no man hath seen or can see* that here engrosses the apostle's contemplation and receives his adoring homage. Observe that the majestic spectacle unfolded, though veiled withal, embodies the conception of everlasting strength. Power belongs supremely to the King immortal. 'It is a flower of His crown imperial', says John Owen. 'If the proudest of creatures go beyond the limits of His permission, He will send worms to eat them up.' His control keeps chaos at bay.

There is a fascinating theory of modern science that primordial light is itself invisible. If so, how fitting an emblem of Deity it becomes. At any rate we know how solar rays can 'chastise inquisitive eyes'. Even so the insufferable brightness engirdling the adytum of Deity may form an inviolable curtain to human sight, avenging every intrusion on its awful privacy with eclipse of vision. 'He clothes Himself with light as with a garment'; but who can stand before its dazzling splendour? A lustre brighter than the sun had once blinded the apostle; but that apocalypse had not rendered Jesus invisible to His prisoner of war. It is otherwise with the glory, dark with excess of brightness, that enspheres absolute Deity. Like a high-tension electric current, that cannot be faced by beings 'whose foundation is in the dust', that transcendent effulgence must perforce consume finite frailty with its radiant infinitude.

vi. 17–19. PARTING ADMONITION TO THE RICH

vi. 17–19. τοῖς πλουσίοις ἐν τῷ νῦν αἰῶνι παράγγελλε μὴ ὑψηλοφρονεῖν μηδὲ ἠλπικέναι ἐπὶ πλούτου ἀδηλότητι ἀλλ' ἐπὶ θεῷ τῷ παρέχοντι ἡμῖν πάντα πλουσίως εἰς ἀπόλαυσιν, ἀγαθοεργεῖν, πλουτεῖν ἐν ἔργοις καλοῖς, εὐμεταδότους εἶναι, κοινωνικούς, ἀποθησαυρίζοντας ἑαυτοῖς θεμέλιον καλὸν εἰς τὸ μέλλον, ἵνα ἐπιλάβωνται τῆς ὄντως ζωῆς.

ὑψηλοφρονεῖν, a compound probably of Pauline mintage, found also in Rom. xi. 20, bases itself on the classical adjective ὑψηλόφρων. The substitution of the abstract πλούτου ἀδηλότης for the simpler Attic τὸ ἄδηλον savours of Latin models, and is paralleled in Plutarch (*Crass.* 2; *Mor.* 112). The entire phrase *affording us all things richly to enjoy* (or *consume*) has its echoes in Philo and Josephus (Wetstein). For ἠλπικέναι see above on iv. 10. ἀγαθοεργεῖν likewise carries the apostle's hallmark; for it has no duplicate except in his own recorded speech in Acts xiv. 17. The rare compound εὐμετάδοτος, *bountiful*, meets us elsewhere only in Marcus Aurelius iii. 14 and Vettius Valens, who uses it seven times. κοινωνικός may signify either *affable* or *generous*, as in the proverb κοινωνικὸς ὁ Ἑρμῆς. An appearance of tautology is avoided by taking it, with Chrysostom, in the sense of *neighbourliness*, borne out by sundry Plutarchean passages (e.g. *Mor.* 703, 757) and the use of the term in Marcus Aurelius. ἀποθησαυρίζειν, a late formation, occurs in Josephus and Valens.

The careful student of this Epistle cannot fail to remark that it exhibits a looser texture than the apostle to the Gentiles usually weaves. The same phenomenon strikes the reader in the closing sections of Romans, and it has given rise to all manner of rash suggestions in regard to their composition. Here, after his flight into the empyrean, Paul is reverting to the topic of wealth already touched on. By this time the Church included opulent members in cities of commercial importance. To them two cautions are addressed; first, not to be purse-proud, and secondly, not to set their confidence on precarious possessions, but on the unchanging Lord whose are the durable riches and whose bounty supplies all His children's needs. Counting their estates a stewardship, let them be rich in good works, open-handed and sympathetic towards their poorer neighbours, laying up treasure not below, but above; for so they will not labour in vain, but obtain a better portion and live a 'life that is life indeed'. ἡ ὄντως ζωή has an incontrovertible claim to be the right reading, and is quite a Pauline coinage. We may compare Peter's ὁ τότε κόσμος and οἱ νῦν οὐρανοί (II Pet. iii. 6 f.) for the idiom employed. Mention has been made earlier of parties who are 'dead while they live'; contrariwise we now view the precious boon of life turned to noble account instead of being thrown away. Of course salvation by works is not taught in this passage, for the works themselves spring from a fountain of love opened up by faith, grateful to overflowing for salvation by grace, secured in Christ to every believer.

vi. 20, 21. CONCLUSION

vi. 20, 21. ὦ Τιμόθεε, τὴν παραθήκην φύλαξον, ἐκτρεπόμενος τὰς βεβήλους κενοφωνίας καὶ ἀντιθέσεις τῆς ψευδωνύμου γνώσεως, ἥν τινες ἐπαγγελλόμενοι περὶ τὴν πίστιν ἠστόχησαν. ἡ χάρις μεθ᾽ ὑμῶν.

παραθήκη, the shorter Herodotean term for a *deposit*, was a business word which can be freely illustrated from the papyri. Dinarchus uses the Attic form metaphorically of children regarded as a sacred trust for the state, and both of them find place in Vettius Valens. ἐκτρέπεσθαι (middle voice with the accusative), *to discountenance, to shun*, is a perfectly classical usage. κενοφωνία, which re-echoes ματαιολογία at the head of the Epistle, can be exemplified only in Dioscorides and one passage of Plutarch (*Mor.* 1069). *The counter-affirmations of knowledge so called* evidently refers to dialectical fencing such as the schoolmen cultivated, what Bacon entitles 'digladiations of subtleties', paraded to glorify their inventor. *Nescio quid grande resonant, nihil tamen subest nisi inanis tinnitus* (Calvin). The immense value attached by the Greek mind to the arts of disputation colours its whole literature, even its tragic muse, with a litigious element that jars on a fastidious taste. The contradictories of Aristotelian logic may be glanced at in the term ἀντιθέσεις; but Marcion's *Antitheses* bore a different signification. ψευδώνυμος exposes the hollowness of the pretension to knowledge affected. So Plutarch writes of a pseudonymous philosopher (*Mor.* 479) and Philo applies the epithet to false gods, in opposition to ὁ ἀληθινὸς θεός (ii. 599).

Soi-disant science or *knowledge* (as it might be rendered) is not a plain reference to Gnosticism (Baur), but points to the quibblings of logical dialecticians, bent on reducing all truth to syllogistic processes or counter-balancings. This vaunted 'scientific thought' is a misnomer, like the pseudonymous δίκη and Προμηθεύς of Aeschylus.

This closing appeal accosts Timothy by name, perhaps to remind him of its honourable etymology. The deposit he is to guard can be nothing else than 'the revelation of Jesus Christ' in all its fulness. He must watch over it like a sentinel or patrol, or the custodian of a precious hoard, not suffering his mind to be distracted with secondary pre-occupations. And as a trustee he must keep to the terms of his trust. 'New light' may court his patronage or subtle logomachies lure him from his proper task. But controversy, though sometimes necessary, not seldom supplants higher matters. If pretension to superior illumination has led many astray, let his evangelist keep aloof from its devious tracks. For ἀστοχεῖν see note on i. 6. ἡ πίστις appears to carry once more an objective sense.

If, with the best uncials, we read μεθ' ὑμῶν, the public destination of this letter seems intimated. The abbreviated greeting finds its counterpart in Colossians and the Second Epistle to Timothy. The spurious subscription from Laodicea (cf. Authorized Version) harks back to Col. iv. 16 for a *pied à terre*.

THE EPISTLE TO TITUS

THERE are more reasons than one for inserting this Epistle between the pair addressed to Timothy. The circumstance that it holds an intermediate station in all likelihood, viewed chronologically, combines with the evidences of affiliation to I Timothy to recommend this order of sequence. The two letters are as nearly allied as the Ephesian and Colossian respectively, though it may be disputed which of them was prior in composition. They include passages that freely reproduce one another; but the Cretan phenomena include a more incipient stage of development than the church of Ephesus exhibits. To borrow the old Huguenot distinction, the former was an *église plantée*, the latter an *église dressée*.

Titus was a comparative veteran in the Lord's service, a Greek convert whose case became at one time crucial (Gal. ii. 3) in regard to the burning question of circumcision. He had been Paul's chosen envoy to the Corinthian church at a critical moment, and his successful delegacy in that affair raised him high in the apostle's regard. To him was entrusted the second Corinthian Epistle (II Cor. viii. 16 ff.); and he reappears as Paul's commissioner to Crete and finally to Dalmatia (II Tim. iv. 10).

i. 1–4. SALUTATION

i. 1, 2. Παῦλος δοῦλος θεοῦ ἀπόστολος δὲ Ἰησοῦ Χριστοῦ κατὰ πίστιν ἐκλεκτῶν θεοῦ καὶ ἐπίγνωσιν ἀληθείας τῆς κατὰ εὐσέβειαν ἐπ᾽ ἐλπίδι ζωῆς αἰωνίου ἣν ἐπηγγείλατο ὁ ἀψευδὴς θεὸς πρὸ χρόνων αἰωνίων,

The lowly title *God's bondservant*, not altogether equivalent to our term *slave*, which Paul here places in the foreground, occurs nowhere else at the head of his Epistles, and would be most unlikely to be set in such relief by any ecclesiastical puppet wearing his mask. κατὰ is of course employed in its usual sense *according to*, notwithstanding the objection of many expositors that an apostolate cannot be regulated by the faith of God's elect. But Paul speaks in this very context of 'the common faith', nor does he claim arbitrary dominion, organ of the

Spirit though he be, over that of his fellow-believers. Had he not pronounced a most solemn curse (Gal. i. 8) on apostles, nay on angels, who should dare to preach 'another gospel'? God's elect are themselves possessors of a God-given faith and taught by His Spirit, and he seeks no higher office than that of sealing their testimony. For they, no less than he, hold fast the truth which holds them in its clasp, walk conformably to its rule, and cherish the same full assurance of hope on the strength of the inviolable faithfulness of the Promiser.

ἐπ' ἐλπίδι is a Pauline phrase (Acts xxvi. 6); and the epithet ἀψευδής, which we find re-echoed in Polycarp's parting prayer, is here rescued from its misguided application to the lying oracles of paganism. It is so used in Herodotus and Euripides (Or. 364). Untrue of false deities, it was grandly appropriate to the God of Truth, pledged to make His every word good. We at once recall the kindred averment of Nu. xxiii. 19 and Heb. vi. 18. The apostle doubtless glances backward to Balaam's declaration (Nu. xxiii. 19): 'God is not a man that He should lie.' Figments befit crooked lips, but the Most High can have no complicity with deceit, which is the very badge of Satan and his crew. Falsehood is impossible to Him because it cannot be an object of His inviolably holy will. Let Titus remember that his mission is not only instinct with the purging influence of true godliness, but embodies a message of unalloyed verity, worthy of the fullest credence and the boldest enunciation. Blass and others regard πρὸ χρόνων αἰωνίων as Latinistic (cf. ante diem tertium Kalendas); but that supposition has been lately challenged and popular examples of its use supplied. The expression appears to be Hebraistic in sense at any rate (meaning 'from eternity'). Chrysostom, where it recurs in II Tim. i. 9, construes it to mean ἀναρχῶς.

Thus Paul opens his Epistle with a reminder to Titus of the august dignity of the Christian revelation in its supramundane source and goal; for eternal life, in all its boundless significance, forms the issue of its anticipations, covenanted from everlasting in the counsels of the Father and the Son. 'A promise', says Thomas Goodwin, 'is the expression of a purpose' on God's part; and so 'the faith of God's elect', seizing the hope set before them, realizes in time the great design of sovereign grace originated before time began in the bosom of the triune Godhead. Faith lays hold of this divine veracity.

i. 3, 4. ἐφανέρωσεν δὲ καιροῖς ἰδίοις τὸν λόγον αὐτοῦ ἐν κηρύγματι ὃ ἐπιστεύθην ἐγὼ κατ' ἐπιταγὴν τοῦ σωτῆρος ἡμῶν θεοῦ, Τίτῳ γνησίῳ τέκνῳ κατὰ κοινὴν πίστιν· χάρις καὶ εἰρήνη ἀπὸ θεοῦ Πατρὸς καὶ Χριστοῦ Ἰησοῦ τοῦ σωτῆρος ἡμῶν.

The phrases κατ' ἐπιταγὴν θεοῦ and ὃ ἐπιστεύθην ἐγώ have already crossed our path in I Tim. i. 1, 11, and the endearing expression γνήσιον τέκνον there conferred on Timothy (cf. Latin germanus) we find here transferred to Titus. According to the critical text, which omits ἔλεος, the apostle's delicate discrimination varies the greeting in that respect insomuch as Titus represents a robuster type of character than his Ephesian colleague. The joint benediction of Father and Son invoked testifies to the equality of the Persons from whom the blessing emanates.

The affirmation here made recalls more than one Pauline passage elsewhere, especially in the Ephesian Epistle. The Father and the Son 'are combined as the common object of every religious aspiration and the common source of every spiritual blessing'. In the gospel committed to the apostle's trust, the divine secret of the ages looms in view, and the allusion to the *common faith*, like Jude's phrase 'the common salvation', stresses its catholic compass and determinate tenor. It offers no preferential tariff to the Jew and no enhanced stipulations to the Gentile; for the kingdom of heaven is opened to all believers. Nay, apostles themselves are saved on the same footing as pariahs and wastrels scouted by polite society. The faith of the whole ransomed host has one object and one ground of confidence and belongs to one genus, however its strength and clarity of vision may admit of gradations. And the Lord's chronometry is perfect (Ex. xii. 41).

i. 5–9. MINISTERIAL QUALIFICATIONS

i. 5. τούτου χάριν ἀπέλιπόν σε ἐν Κρήτῃ, ἵνα τὰ λείποντα ἐπιδιορθώσῃ καὶ καταστήσῃς κατὰ πόλιν πρεσβυτέρους, ὡς ἐγώ σοι διεταξάμην·

The position of χάριν after its case marks a literary document; for this nicety is generally shelved in the papyri. The neuter sense of λείπειν, *to be lacking*, was common, though perhaps most usually in the middle voice. ἐπιδιορθοῦν rarely occurs elsewhere save in an inscription, and in a substantival form in Longinus. But Philo uses this very phrase for the more classical ἐπανορθοῦν (ii. 535). It means *to set to rights, rectify*; for Titus was commissioned to appoint presbyters for the Cretan flocks, as Paul proceeds to state, κατὰ πόλιν (Acts xx. 23; Calvin *oppidatim*). In each town he was to ordain pastors, presumably over the local churches scattered here and there, according to instructions already imparted to him ere the apostle left the island. A visit of Paul to Crete has evidently taken place, and the wording contrasts with the language of I Timothy, which, as we have seen, does not necessarily imply a recent sojourn of Paul in Ephesus.

i. 6. εἴ τίς ἐστιν ἀνέγκλητος, μιᾶς γυναικὸς ἀνήρ, τέκνα ἔχων πιστά, μὴ ἐν κατηγορίᾳ ἀσωτίας ἢ ἀνυπότακτα.

We observe here just that amount of repetition of Timothy's instructions, relieved by minor variations, which indicates one and the same author. But why any forger should thus dovetail his fabrication in three sections, forming a chequerwork partly corresponding, partly divergent, as if to multiply the risk of detection by complicating the particulars, it would be hard to explain. ἀνέγκλητος, a classical word for *irreproachable*, we have seen applied as a touchstone for deacons in I Tim. iii. 10. The phrase μιᾶς γυναικὸς ἀνήρ has been there discussed (see p. 50). In the mention of a well-ordered family we notice a change of wording due to the more intractable Cretan features. A pastor's children must not be insubordinate nor chargeable with being ne'er-do-weels. ἀσωτία combines the spendthrift and the rake as in the picture of the prodigal son. Their misconduct reflects on the home discipline (Pr. xxviii. 7).

i. 7–9. δεῖ γὰρ τὸν ἐπίσκοπον ἀνέγκλητον εἶναι ὡς θεοῦ οἰκονόμον, μὴ αὐθάδη, μὴ ὀργίλον, μὴ πάροινον, μὴ πλήκτην, μὴ αἰσχροκερδῆ, ἀλλὰ φιλόξενον, φιλάγαθον, σώφρονα, δίκαιον, ὅσιον, ἐγκρατῆ, ἀντεχόμενον τοῦ κατὰ τὴν διδαχὴν πιστοῦ λόγου, ἵνα δυνατὸς ᾖ καὶ παρακαλεῖν ἐν τῇ διδασκαλίᾳ τῇ ὑγιαινούσῃ καὶ τοὺς ἀντιλέγοντας ἐλέγχειν.

Obviously the πρεσβύτερος and ἐπίσκοπος are synonymous in this passage, for the titles are simply interchanged. So, among others,

Theodoret of Antioch remarks on this text, ἐντεῦθεν δῆλον ὡς τοὺς πρεσβυτέρους ἐπισκόπους ὠνόμαζον. *God's steward* or *house-ruler* bespeaks one of Paul's favourite conceptions of the Christian minister. αὐθάδης (Luther, *eigensinnig*), meaning *self-willed*, *headstrong*, a stubborn assertor of his own private piques or rash verdicts; ὀργίλος, meaning *choleric*, *peppery*. Obstinacy and snappishness are very undesirable traits in one who has to conciliate minds of various complexion. The other deprecated characteristics we have met with before. Notice the Pauline *penchant* for tabulation. There follow the positive constituents of a minister of the gospel, likewise ranged in order, some fresh, some reiterated. ἐγκρατής alone calls for remark, being a classical term expressive of self-control, especially in regard to sensuous appetites.

The apostle subjoins an injunction not specified in Timothy respecting the probationer's tenacity of convictions. It would almost seem as though the πιστὸς λόγος κατὰ τὴν διδαχήν, presented as a familiar standard of sound doctrine, must have by this time assumed a written shape. If so, the phrase may cast light on the five 'faithful sayings' of these Epistles, which wear the guise of quotation more or less documentary. The candidate must be competent to exhort his fellow-believers in the truth and to cope with and confute gainsayers. Here we have a mental as well as moral standard made obligatory in a teacher of others. For Paul was anything but a fanatic, as his entire career demonstrates. ἀντέχεσθαι with the genitive is excellent Attic Greek for *cleaving fast to*.

i. 10–16. THE CRETAN CHARACTER

i. 10, 11. εἰσὶν γὰρ πολλοὶ καὶ ἀνυπότακτοι, ματαιολόγοι καὶ φρεναπάται, μάλιστα οἱ ἐκ περιτομῆς, οὓς δεῖ ἐπιστομίζειν, οἵτινες ὅλους οἴκους ἀνατρέπουσιν, διδάσκοντες ἃ μὴ δεῖ αἰσχροῦ κέρδους χάριν.

The apostle now adverts to the notorious ill repute of the Cretans for dissimulation and bad character in general. A spirit of unruliness, already signalized in family life, and of prattle and fraudulency prevails, not least among the Judaizing proselytizers. It must be curbed; for its fruits are in the highest degree pernicious. We have had ματαιολογία in I Tim. i. 6. The adjectival form also occurs in Vettius Valens (301). φρεναπατᾶν in the verbal shape, unknown elsewhere, meets us as an adjective in Gal. vi. 3; the noun occurs once in a lyrical fragment of the papyri, and appears to convey the active sense of *cheats, cozeners*. The picturesque image of muzzling contained in ἐπιστομίζειν dates from the era of Attic purity, and had even then acquired the broader sense of silencing by force of reason (Plat. *Gorg.* 482). οἵτινες has its usual suggestion of *quippe qui*. ἀνατρέπειν is excellent Greek for *to upset, subvert*. Plutarch uses the noun ἀνατροπεύς figuratively for an over-turner. We should doubt whether any distinction can be drawn between ἃ μὴ δεῖ and ἃ οὐ δεῖ in this context, when the negative μή was encroaching on the province of its rival. αἰσχρὸν κέρδος is written as two words because the literal meaning has stress laid upon it.

The sketch here drawn of these rather despicable sheepstealers from the Christian fold reminds one of sundry modern cults of dubious creed which hang on the Church's skirts with similar aims in our own times. The forte of those sophisters lies in a deceptive volubility, hollow yet seducing, which needs a check to be set upon it; for its sedulous canvass entraps entire households with the bait of its deleterious wares, propagated in specious wise for self-seeking or mercenary ends. A sad picture! Some of its darker features reflect the debased moral atmosphere of the insinuating parties. Polybius (vi. 46) notes the supreme addiction of the Cretan to 'base gain'; and the Jewish element was very strong in the island.

i. 12. εἰπέν τις ἐξ αὐτῶν, ἴδιος αὐτῶν προφήτης

Κρῆτες ἀεὶ ψεῦσται, κακὰ θηρία, γαστέρες ἀργαί.

ἡ μαρτυρία αὕτη ἐστὶν ἀληθής.

Mendax, venter iners, semper mala bestia Cres est runs the Latin hexameter corresponding.

To obviate any charge of calumniation, the apostle cites, to substantiate his indictment, the testimony of Epimenides, a venerable figure in the traditions of the islanders, to their bad character. Some would transfer the sentiment to the later Callimachus, who cites half the line in a hymn to Zeus, and allege its Attic diction in proof, but many Homeric verses are cast in the same mould,[1] and both classical

---

[1] Hesiod's hemistich κάκ' ἐλέγχεα, γαστέρες οἶον (*Theog.* 26) might well be its model. See further N. B. Stonehouse, *The Areopagus Address* (Tyndale Press, 1949), pp. 18, 34; F. F. Bruce, *The Acts of the Apostles* (Tyndale Press, 1951), pp. 335 f., 338 f.

and patristic testimony weigh in the other scale. The title of *prophet* clung to Epimenides throughout Greek literature; it is endorsed by Plato. The commentators take the term quite seriously; but we cannot help surmising that Paul wrote 'a prophet *of their own*' with a twinkle in his eye. For he has them on the horns of a dilemma, remarked by Plutarch and Cicero (*Acad.* ii. 29). If they endorse the statement, they own their ethical degradation; if they repudiate it, they make their chosen seer a liar and brand the patron saint of Crete with the stigma of mendacity. Basil employs the same poser to David's outburst: 'all men are liars'.

In point of fact, the declaration had been abundantly verified. The very claim of Crete to contain the tomb of Zeus supplied one evidence of it, and the Greek tongue another; for κρητίζειν means *to lie* and κρητισμός (Plut. *Aem.* 26) denotes *falsehood*. πρὸς Κρῆτα κρητίζειν in Polybius (viii. 19) is *to meet craft with craft*. Ovid and Lucian tell the same tale. κακὰ θηρία became the Roman objurgation *mala bestia*, and γαστέρες ἀργαί, *sluggard paunches*, might be more plainly rendered 'lumpish greedy-guts'. Evidently the Cretan censor intends his lash to draw blood!

i. 13, 14.   δι' ἣν αἰτίαν ἔλεγχε αὐτοὺς ἀποτόμως, ἵνα ὑγιαίνωσιν ἐν τῇ πίστει, μὴ προσέχοντες Ἰουδαϊκοῖς μύθοις καὶ ἐντολαῖς ἀνθρώπων, ἀποστρεφομένων τὴν ἀλήθειαν.

δι' ἣν αἰτίαν, an innovation in Paul's diction found also in Luke, seems suggested by growing familiarity with the Latin *quamobrem*. ἀποτόμως, *pungently* or (with surgical allusion) *incisively*, recalls II Cor. xiii. 10.

Titus is bidden to reprimand the mutinous Cretan temperament without compunction. In politer Ephesus such plain-spokenness might have been unsuitable. Here 'stablishment in the faith', probably used objectively, demands firm reprehension. Plutarch thus employs ἀνατομία (*Mor.* 13) to denote trenchant penalty administered to a restive urchin. They must not be suffered to gull their fancies with Jewish fables, nor act the part of renegades by espousing the cajoleries of seducers. No quarter must be shown to mercenary false guides. Their too facile dupes needed sharp castigation, if the recusants were to be preserved from perversity of judgment.

The Judaical school of these propagandists is apparent, and their substitution of human precepts for divine takes after Pharisaical precedents. But God's truth must not thus be bartered for the fallacies and fables of men. Fallible sanctions cannot usurp the place of infallible.

i. 15. πάντα καθαρὰ τοῖς καθαροῖς· τοῖς δὲ μεμιαμμένοις[1] καὶ ἀπίστοις οὐδὲν καθαρόν, ἀλλὰ μεμίανται αὐτῶν καὶ ὁ νοῦς καὶ ἡ συνείδησις.

It is characteristic of the apostle Paul to enunciate broad generalizations. Jewish teachers were perpetually engrossed with alleged impurities. Peter had to be taught a more spiritual valuation of purity on the housetop at Joppa, taught the Master's lesson that the heart and not the hand or the mouth constitutes the organ of cleanness or uncleanness. Ceremonialism ever tends to exalt the seen above the unseen, form above substance, semblance above being. Paul cuts at the root of this delusion by laying down the principle that to the pure all things are pure. He had said as much in his letter to the Romans (xiv. 20) in regard to meats. The stainless Son of God was not contaminated by the proximity of Satan nor by touching the ostracized leper. Fire can kindle only on combustible material, and to the truly chaste soul impure suggestions convey no taint of allurement. We are not to seek haunts of vice to show our powers of resistance, any more than Daniel entered the lions' den of his own motion; yet when flung into it for fidelity to Jehovah he took no harm by the exposure. From the ritual domain this aphorism raises the question to the spiritual sphere, where distinctions of meats or rubrics vanish out of sight.

But the apostle carries the war into the enemy's country when he adds that to the polluted and unbelieving nothing is pure. Their labour of purification is lost labour. The outside of the platter may be assiduously cleansed, but within it is full of dead men's bones, and its touch is defilement. The *cloaca* lies underneath the surface and its main arteries infect the unregenerate mind and conscience. *Malus animus omnia in mala vertit* (Seneca, *Ep. Mor.* xvi. 3). We agree with M. & M. that the full significance of the term συνείδησις in St Paul's writings cannot be paralleled from Greek philosophy; for the word has no currency in Epictetus or Marcus Aurelius. Christianity has 'baptized it with a

---

[1] The more correct μεμιασμένοις lacks uncial support. This form appears also in Josephus and the Apocrypha.

deeper connotation'. In Menander's famous iambic, ἅπασιν ἡμῖν ἡ συνείδησις θεός, it bears apparently the sense of reflexive consciousness. Vettius Valens (210) approximates more closely to the concept of a moral sense, but his date is post-Christian.

How true it is that, whereas converse with the Lord clarifies moral perceptions, an unbelieving heart waxes more and more obtuse, and a sinful course of life ossifies the very organ by which sin is detected. Such a man's moral condition vitiates by degrees his intellectual appraisements.

i. 16. θεὸν ὁμολογοῦσιν εἰδέναι, τοῖς δὲ ἔργοις ἀρνοῦνται, βδελυκτοὶ ὄντες καὶ ἀπειθεῖς καὶ πρὸς πᾶν ἔργον ἀγαθὸν ἀδόκιμοι.

Paul proceeds to unmask these smooth dissemblers. Outwardly they may pose as devout characters, but their acts belie their words. βδελυκτός, a very strong term like *execrable* or *loathsome*, expresses disgust at their hypocrisy and ἀπειθής sets their mutinous bias in relief, intractable to the yoke of grace. ἀρνεῖσθαι θεόν may be said to appertain to Christian phraseology; for its use with a personal object cannot be exemplified from ordinary Greek literature. Josephus writes (*Ap.* i. 22) ἀρνούμενοι τὰ πατρῷα with the meaning *disowning*; but profane usage restricts the expression to things. ἀδόκιμος is an undeniable Paulinism. The adjective was applied to coins below standard weight (Epict. i. 6) and to anything discredited as worthless. So Paul uses it in the passage in I Corinthians (ix. 27) where the Authorized Version loosely translates it 'a castaway'. Xenophon (*Lac. Pol.* iii) reprobates cowards in Sparta and Lucian (*Deor. Concil.* xv) rejected candidates with this epithet. Josephus too (*B.J.* i. 26) opposes the term to δεδοκιμασμένος, 'accredited'.

These interlopers make glib avowal that they 'know God'; but when the tree is judged by its fruits, their corrupt practices reveal them as counterfeit lip-homagers whose lives confute their glib professions. No sterling good works secure their support or patronage. Their stock-in-trade consists wholly and solely in plausible verbiage. The species is by no means extinct!

ii. 1–8. ADMONITIONS TO SENIORS AND JUNIORS

ii. 1, 2. σὺ δὲ λάλει ἃ πρέπει τῇ ὑγιαινούσῃ διδασκαλίᾳ, πρεσβύτας νηφαλίους εἶναι, σεμνούς, σώφρονας, ὑγιαίνοντας τῇ πίστει, τῇ ἀγάπῃ, τῇ ὑπομονῇ·

The old distinction between λαλεῖν, *to chatter*, and λέγειν, *to speak*, was almost obliterated in Hellenistic Greek, as may be seen in the New Comedy, though λαλεῖν still indicates vocal utterance and λέγειν regular discourse (cf. Latin *sermo*). These informal instructions would most naturally fall under the less elaborate term. The category of sound or wholesome teaching, which we have already remarked in I Tim. i. 10 as a fresh figure characteristic of the Pastoral Epistles, here meets us again. It is one of several signs of a consolidated rule of faith synchronous with a development of church organization, but not therefore to be ascribed to a sub-apostolic era. Cf. Rom. xvi. 17.

πρεσβύτης, the sixth of the seven ages of man in Hippocrates, represents the greybeards of the flock, just as the succeeding πρεσβῦτις denotes the 'mothers in Israel'. The quality of *sober-mindedness* (νηφάλιος) was among those pronounced requisite for the pastor and deacon (I Tim. iii. 2, 11). Gravity and self-respect befit seniority of station and that trait of discretion that should be learnt in the school of experience. Their faith (here subjective) and love and *steadfastness* (ὑπομονή) should yield evidences of maturity and vigour.

ii. 3–5. πρεσβύτιδας ὡσαύτως ἐν καταστήματι ἱεροπρεπεῖς, μὴ διαβόλους, μηδὲ οἴνῳ πολλῷ δεδουλωμένας, καλοδιδασκάλους, ἵνα σωφρονίζωσιν τὰς νέας φιλάνδρους εἶναι, φιλοτέκνους, σώφρονας, ἁγνάς, οἰκουργούς, ἀγαθάς, ὑποτασσομένας τοῖς ἰδίοις ἀνδράσιν, ἵνα μὴ ὁ λόγος τοῦ θεοῦ βλασφημῆται.

κατάστημα (cf. Latin *incessus*) expresses a dignified *carriage*, such as becomes an elderly matron. Thus Aristeas (122) and Lucian (*Hermot.* 18) employ the phrase τὸ μέσον κατάστημα for sedateness of mien. Similarly Plutarch of Marcellus (23), and Josephus writes ἀτρεμαῖον κατάστημα (*Antiq.* xv. 7), meaning *intrepid demeanour*, in description of the death of Mariamne, wife and victim of Herod the Great. Plutarch even employs the curious adjective καταστηματικός in the sense of *staid.* ἱεροπρεπής is pure Attic (M. & M. blunder here), in fact a Platonic vocable (*Theag.* 122), sometimes associated with temple accessories, but capable of a wider scope. Cf. Philo ii. 529; Plut. *Mor.* 11; Menander (Allinson, p. 346). Some ardent sacerdotalists have tried to discover an embryo order of nuns in this innocent epithet. As well extract sunbeams from cucumbers, after Swift's Laputan model! The word may be rendered *decorous* or *of reverend aspect.* From the inhibited foibles of tale-telling and wine-bibbing it is plain that the Cretan women were not modelled on the conventual ideal. The figurative use of δουλόω has plenty of classical precedent and is no second-century usage, as Dr Harrison would fain make out because he finds the same metaphor in Dio Cassius. καλοδιδάσκαλος is an ἅπαξ εἰρημένον and σωφρονίζειν a classical verb for indoctrinating, employed by Xenophon for the curbing of a horse (*Hier.* 10), and by Plutarch (*Mor.* 641 and again 784), as here with an infinitive, of *schooling* some one in a needed lesson.[1] φίλανδρος and φιλότεκνος have literary associations and are common on epitaphs. οἰκουργός is so rare a term that the sole known instance of its occurrence elsewhere is in Soranus, a second-century medical writer. But it is much the best supported reading and the significance of *home-worker* suits the context well and was little likely to arise from the more usual alternative reading οἰκουρούς, *keepers-at-home.* Yet the latter is classically descriptive of the mistress of the house (cf. Eur. *Or.* 928), and frequent in Plutarch (*Cam.* 11, *Nic.* 5), who uses the phrase οἰκουρίαν φρονεῖν for 'minding house-keeping' (*M. Ant.* 10) or being domesticated. The verb οἰκουρεῖν carries the like meaning.

These counsels explain themselves. Propriety of deportment adorns grey hairs, and gives weight to advice tendered to more youthful companions. Intemperance must have been rife in Crete to render the warning against thraldom to the wine-cup needful. Yet the limitation imposed cannot be deemed severe. It was *vin coupé* that was commonly drunk. The domestic sphere reappears here as woman's natural domain —marriage is assumed—and her special conjunction with husband and

---

[1] Notwithstanding uncial support, we hold the subjunctive σωφρονίζωσιν to be the correct reading here. Surely no writer would introduce ἵνα twice in the same sentence, once with a verb in the indicative and once with the subjunctive. o (ου) and ω are constantly confused in late Greek MSS.

children noted. To the former her nuptial tie entails a bond of allegiance for conscience' sake, as an element in her Christian profession the absence of which provokes adverse remark.

ii. 6–8. τοὺς νεωτέρους ὡσαύτως παρακάλει σωφρονεῖν, περὶ πάντα σεαυτὸν παρεχόμενος τύπον καλῶν ἔργων, ἐν τῇ διδασκαλίᾳ ἀφθορίαν, σεμνότητα, λόγον ὑγιῆ ἀκατάγνωστον, ἵνα ὁ ἐξ ἐναντίας ἐντραπῇ μηδὲν ἔχων λέγειν περὶ ἡμῶν φαῦλον.

τύπος, meaning *pattern*, we have already commented on in I Tim. iv. 12. In Paul's compressed style παρεχόμενος must be repeated with the second branch of the sentence. ἀφθορία, certainly the correct reading, presents us with another ἅπαξ εἰρημένον; but the adjective ἄφθορος, meaning *chaste* (Est. ii. 2, LXX), is found as the masculine counterpart of παρθένος. *Untaintedness* of doctrine is what Titus is urged to exhibit. σεμνότης, *dignity*, almost *self-respect*, a Roman quality *par excellence*, had attracted Aristotle's attention (1192, 1233) in his ethical philosophy; he defines it as the μεσότης αὐθαδείας καὶ ἀρεσκείας, the mean between pig-headedness and pliability. But it conveys in later usage a certain tone of moral elevation which baffles a translator, *high-mindedness* being the nearest equivalent. The correspondent Latin *gravitas* was a necromantic term to the Roman ear. The rare compound ἀκατάγνωστος, *irreproachable*, meets us chiefly in inscriptions. ὁ ἐξ ἐναντίας is Pauline shorthand for *the adverse party*. ὁ δι' ἐναντίας occurs in the papyri and later in Sextus Empiricus. Blass remarks that 'the ellipse is obscure'; probably χώρας in the sense of *post* should be supplied. ἐντρέπεσθαι in the sense of *being put to shame* pertains to the Koiné vocabulary and can be illustrated from the papyri; but sporadic instances of its occurrence are met with in Polybius (vii. 12) and Plutarch (*Mor.* 560).

Titus himself, though presumably of middle age, is here urged to set the juniors an example of godly demeanour, and train them in soundness of speech and sobriety of carriage, so that they may furnish no mark for an enemy to fire at. By the grace of God even Cretan levity might be replaced by spiritual steadfastness and solid worth, and present no visible target for ridicule. To Paul the gospel is always 'the power of God', a sovereign catholicon for all the diseases flesh is heir to. *Purgatio pessimi optima!*

ii. 9, 10. DIRECTIONS TO SERVANTS

ii. 9, 10. δούλους ἰδίοις δεσπόταις ὑποτάσσεσθαι, ἐν πᾶσιν εὐαρέστους εἶναι, μὴ ἀντιλέγοντας, μὴ νοσφιζομένους, ἀλλὰ πᾶσαν πίστιν ἐνδεικνυμένους ἀγαθήν, ἵνα τὴν διδασκαλίαν τὴν τοῦ σωτῆρος ἡμῶν θεοῦ κοσμῶσιν ἐν πᾶσιν.

According to J. H. Moulton these loose infinitives are substitutes for the imperative mood, an idiom familiar to Homeric students and customary in brief announcements of edicts or regulations. There are pure imperatival infinitives in the New Testament which it would be hard to eliminate (e.g. Phil. iii. 16); but why should they be needlessly multiplied? Here we may bring ὑποτάσσεσθαι readily under the regimen of παρακάλει supra. εὐάρεστος, a favourite Pauline vocable, can be quoted from Philo, Marcus Aurelius (vi. 30) and the papyri, as well as the LXX.[1] νοσφίζεσθαι is the regular term for petty larcenies, *filching*, etc. ἐνδείκνυσθαι meaning *to exhibit* is excellent classical Greek and exclusively Pauline (except Hebrews) in the New Testament. πίστις, *fidelity*, here wears a subjective aspect. The ascription of the title *Saviour* to God we have already noticed on i. 3; here it is set over against the selfsame title applied to Christ in verse 13.

The points in the servant's behaviour selected for remark here differ from those noticed in I Timothy. They consist of three main elements.

(1) *Subordination.* Compliance with their master's wishes and injunctions ought not to be slack or half-hearted. Their station entails obedience to his directions.

(2) *Good temper.* The services they render should not be grudging, nor performed with a sullen mien, and they must not allow themselves to dispute with or contradict their employers. Luther's picturesque version reads *widerbellend.* Most of these servants were slaves, but pert Greek slaves in particular often took unwarrantable liberties of argumentation with their masters and mistresses.

(3) *Honesty.* Opportunities of small peculation not seldom presented themselves, and to those unjustly deprived of freedom petty larcenies might seem to be a fair retaliation for the wrongs they suffered. But a Christian servant has to pay heed to the will of a higher Master,

---

[1] Applied to things it signified *agreeable.* So Vettius Valens of wine (221).

and his task is to adorn the doctrine of which he is a confessor in all respects, to show forth the praises of his Overlord, to witness to the sanctifying influence of the grace of God in the humblest estate, perhaps to do for a master spiritually what the Israelitish maid did for Naaman physically by becoming the instrument of his cure from leprosy.

ii. 11–15. THE LIFE CONSONANT WITH THE DISPENSATION OF GRACE

ii. 11-13. ἐπεφάνη γὰρ ἡ χάρις τοῦ θεοῦ σωτήριος πᾶσιν ἀνθρώποις, παιδεύουσα ἡμᾶς ἵνα ἀρνησάμενοι τὴν ἀσέβειαν καὶ τὰς κοσμικὰς ἐπιθυμίας σωφρόνως καὶ δικαίως καὶ εὐσεβῶς ζήσωμεν ἐν τῷ νῦν αἰῶνι, προσδεχόμενοι τὴν μακαρίαν ἐλπίδα καὶ ἐπιφάνειαν τῆς δόξης τοῦ μεγάλου θεοῦ καὶ σωτῆρος ἡμῶν Ἰησοῦ Χριστοῦ,

The Authorized Version goes wrong here. σωτήριος followed by a dative case, like *salutaris* in Latin, is a classical idiom as old as Thucydides (vii. 64) and specially favoured by Plutarch, for *bringing deliverance to*. Here perhaps we may render *of saving efficacy for*, since salvation acquires so much deeper a meaning under New Testament influence. The connecting link γάρ may be understood to refer to the variety of directions given, extending to old and young and to the spurned class of slaves, inclusive even of ill-savoured Crete.

ἀρνεῖσθαι, *to renounce*, with an impersonal object, has classical precedents and is used by purists like Josephus (ἀρνούμενοι τὰ πατρῷα, *Ap.* i. 22). ἀσέβεια of course forms the classical expression for *impiety*. κοσμικός as a religious term has a decidedly Hebrew ring. We find it used elsewhere (Heb. ix. 1) only of the mundane sanctuary of the old covenant. In Plutarch and Vettius Valens it has a hemispherical reference, but Josephus in one passage (*B.J.* iv. 5) employs the expression ἡ κοσμικὴ θρησκεία of the temple worship, yet apparently in a different sense, 'world-wide'. Here *worldly* has assumed its Christian connotation.

ἐπιφάνεια properly signifies a divine manifestation, though sometimes applied in adulation to the Roman Emperors, whose virtual apotheosis was a contrivance of statecraft. Paul has already used it of the Second Advent in II Thes. ii. 8 in lieu of the alternative παρουσία and here it follows by a natural sequence the cognate verb at the head of the sentence.

That it should be identified with the preceding 'blessed hope'[1] may be inferred from the omission of the article before ἐπιφάνειαν, and the selfsame reason warrants the conclusion that the 'great God and our Saviour Jesus Christ' denotes one and the same Person. What is known as Granville Sharp's rule on this point has been widely challenged since Bishop Middleton wrote his well-known work on *The Greek Article in the New Testament*. But though that rule may not be stringently observed in later Greek writers, it certainly holds as a correct idiom of the language.[2] Middleton had produced a number of crucial instances from both Attic and Hellenistic authors and, what is more notable, from the New Testament itself, in which nouns linked together by one article designate the same subject, especially in the singular number (e.g. Mk. vi. 3; Acts iii. 14; Heb. iii. 1; Rev. i. 9). Thus, on the one hand, when Plutarch writes in his *Life of Cicero* Ῥώσκιος ὁ υἱὸς καὶ κληρονόμος τοῦ τεθνηκότος, he is speaking of one person, not two; and on the other, when Matthew mentions ὁ ἐθνικὸς καὶ ὁ τελώνης (xviii. 17) and Luke ὁ βασιλεὺς καὶ ὁ ἡγεμών (Acts xxvi. 30) they are differentiating two personalities. The main objection to conforming the present example to the rule lies in the assumption that σωτὴρ ἡμῶν is tantamount to a proper name, in which case the rule need not apply. Winer also advances the merely subjective ground of his 'dogmatic conviction' that Paul could not have called Christ 'the great God'. To which we might rejoin that the unique title *great*, not used elsewhere of the Deity by him, points to a speciality of meaning, and that the term ἐπιφάνεια is in no instance applied to God the Father. J. H. Moulton (*Grammar of New Testament Greek*, i, p. 84) has the candour to admit how much can be said in favour of regarding this clause as a second predicate. He points out an exactly similar formula, τοῦ μεγάλου θεοῦ εὐεργέτου καὶ σωτῆρος, applied to the deified Ptolemies, where only one person is concerned. The Greek Fathers understand the phrase of Christ, and they must have been able to appraise a Greek idiom. More-

---

[1] It is curious that almost all the older expositors take the 'blessed hope' to be eternal life as in i. 2; but the absence of the article militates against their view. The hope spoken of is plainly objective.

[2] See A. T. Robertson, *Grammar of the Greek New Testament*, pp. 785 ff.

over the papyri attest the employment of the phrase 'our great God and Saviour' among Hellenistic Christians.

The thought here set in relief starts from the proposition of the un-restricted nature of the gospel dispensation, stretching its stakes to every kindred and tribe under heaven, and exerting a renovating power wheresoever it comes. It tutors its recipients to a sober, just and godly manner of life, by teaching them not merely to eschew evil but to pursue after integrity and holiness, with an outlook that embraces the future as well as the present. One transforming epiphany has already taken place in the coming of the Son of God, an avatar of grace in-carnate; but a Second Advent, a more glorious epiphany of adjudica-tion, impends, when Christ shall appear in the glory of the Father, crowned with the full insignia of Deity. We hold that it is just because the Father has been entitled Saviour in verse 10 that the co-equal Son shines forth so radiantly in the vestments of Godhead in verse 13. For the ascription of salvation to both Persons interchangeably in a sixfold repetition cannot be accidental in this Epistle, in each chapter of which first the Father and then the Son receives the title of Saviour. This fact surely reinforces the exegesis which finds a studied assertion of the Redeemer's Deity in this passage. In any interpretation Father and Son are placed, be it observed, on an equal footing. The glory of the One irradiates likewise the Other. It was on this text that John Selden pillowed his head on his deathbed.

ii. 14, 15. ὃς ἔδωκεν ἑαυτὸν ὑπὲρ ἡμῶν, ἵνα λυτρώσηται ἡμᾶς ἀπὸ πάσης ἀνομίας καὶ καθαρίσῃ ἑαυτῷ λαὸν περιούσιον ζηλωτὴν καλῶν ἔργων. ταῦτα λάλει καὶ παρακάλει καὶ ἔλεγχε μετὰ πάσης ἐπιταγῆς· μηδείς σου περιφρονείτω.

The appellation *Saviour*, as assigned to Christ in verse 13, suggests further amplification; for the theme is one that always stirs the apostle's emotions. He gave *Himself* for us, the grandest of all gifts. No doubt ὑπέρ has a wider scope than ἀντί and may usually be rendered 'on behalf of'; but we are glad that M. & M. grant that, like the sister preposition, it may carry the meaning *instead of.* As this conclusion has been widely challenged, we refer the reader to a brief excursus on that point appended at the close of the chapter.[1]

[1] See pp. 110–112.

λαὸς περιούσιος, the LXX rendering of 'am segullah from Ex. xix. 5 onwards, the title of the Lord's 'peculiar treasure', conferred on Israel, a people of His own reservation or possession, *peculium Dei*, Luther's *Volk zum Eigentum*, does not easily explain itself. περιούσιος naturally signifies supernumerary; but Peter's modification of the phrase, λαὸς εἰς περιποίησιν (I Pet. ii. 9), fixed the other sense, drawn from the LXX, upon it. (See Lightfoot, *On a Fresh Revision*, App. 1.) No example of the word elsewhere has been discovered, and it continues in the diminished list of Jewish-Greek formations. ζηλωτής with the genitive has a thoroughly Pauline ring (Acts xxii. 3; 1 Cor. xiv. 12; Gal. i. 14). It is quite classical and inscriptional too. ἐπιταγή, as already noted, constitutes an exclusively Pauline vocable. περιφρονεῖν forms a substitute, comparatively rare, for the common καταφρονεῖν.

Christ's glorious self-oblation on our behalf, His offering up of His whole Self in our room, had for its end our redemption from all law-breaking, the purgation of our entire beings from contrariety to God's holy will, our sanctification unto Him as His peculiar portion, emulous of works of goodness acceptable in His sight, renewed in His image, not a mere relinquishment of crooked and rebellious ways, but a fervent espousal of His pristine design when He made man upright and obedient. Believers have free will to that which is spiritually good. Sin alone renders men contemptible, holiness alone honourable. 'No unholy person', says John Owen, 'can have any sure evidence of his interest in the oblation of Christ.'

The concluding counsel, *let no man make light of thee*, does not reproduce the reference in Timothy to youthfulness; for Titus was evidently an older man; but puts him on his guard against the petulance of the Cretan temperament.

NOTE ON THE MEANING OF ΥΠΕΡ IN CERTAIN CONTEXTS

We need not concern ourselves with the ordinary use of ὑπέρ with the genitive to express the sense *concerning*, *in regard to*, nor dwell on the closer tie which we recognize in its frequent employment to denote, like ἕνεκα, *for the sake of*. It seems as if that arose from such an image as ὑπερασπιστής, ὑπερασπίζειν, that of standing over a person to shield him. It is the yet stricter bond which ὑπέρ is capable of cementing to which we would draw attention, that of vicarious action performed in the place of another. This connotation has indeed been peremptorily rejected in certain quarters and tamely surrendered in others; but on a survey of the field impartial inquirers will admit its existence. We can adduce only a few samples out of many of its occurrences. It does not characterize a single phase or epoch of Greek literature, but diffuses itself through them all.

ἀντί is the typical preposition descriptive of substitution. That is beyond gainsaying. Perhaps it may be alleged of ὑπέρ in the special sense to which we refer that it rather expresses *representation*. Trench cites from Tischendorf the judicious award: '*pro coniuncta significatione et commodi et vicarii ab apostolo adhibita est praepositio ὑπέρ.*' In most cases it may be translated *for the sake of*; but in other contexts the notion of sponsorship seems uppermost. Take crucial instances from the New Testament itself. Caiaphas declares it to be expedient that one man should die in lieu of (ὑπέρ) the nation (Jn. xi. 50), manifestly by way of scapegoat. Paul proclaims that Christ was made a curse for us (ὑπὲρ ἡμῶν—Gal. iii. 13), and yet more explicitly that One died for all (ὑπὲρ πάντων) and that therefore the 'all' signified died in Him (II Cor. v. 15). He protests that he would gladly have retained Onesimus to minister to him ὑπὲρ σοῦ, that is, in Philemon's place. Cf. Is. xliii. 3, LXX ἄλλαγμα ὑπὲρ σοῦ, 'in thy stead'.

This pregnant signification of ὑπέρ is no dubious provincialism. It finds sanction in all quarters, at any rate as a 'resultant meaning'. Plato himself, the cynosure of literary Attic, uses ἀποκρίνεσθαι ὑπέρ (*Gorg.* 515, *Rep.* 476) for answering in the room of another, and makes a speaker define λέγειν ὑπὲρ ἐμοῦ (*Symp.* 185) as ἐν τῷ σῷ μέρει. So again in his *Theaet.* 162, ἐρεῖ Πρωταγόρας ἤ τις ἄλλος ὑπὲρ αὐτοῦ. Elsewhere Plato interchanges ὑπεραποθνῄσκειν with προαποθνῄσκειν (*Symp.* 208) in reference to the story of Alcestis. We turn to the play of Euripides bearing that title and find ἀντί, ὑπέρ and even περί alike employed to depict her vicarious death. Observe that no verb ἀντιθνῄσκειν was deemed requisite in such cases. Similarly in his *Heracleidae* the proffer of a vicarious death for the suppliants is voiced successively by means of the prepositions ἀντί, ὑπέρ and πρό (453, 545, 622), and the sacrifice of Iphigenia (*El.* 1026) expressed thus: ἔκτεινε μίαν ὑπὲρ πάντων. In like manner Antilochus, who dies to save his father's life, according to Pindar (*Pyth.* vi. 30), ὑπερέφθιτο πατρός, and in Xenophon's allusion (*Cyr.* i. 14) is spoken of as τοῦ πατρὸς ὑπεραποθανών. In his *Agesilaus* (i. 24) his phrase runs, τὸν ὑπὲρ αὐτοῦ ἀποθανούμενον. This identification of ὑπέρ with proxyship persists in the Hellenistic era. Plato's formula for a reply through another's lips reappears as late as Lucian (*Jup. Confut.* 15, 18, *Hermot.* 55). Elsewhere (*Pisc.* 8), in a choice of one to speak on behalf of all as their representative, the expression he employs is ἕνα χειροτονεῖν ὑπὲρ ἀπάντων. So Philo (ii. 325) uses ἀποθνῄσκειν ὑπέρ of a substitutionary death and interprets it (327) by ἕτερον ἀνθ᾽ ἑτέρου κτείνειν. And Plutarch, relating the story of the Spartan 'forlorn hope' who proclaimed ὑπὲρ αὐτῶν ἤλθομεν ἀποθανούμενοι (*Mor.* 236), uses Philo's ἀποθνῄσκειν ὑπέρ repeatedly, and says of Aratus (17) ἐκινδύνευε μόνος ὑπὲρ πάντων and of Aemilius (*Mor.* 198) τὴν νέμεσιν ὑπὲρ πάντων αὐτὸς ἀναδέδεκται. Dionysius of Halicarnassus moreover writes of filling gaps in the ranks (viii), ὑπὲρ τῶν ἀποθανόντων στρατιωτῶν ἑτέρους καταγράφειν just as Plato (878) had used ὑπέρ of a soldier required to serve in lieu of one he had maimed. Appian (*B.C.* iii. 8) has the locution δίκας ἀπαιτήσω ('I will pay the penalty') μόνος ὑπὲρ ἀπάντων. Here are specific transferences of liabilities.

Were further proof necessary, we might point out that ὑπέρ is the current term in the case of hostages as well as ransoms or replacements. Plutarch lauds Antigonus (*Demetr.* 51) because he was ὁμηρεύειν ἕτοιμος αὐτὸς ὑπὲρ τοῦ πατρός. Finally it is the preposition employed when a person writes or signs in the name of an illiterate. In the papyri the form used is ἔγραψα ὑπὲρ αὐτοῦ ἀγραμμάτου. We could adduce other Hellenistic examples, but enough has been said to sustain our thesis. We may render it 'on behalf of', if we so please; but it is plain that it can be used more restrictedly to indicate one or more speakers or actors singled out to take the place of others. The nexus may be that of interchange of parts.

iii. 1, 2. DEMEANOUR TO THE OUTSIDE WORLD

iii. 1, 2. ὑπομίμνῃσκε αὐτοὺς ἀρχαῖς ἐξουσίαις ὑποτάσσεσθαι, πειθαρχεῖν, πρὸς πᾶν ἔργον ἀγαθὸν ἑτοίμους εἶναι, μηδένα βλασφημεῖν, ἀμάχους εἶναι, ἐπιεικεῖς, πᾶσαν ἐνδεικνυμένους πραΰτητα πρὸς πάντας ἀνθρώπους.

ὑποτάσσεσθαι=*loyal subjection*; πειθαρχεῖν regards conformity to regulations. βλασφημεῖν here of course bears its secondary meaning, *slander*. For ἄμαχος and for ἐπιεικής cf. I Tim. iii. 3. πραΰτης is the later form of the classical πραότης. Note the characteristically Pauline πᾶσαν with an abstract term. Cf. Acts xx. 19; II Cor. viii. 7, xii. 12; I Tim. iii. 4; II Tim. iv. 2; Tit. ii. 15. In these succinct instructions of a more general scope Paul bids Titus remind his Cretan flocks to obey the civil authorities as law-abiding citizens. Doubtless the democratic spirit of the island, noticed by Polybius, and the factious tendencies noted by Plutarch (*Mor.* 490), rendered these counsels timely. They were not to stand aloof from any praiseworthy enterprise, nor to indulge in censorious language, but were to curb their pugnacious tendencies and to display suavity of temper towards all men. Very essential advice in such a turbulent environment! True religion does not adopt the arts of the agitator, but upholds law and order.

iii. 3. THE CONTRAST BETWEEN PAST AND PRESENT

iii. 3. ἦμεν γάρ ποτε καὶ ἡμεῖς ἀνόητοι, ἀπειθεῖς, πλανώμενοι, δουλεύοντες ἐπιθυμίαις καὶ ἡδοναῖς ποικίλαις, ἐν κακίᾳ καὶ φθόνῳ διάγοντες, στυγητοί, μισοῦντες ἀλλήλους.

πλανᾶσθαι may be middle or passive; either sense would suit this context. δουλεύειν ταῖς ἡδοναῖς—alleged to be non-Pauline—is a stock phrase in Greek ethics. ποικίλος signified *shifting* or possibly *volatile*, a meaning exemplified as early as Aristotle. Vettius Valens couples ποικίλοι with ἄστατοι ταῖς γνώμαις (45, 7). We have met the phrase βίον διάγειν in I Tim. ii. 2; here the equally classical διάγειν alone is employed. The rare στυγητός, *detestable*, has a poetical ring, like the old English word *fulsome* used in this sense.

It is St Paul's manner to lay stress on the folly and delusion of the natural heart and its thraldom to a train of 'pleasures with mutable faces', to borrow Sir Thomas Browne's figure, and to stigmatize the malice and jealousy it breeds and the seething cauldrons of hatred it foments. The exposure of its noxious workings is meant to inspire disgust, yet he does not adduce it misanthropically, but as a foil to the heavenly lustre of the epitome of the gospel of redeeming love which in grateful contrast follows in its wake.

iii. 4–7. THE GLORY OF THE GOSPEL OF GOD'S GRACE

iii. 4–7. ὅτε δὲ ἡ χρηστότης καὶ ἡ φιλανθρωπία ἐπεφάνη τοῦ σωτῆρος ἡμῶν θεοῦ, οὐκ ἐξ ἔργων τῶν ἐν δικαιοσύνῃ ἃ ἐποιήσαμεν ἡμεῖς ἀλλὰ κατὰ τὸ αὐτοῦ ἔλεος ἔσωσεν ἡμᾶς διὰ λουτροῦ παλιγγενεσίας καὶ ἀνακαινώσεως Πνεύματος Ἁγίου οὗ ἐξέχεεν ἐφ' ἡμᾶς πλουσίως διὰ Ἰησοῦ Χριστοῦ τοῦ σωτῆρος ἡμῶν, ἵνα δικαιωθέντες τῇ ἐκείνου χάριτι κληρονόμοι γενηθῶμεν κατ' ἐλπίδα ζωῆς αἰωνίου.

χρηστότης is a word confined in the New Testament to six of Paul's Epistles. It belongs to literary Hellenistic and is defined by Jerome as a spontaneous disposition to bless (Trench). *Benignity* is the nearest English equivalent. Plutarch, Lucian, Philo and Josephus, all of them conjoin it with φιλανθρωπία to express the conception of sincerest benevolence; in fact, Plutarch (*Num.* 4) and Marcus Aurelius (viii. 34) use this concept to denote God's kind dealings with man. τὰ ἔργα τὰ ἐν δικαιοσύνῃ are works performed indefectibly, like the angelic ministries, from right motives and with perfect rectitude. The critical text reads τὸ ἔλεος, a form supported by examples in the LXX and Polybius. Alford and other commentators assume that λουτρόν designates the material apparatus of baptism, discarding the rendering *washing*, accepted by the Authorized Version and Revised Version. But as Doddridge long ago remarked, the version *laver* lacks corroboration, except in patristic treatises, coloured by the dogma of baptismal regeneration, and the LXX term thus translated is λουτήρ, which undoubtedly signifies a bathing-tub (L. & S.). We are glad that both M. & M. and Dr Lock in the I.C.C. incline to the translation *washing* or *water for washing*. It is chiefly in the plural that the word means *baths*. For the active sense of washing there is abundant evidence throughout Greek literature. We might instance Eur. *Hec.* 780, *El.* 794; Soph. *El.* 84, 1139, *Oed. in Col.* 1599; Aristoph. *Lys.* 377; Herodotus

vi. 52; Plat. *Crat.* 405; Xen. *Cyr.* vii. 5, 59, *Oecon.* ix. 7; Plut. *Mor.* 652, *Poplic.* 19; LXX Ct. iv. 2; Homeric *Hymn to Demeter* 50; in the Mysteries Inscription ἀλείμματος καὶ λουτροῦ, a combination met with in Plutarch (*Alex.* 40, *Marcell.* 17), and Justin Martyr's τὸ λουτρὸν ποιοῦνται (*Apol.* 61).

παλιγγενεσία has two aspects, the cosmic and the spiritual. To the Stoic it connoted a periodic revivification of nature; but Christianity personalizes its significance by relating it to the new birth. In Mt. xix. 28 indeed it retains much of its Greek associations; but here it denotes the work of the Spirit in regeneration, the new creation within. ἀνακαίνωσις (Rom. xii. 2) expresses the process of the renovation of the divine image, as Trench has observed. It is a characteristically Pauline locution for the second constituent element in the work of the Holy Ghost in the believer's soul.

The attraction of the relative οὗ to the case of its antecedent is of course normal. κληρονόμος recalls Rom. viii. 17. Here for the third time the apostle honours the Son as he honours the Father by bestowing on both Persons the appellation of Saviour.

The demand for a sample of undeniably Pauline theology from the Pastorals is fully met by this 'Gospel in a nutshell'. Not a programme of 'work and win', but of 'take and have' constitutes its very keystone. The water of life is not on sale, but on draught! Salvation by grace stands forth in clearest relief in the language employed, which effectually excludes all glorying on man's part and denies to any stock of good works amassed by any sinner a 'merit of congruity' drawing forth the riches of divine mercy. On the antitypical day of atonement no work is to be done but that of the Lamb of God, *Ipse Sacerdos*, *Ipse Hostia*, on whom hinges the whole onus of expiation. The use of the term *justification* evinces that the sacred writer is dealing with the relation of the offending parties to the majestic standard of the divine Law, and corroborates the impression that far profounder issues than a sacramental observance engross the apostle's mind. That baptism has a symbolic reference to cleansing we do not deny; but a spiritual economy cannot be tied to a material agency as an indispensable channel of grace. How can a sign engross the virtue of the thing signified? Salvation by occult qualities is a pagan conception which Rome has annexed and evolved with characteristic effrontery. The sacraments are not primaries but satellites in the gospel firmament. So Calvin styles baptism 'an accessory to the gospel'. Even under the old covenant ceremonial rites were not accepted in lieu of moral and spiritual affections or identified with them; and Christ Himself (Mt. xv. 1–20) denies to lustrations any power of spiritual purgation. Who can deny that a *radical* change of heart and life is here predicated, paramount and permanent in its character?

The law of the Lord is perfect and the obligation to conformity with it rests on every moral agent by virtue of his relationship to a holy Creator and Benefactor. We have all broken that law and are verily guilty; but pardon is freely bestowed on the believer who appropriates Christ's atoning sacrifice by that saving faith which unites him with his Kinsman-Redeemer. God justifies the ungodly, not because of compensatory works of theirs wrought in reparation for their guilt, but in view of the righteousness of Him who has spontaneously assumed and discharged their liabilities. But justification includes more than clearance at the bar of justice. The penalty of the law is fully met; but the Saviour's spotless obedience is also transferred to our account. We are made partakers of the inheritance of the saints in light, sons of God and expectants of glory by investment with His righteousness, heirs of eternal life as well as forgiven offenders. In Wesley's language:

> The mystery of redemption this,
> This the Saviour's strange design:
> Man's offence was counted His,
> Ours His righteousness divine.

Thus infinity comes to our relief and rescue. We can feel the throb of Paul's heart whenever he touches on this sweetest and sublimest of all themes, never to be sounded by finite plummet and never to be exchanged for any counterfeit gospel!

iii. 8–11. EPITOME OF COUNSELS

iii. 8.   πιστὸς ὁ λόγος, καὶ περὶ τούτων βούλομαί σε διαβεβαιοῦσθαι, ἵνα φροντίζωσιν καλῶν ἔργων προΐστασθαι οἱ πεπιστευκότες θεῷ. ταῦτά ἐστιν καλὰ καὶ ὠφέλιμα τοῖς ἀνθρώποις.

The peculiar expression, πιστὸς ὁ λόγος, which meets us here for the fourth time, seems to refer to the foregoing sentence (so the Sinaitic uncial and Chrysostom construe it), which once more wears the air of a catechetical or credal extract, apostolically endorsed. The practical exhortation appended presents the usual insistence on a true Christian walk as well as a verbal profession, the concomitant of the title to salvation presumed. The most doctrinal of all Paul's Epistles closes with a comprehensive assemblage of ethical injunctions, summed up in the words: 'let us walk in seemly wise' (εὐσχημόνως, Rom. xiii. 13). προΐστασθαι (cf. προστάτης) probably indicates *to be forward* or perhaps *foremost* in good works, a not uncommon sense of the verb, akin to the Latin *praestare*. Another meaning, *to carry on honest businesses*, has been advocated. The verb can convey that idea, exemplified in Plutarch and the papyri; but καλός is not the right adjective in such a connection, and the phrase is one statedly used for 'good works'.

iii. 9–11. μωρὰς δὲ ζητήσεις καὶ γενεαλογίας καὶ ἔριν καὶ μάχας νομικὰς περιΐστασο, εἰσὶν γὰρ ἀνωφελεῖς καὶ μάταιοι. αἱρετικὸν ἄνθρωπον μετὰ μίαν καὶ δευτέραν νουθεσίαν παραιτοῦ, εἰδὼς ὅτι ἐξέστραπται ὁ τοιοῦτος καὶ ἁμαρτάνει, ὢν αὐτοκατάκριτος.

W. & H. oust the old reading ἔρεις here and elsewhere; but it has considerable uncial support, and a singular noun inserted amid a batch of plurals reads harshly. περιΐστασθαι, meaning *shun, avoid*, a locution censured, yet used, by Lucian (*Hermot.* 86), belongs to the later Hellenistic, occurring in Philodemus (*Rhet.* 258, 384), Josephus (*B.J.* ii. 8) and Marcus Aurelius (iii. 4). αἱρετικὸς ἄνθρωπος signifies much what we call a *cliquist* or opinionative propagandist who promotes dissension by his pertinacity. At this stage it has not acquired the subsequent connotation of *heretic*, but is travelling in that direction. For παραιτεῖσθαι cf. I Tim. iv. 7. ἐκστρέφεσθαι was a medical term for dislocation, used by the LXX to stigmatize perversity of behaviour. Plutarch has the phrase ἐκστροφὴ τοῦ λόγου for an inversion of language. Alford has noted how characteristic ὁ τοιοῦτος is of Paul's diction. αὐτοκατάκριτος is counted ἅπαξ εἰρημένον by M. & M.; but Philo uses it in a fragment preserved by John of Damascus. μάταιος with two terminations has classical precedent, and the heteroclite combination εἷς καὶ δεύτερος is found in Herodian and Galen.

The ransackers of genealogical mysteries here censured are evidently akin to, but more culpable than, those rebuked in the opening verses of I Timothy. It is a token of Jewish circles that they are charged with a propensity to skirmishes relative to the Law. The vanity of these debates sufficiently condemned their promoters, the more fanatical of whom seem to have formed cabals of their own apart from the congregations for the pursuit of their aimless, profitless word-spinning. If they persist in the teeth of expostulation and warning, let them be wholly discountenanced, as parties out of touch with truth, perverted in outlook and at war with their own professions. As they cannot plead ignorance in excuse, their own conduct or consciences must needs reproach them. We are reminded of Peter's sentence (II Pet. ii. 21): 'better not to have known the way of righteousness than after knowing it to turn away from the holy commandment', whether to sheer sensuality or to empty quibblings that starve the soul that makes them its diet.

iii. 12–15. PERSONALIA

iii. 12–14. ὅταν πέμψω Ἀρτεμᾶν πρὸς σὲ ἢ Τυχικόν, σπούδασον ἐλθεῖν πρός με εἰς Νικόπολιν, ἐκεῖ γὰρ κέκρικα παραχειμάσαι. Ζηνᾶν τὸν νομικὸν καὶ Ἀπολλὼν σπουδαίως πρόπεμψον ἵνα μηδὲν αὐτοῖς λείπῃ. μανθανέτωσαν δὲ καὶ οἱ ἡμέτεροι καλῶν ἔργων προΐστασθαι εἰς τὰς ἀναγκαίας χρείας, ἵνα μὴ ὦσιν ἄκαρποι.

These verses require little comment. Of Artemas nothing authentic is known, though later days raised him to the episcopate. The name appears to be a curtailed form of Artemidorus. Tychicus, 'casual' by etymology, finds mention in Acts xx. 4 as 'an Asian', namely a native of Asia Minor, who accompanied Paul on his last visit to Jerusalem. We next learn of him as a faithful ministrant to the apostle during his first Roman imprisonment (Eph. vi. 21; Col. iv. 7) and his envoy to the churches in proconsular Asia. Now he is nominated to relieve Titus of his Cretan charge ere long. Once again we find this trusty envoy beside his principal in his final confinement and designated to take Timothy's place in Ephesus (II Tim. iv. 12). {Titus is likewise bidden to further 'Zenas the legalist' and Apollos the Alexandrian on their way when he travels to Nicopolis, probably the city of that name in Epirus associated with Epictetus. Whether ὁ νομικός denotes an ex-rabbi or a Roman lawyer (*iuris consultus*) remains uncertain. This name likewise may be an abbreviation of Zenodorus. The Gospels show that νομικός was in use to describe the class more precisely entitled νομο-διδάσκαλος; but in the papyri it indicates one versed in Roman juris-prudence. So Plutarch applies the term to Mucius Scaevola (*Sull.* 36) and to a legal aspirant snubbed by Cicero (*Cic.* 26). κέκρικα recalls I Cor. ii. 2. So Polybius. προπέμπειν means *escort*, not as in the Authorized Version 'bring'. παραχειμάζειν (Plut. *Sert.* 3) is the classical term for *spending the winter* at a place. οἱ ἡμέτεροι, *our people*, seems suggested by the military and philosophical use of *nostri* in this manner in Caesar and Cicero, and not quite unknown to Attic Greek (Plat. *Menex.* 248). An example in the papyri (M. & M.) is evidently derived from that source; the phrase occurs in Philodemus (*Rhet.* iii, p. 8), Philo (*Leg. ad Gaium*, 28) and Strabo (i. 2, vi. 3). We take ἀναγκαῖαι χρεῖαι to signify *necessitous cases* or *necessities*, a sense in which Diodorus and Philo employ the expression (Wetstein).

iii. 15. ἀσπάζονταί σε οἱ μετ᾽ ἐμοῦ πάντες. ἄσπασαι τοὺς φιλοῦντας ἡμᾶς ἐν πίστει. ἡ χάρις μετὰ πάντων ὑμῶν.

The final salutation of this more succinct Epistle follows the precedent of former Letters by transmitting a double greeting from himself and his unknown fellow-travellers, sufficiently numerous to be comprised under the title *all*. ἐν πίστει may doubtless be rendered *in the faith*, the article being dropped after a preposition. But οἱ φιλοῦντες ἐν πίστει so much resembles the last sentence of Ephesians (vi. 24), where we read οἱ ἀγαπῶντες ἐν ἀφθαρσίᾳ, that we incline to translate it adverbially, as that is generally done, in some such way as *faithfully*. *Grace be with you all* is Paul's established sign manual (II Thes. iii. 18). The plural *all of you* shows that the Letter was more than a private document. The subscription from Nicopolis (cf. Authorized Version) carries no authority.

THE SECOND EPISTLE
TO TIMOTHY

THIS parting letter of so signal a wooer of souls and warder of saints is invested with a tenderness and pathos incapable of fabrication. Most of those who cast suspicion on the genuineness of the Pastoral Epistles as a whole are compelled by the force of evidence that cannot be ignored to acknowledge the presence therein of passages obviously Pauline in conception and expression. And as the notion to which they cling of a patchwork interlaced with authentic fragments has not a shred of documentary evidence to rest upon, but is subjectively excogitated and backed only by arguments drawn from a search governed by initial prepossessions, it may be treated as an *idolon tribus*, too arbitrary to call for detailed confutation. For the same external proof which ratifies the admittedly Pauline ingredients sustains those paragraphs to which they take exception. As an historical document this Epistle, like its two brethren, comes before us in no fragmentary shape, but as an integral consignment from antiquity.

The apostle's condition has obviously changed for the worse. No longer can he write of his free movements and cherished plans; for a final arrest has been laid on his activities. This he recognizes in a way that sets this incarceration in a class by itself. It cannot be identified with the first Roman imprisonment for the simple reason that it wears an entirely different colouring. The charge against him now is of so grave a cast that it affords no hope of escape from a capital sentence. Judgment has been deferred, but the issue can no longer be deemed doubtful. If Timothy is to see his principal again, he must hasten to Rome for a farewell interview. To understand the tone and purport of the Letter, these considerations must be constantly borne in mind.

i. 1, 2. SALUTATION

i. 1, 2. Παῦλος ἀπόστολος Χριστοῦ Ἰησοῦ διὰ θελήματος θεοῦ κατ᾿ ἐπαγγελίαν ζωῆς τῆς ἐν Χριστῷ Ἰησοῦ Τιμοθέῳ ἀγαπητῷ τέκνῳ· χάρις ἔλεος εἰρήνη ἀπὸ θεοῦ πατρὸς καὶ Χριστοῦ Ἰησοῦ τοῦ κυρίου ἡμῶν.

The salutation deviates slightly from former models. I Corinthians, Ephesians and Colossians parallel the phrase διὰ θελήματος θεοῦ, expressive of the solid foundation on which Paul's apostolate was reared; whilst κατ᾿ ἐπαγγελίαν ζωῆς recalls the statement of Tit. i. 2 respecting the pre-mundane divine engagement to bestow life eternal on the heirs of salvation. The apostle magnifies his office to give weight to his message.

Timothy, here styled ἀγαπητός, is, as it were, pressed to his heart once more by the most endearing epithet he can cull. 'Love never faileth.' The insertion of *mercy* in the greeting along with grace and peace has been remarked at the opening of the first Epistle.

i. 3–10. A PERSONAL REMINDER

i. 3–5. χάριν ἔχω τῷ θεῷ, ᾧ λατρεύω ἀπὸ προγόνων ἐν καθαρᾷ συνειδήσει, ὡς ἀδιάλειπτον ἔχω τὴν περὶ σοῦ μνείαν ἐν ταῖς δεήσεσίν μου, νυκτὸς καὶ ἡμέρας ἐπιποθῶν σε ἰδεῖν, μεμνημένος σου τῶν δακρύων, ἵνα χαρᾶς πληρωθῶ ὑπόμνησιν λαβὼν τῆς ἐν σοὶ ἀνυποκρίτου πίστεως, ἥτις ἐνῴκησεν πρῶτον ἐν τῇ μάμμῃ σου Λωΐδι καὶ τῇ μητρί σου Εὐνίκῃ, πέπεισμαι δὲ ὅτι καὶ ἐν σοί.

χάριν ἔχειν (cf. Latin *gratiam habere*) takes the place of the verb εὐχαριστεῖν. It is of course quite literary, more so in fact than the other expression. We have had it before in I Tim. i. 12. ἀπὸ προγόνων of ancestral relations occurs in the papyri. A passage in Plato (*Laws*, 931) shows that the noun may refer to immediate forbears. ἀδιάλειπτος we recognize as a Pauline adjective and adverb (Rom. i. 9, ix. 2; I Thes. i. 2, ii. 13, v. 17). For the order νυκτὸς καὶ ἡμέρας see I Tim. v. 5. ἐπιποθεῖν, similar in meaning to Latin *desiderare*, is, with its substantives, almost confined in the New Testament to Paul's writings; it conveys the idea of *yearning* (cf. Rom. i. 11). The phraseology ὑπόμνησιν λαβών suggests, as Bengel observes, that a reminder of Timothy had just reached the apostle in his cell. μάμμη, a pet name like 'grannie' for grandmother, was rejected by the Atticists in favour of τήθη, but has a place in Plutarch and Philo, and abounds in the papyri.

We have here a capital instance of the apostle's individualizing propensity, and nice appreciation of personal traits. Paul claims for himself the credit of a clear conscience and for his ancestors, as God-fearing characters, however incompletely enlightened. So he had testified before Felix (Acts xxiv. 16). A man may well be thankful when he comes of a godly stock, when the family traditions are of a devout stamp. Grace does not 'run in the blood' but sober-mindedness may be inherited and fostered by parental example, and be a factor for good and a ground of thanksgiving.

The tears Timothy had shed at bidding the apostle good-bye linger in his recollection, and carry his thoughts back to bygone days, when his disciple had been a youngster at home in Lystra. We picture him a docile and somewhat shy and reticent fondling of his grandmother and mother, whose name we might transliterate into Victoria. His father was a Greek, but of him there is no mention, whilst these two saintly women are enshrined in Holy Writ. Their piety must have been of an eminent type to obtain so cordial a recognition. They were 'Israelites indeed', like Nathanael, ready for the seed of the kingdom, when it fell in the soil of their hearts. πέπεισμαι ὅτι is a thoroughly Pauline phrase for full conviction (Rom. viii. 38).

i. 6. δι' ἣν αἰτίαν ἀναμιμνήσκω σε ἀναζωπυρεῖν τὸ χάρισμα τοῦ θεοῦ ὅ ἐστιν ἐν σοὶ διὰ τῆς ἐπιθέσεως τῶν χειρῶν μου·

δι' ἣν αἰτίαν has Attic authority and as a link of connection is met with in the Acts; but its triple occurrence in the Pastorals alone may possibly be a sign of recent Latin associations, since *quamobrem* is such a favourite Roman conjunction. The metaphor embodied in ἀναζωπυρεῖν, of which this is the sole New Testament example, is found in the LXX, and does not lack classical precedent in Plato (*Rep.* 527). Plutarch uses it (*Mor.* 1095) of rekindling faded emotions, and Josephus not infrequently, in one instance (*B.J.* i. 22) of the reawakening of a love-passion. We have already remarked (I Tim. iv. 14) the peculiarly Pauline stamp of the term χάρισμα, *gift of grace.*

The apostle's solicitude for Timothy's spiritual health finds vent in an exhortation to revivify the fire burning on the altar of his soul, and in order to animate his zeal puts him in mind of the fervour of his youth and the special enduement of the Spirit bestowed on him at the hour of his self-dedication to his life-work, when Paul's hands were laid on the probationer's bowed head. Hypercritical minds fancy they can detect a discrepancy between the act of the presbytery in I Tim. iv. 14 and the statement advanced here. But whilst the rite of ordination may have pertained officially to them, it stands to reason that, his spiritual father being present and invested with full apostolic authority, he would bear part in the solemnity. We can discover, however, no veiled rebuke in this passage administered to Timothy's assumed lassitude. Every Christian needs to be reminded of the 'love of his espousals' and of the ardency of his first aspirations in his Master's service, which many a chilling experience has since tended to enervate. Ephesus with its cinders of carping criticism in default of the cheering glow of Paul's ardency may have proved rather a damper to his susceptible disciple.

i. 7. οὐ γὰρ ἔδωκεν ἡμῖν ὁ θεὸς πνεῦμα δειλίας ἀλλὰ δυνάμεως καὶ ἀγάπης καὶ σωφρονισμοῦ.

The apostle's penchant for generalizations is well known, and this verse furnishes an instance of it. We do not think that he is hinting at his lieutenant's pusillanimity, as some suppose; far from it. Had he received news of that, he would have expostulated with him sharply; for innuendoes are not at all in Paul's style. The negative clause serves as a foil to the positive. The Lord's soldier has not been empowered from on high that he may display a shrinking, dastardly, apologetic bearing, but that he may stand to his guns like one 'valiant for truth'. A man in Christ counts for more than a man by himself. He enjoys a grand alliance and unseen resources. The love spoken of may be a loving spirit towards others, but that must flow from a diviner well-spring. Love to Christ induces impassioned devotion, love to Him for whom no sacrifice of self-pleasing we can make deserves the name, as Livingstone once wrote, when ranged side by side with His sacrifice for us. σωφρονισμός conveys a stronger sense than the σωφροσύνη of the first Epistle. It expresses *self-command* or *self-discipline* (cf. Plut. *Mor.* 653). The verb σωφρονίζειν is employed by Xenophon (*Hier.* 10)

and Plutarch (*Mor.* 641) of curbing a skittish horse. The mastery of
self needs much grace to effect and yet more grace to preserve intact,
and in this respect Timothy may have been constitutionally infirm. To
control others we must first learn to control ourselves and our impulses.
Trapp styles this armour of strong-mindedness our *aes triplex*.

i. 8–10a. μὴ οὖν ἐπαισχυνθῇς τὸ μαρτύριον τοῦ κυρίου ἡμῶν μηδὲ
ἐμὲ τὸν δέσμιον αὐτοῦ, ἀλλὰ συνκακοπάθησον τῷ εὐαγγελίῳ κατὰ
δύναμιν θεοῦ τοῦ σώσαντος ἡμᾶς καὶ καλέσαντος κλήσει ἁγίᾳ, οὐ κατὰ
τὰ ἔργα ἡμῶν ἀλλὰ κατὰ ἰδίαν πρόθεσιν καὶ χάριν τὴν δοθεῖσαν ἡμῖν
ἐν Χριστῷ Ἰησοῦ πρὸ χρόνων αἰωνίων, φανερωθεῖσαν δὲ νῦν διὰ τῆς
ἐπιφανείας τοῦ σωτῆρος ἡμῶν Χριστοῦ Ἰησοῦ,

The classical verb ἐπαισχύνεσθαι, here passive in form, but active in
syntax, receives no illustration from the papyri, but occurs in the
Gospels and in Romans and Hebrews. The negative is far from implying
that Timothy had shown symptoms of invertebracy. Paul is fond of
the figure meiosis. When he tells us that he is 'not ashamed of the
gospel', who imagines that he means anything less than when he says
that he glories in the cross? συνκακοπαθεῖν, *brook hardship with me*,
seems a new coinage of the apostle, here and in ii. 3. Later in this
Epistle he writes κακοπαθεῖν (see for meaning ii. 9). πρόθεσις, similar
in meaning to Latin *propositum*, used of the divine purpose in Romans
and Ephesians, strikes a familiar chord. The noun acquires this later
sense in Polybius and Philo. We have met πρὸ χρόνων αἰωνίων in
Tit. i. 2. ἐπιφάνεια has reference here (cf. Tit. iii. 4) to the first advent
of Jesus Christ.

The apostle, as he approaches the vital centre of Christian truth,
characteristically launches forth into a periodic sentence which he
scarcely rounds off. Timothy must 'hold the fort' committed to his
trust without flinching and not dream of discountenancing the forlorn
state-prisoner at Rome. So many of whom better things might have
been expected had been showing the white feather that we cannot
wonder at this earnest appeal, designed to brace his deputy's spiritual
muscle. Less sturdy in temperament than Titus, he needed more
specific incitement to gird up his loins for the race he had to run. How
like Paul to repeat the title he had appropriated to himself in Ephesians
(iii. 1) and Philemon (1, 9) of *the Lord's prisoner*, not Nero's! That

persuasion transfigured his bonds into badges of distinction. Suffering for the gospel's sake raises a believer to the rank of the heavenly legion of honour. Paul's worn eyes flash and his weather-beaten visage clears at the mention of his gospel, and he has to unfold the precious scroll once more and feast his soul upon it. Implicit in its message of salvation lies hid the power of God. An almighty hand has rescued us from the sphere of the precarious and planted us in its impregnable stronghold. Cannot He who saves keep? Has He not cast over us a spell of irrevocable fixity? Then sounds the Pauline keynote, 'not according to our works but according to His own purpose and grace bestowed on us in Christ'. It is a sign of Paul's hand, as we have remarked in Titus, to give the Son the appellation of Saviour after giving it to the Father. That the homage here paid to the sovereign grace of God accords with his inmost convictions who can dispute? The Lord's choices have their unfathomable grounds, but they are not founded on the innate eligibility of the chosen. The effectual call of His Spirit opens both the outer door of the understanding, as Boston puts it, and the inner door of the will.

i. 10b. καταργήσαντος μὲν τὸν θάνατον, φωτίσαντος δὲ ζωὴν καὶ ἀφθαρσίαν διὰ τοῦ εὐαγγελίου,

Of true eloquence it has been remarked that like Virgil's Fame, *vires acquirit eundo*. 'E'en in our ashes live their wonted fires'; and Paul's fervent spirit kindles into lambent incandescence at the mention of so transcendent a theme as his unique gospel. In a sentence already packed with meaning he inserts this glowing parenthesis in honour of his beloved Lord, heightening its effect by the employment of his favourite vocable καταργεῖν. That verb recurs in his Epistles no fewer than twenty-five times (indeed only once besides in its metaphorical sense in the New Testament). It is a rare term, found once in Euripides (*Phoen.* 753), but scarcely elsewhere outside the papyri, and best understood by scanning the various meanings of the adjective ἀργός, such as *lying fallow*, *fruitless* (Isocr., Plut., Joseph.), or *unserviceable* in Marcus Aurelius (xii. 6) of the left hand; or Philodemus's (*Rhet.* i. 354) use of ἄπεργος for *obsolete*. In Paul's mouth it means *to render nugatory*, *frustrate*, *quash*, *dismantle*. It may be rendered *disempowering* or *nullifying* death, here almost personified by the insertion of the article.

The underlying thought is that of invalidating or, more literally, putting out of gear (M. & M.). φωτίζειν, *to bring to light, disclose*, is a Polybian expression, found also in Lucian (*Calumn.* 32) and in Vettius Valens (173, 271, 359). The enigmas of the Old Testament are unravelled in the New. Its dark oracles are lit up with a 'glory that excelleth' when set in its brighter lustre.

Christ has disarmed the last enemy, and rendered its dreaded sting innocuous; His revelation of everlasting bliss and peace has robbed the king of terrors of his threatening mien. Jesus died our deserved death for us as believers, and we only fall asleep, because He has tasted all its bitterness in our stead. Hence the inextinguishable joy and triumphant outlook of His followers, even on the rack or at the stake. They are not death's prey, but death itself is *theirs*, transferred from the debit to the credit side of their ledger.

i. 11, 12. AN EXEMPLIFICATION IN HIS OWN CASE

i. 11, 12. εἰς ὃ ἐτέθην ἐγὼ κῆρυξ καὶ ἀπόστολος καὶ διδάσκαλος. δι᾽ ἣν αἰτίαν καὶ ταῦτα πάσχω, ἀλλ᾽ οὐκ ἐπαισχύνομαι, οἶδα γὰρ ᾧ πεπίστευκα καὶ πέπεισμαι ὅτι δυνατός ἐστιν τὴν παραθήκην μου φυλάξαι εἰς ἐκείνην τὴν ἡμέραν.

To enforce his solemn charge, the apostle, conscious of his approaching end, bears personal testimony to his own unshaken trust and confidence in his heavenly Warder. First of all he repeats *totidem verbis* the declaration of his first Epistle (ii. 7) that he owed his office to divine appointment, with the omission of the affidavit, 'I lie not', needless where its challengers are lost sight of and he is writing a more confidential letter. Were it not for that sense of delegation that sustains him, and the assurance that his bonds enter into the divine purpose, his fortitude might give way; but, as it is, he knows with an intimacy blessedly real the faithfulness of his Sponsor and has not a shadow of doubt that He will guard the deposit he has placed in His hands inviolate till the day of settlement ever pending. His Lord's potency to fulfil all His engagements admits of no question. παραθήκη is the curtailed form of the full term for a legal deposit παρακαταθήκη, and plentiful examples of it may be met with in the papyri. It has already crossed our path in

I Tim. vi. 20 and was of old standing enough to find place in the Ionic of Herodotus.

What is the deposit here referred to? Some interpret it of the evangel just mentioned, the message entrusted to his charge; but surely the resonant note struck accords with a more personal allusion. The apostle is looking at home. Philo applies the term to the soul (ii. 37), our costliest treasure, and it is that entrustment the saints, especially in prospect of taking flight, commit into Immanuel's steadfast hands. When Dr James Alexander of Princeton lay on his death-bed his wife quoted these words in an inexact form: 'I know in whom I have believed.' Her husband gently corrected her version. He would not let even a preposition creep between his soul and his Saviour. Faith of the true strain makes straight for Christ; for it is certain of His ability to secure the sheep of His pasture from all despoilers unto the end. *That* tremendous day of settlement is ever present to St Paul's far-seeing vision.

i. 13, 14. HOLD FAST THE TRUTH

i. 13, 14. ὑποτύπωσιν ἔχε ὑγιαινόντων λόγων ὧν παρ' ἐμοῦ ἤκουσας ἐν πίστει καὶ ἀγάπῃ τῇ ἐν Χριστῷ Ἰησοῦ· τὴν καλὴν παραθήκην φύλαξον διὰ πνεύματος ἁγίου τοῦ ἐνοικοῦντος ἐν ἡμῖν.

We have had ὑποτύπωσις in I Tim. i. 16, where see note. Whatever may be its precise sense there, the signification of a *summary*, *outline*, which Galen assigns to the word, best tallies with this context. Sextus Empiricus repeatedly uses it in that acceptation. If so, it presents yet another sign that epitomes of the Christian faith were beginning to pass current. λόγοι in the plural would naturally mean *propositions* in such a connection. It may be incorrect, as Ellicott urges, to translate ἔχε *hold fast* (Authorized Version); but evidently the weak sense put upon it by Alford and others is mistaken. They forget that it stands in the imperative mood in this instance, and is coupled with the strong term φύλαξον.

τὴν καλὴν παραθήκην we take to mean *thy goodly deposit*. In this case the figure does seem to indicate the revelation of divine truth consigned to Timothy's custody, and if the parallelism of meaning in verses 12 and 14 be insisted upon, that must be its interpretation in the preceding sentence. Possibly the two lines of thought may be combined, if we regard the preacher's soul as the casket of his message, deposited both with him and in him, an image familiar to Philo. Mark the suppression of the articles in the earlier part of the sentence, not easy to explain except as indications of expedition on the part of the writer, similar to our own habit in English of curtailing 'the grace of God' into 'God's grace'. Paul resorts to this mode of condensation occasionally; cf. Eph. vi. 17, 18. ἐνοικεῖν is an exclusively Pauline verb in the New Testament.

i. 15–18. THE APOSTLE'S LONELINESS

i. 15–18. οἶδας τοῦτο ὅτι ἀπεστράφησάν με πάντες οἱ ἐν τῇ Ἀσίᾳ ὧν ἐστιν Φύγελος καὶ Ἑρμογένης. δῴη ἔλεος ὁ κύριος τῷ Ὀνησιφόρου οἴκῳ, ὅτι πολλάκις με ἀνέψυξεν, καὶ τὴν ἅλυσίν μου οὐκ ἐπαισχύνθη[1] ἀλλὰ γενόμενος ἐν Ῥώμῃ σπουδαίως ἐζήτησέν με καὶ εὗρεν ⸺ δῴη αὐτῷ ὁ κύριος εὑρεῖν ἔλεος παρὰ Κυρίου ἐν ἐκείνῃ τῇ ἡμέρᾳ· ⸺ καὶ ὅσα ἐν Ἐφέσῳ διηκόνησεν, βέλτιον σὺ γινώσκεις.

We have met ἀποστρέφεσθαι with the accusative in Tit. i. 14. Nothing can be told concerning Phygelus and Hermogenes, the latter a name of pagan origin extant in the papyri. δῴη with *iota subscript* is, of course, an optative form equivalent to δοίη. ἀναψύχειν, meaning *to refresh*, is a classical word, borrowed by the LXX. The singular ἅλυσις has been thought to refer to the chain binding the prisoner's wrist to a soldier who guarded him, or combined with a wooden collar (κλοιός) as we find it in Lucian's *Toxaris* (33). Cf. Joseph. *Antiq.* xviii. 6, *B.J.* iv. 10; Sen. *Ep.* 5.

Intensely sympathetic souls crave sympathy in return. Christ Himself in Gethsemane yearned for the comradeship of Peter, James and John. Paul had been undergoing close confinement on a capital charge unrelieved by any prospect of vindicating his innocence; but the bitterest ingredient in his cup consisted of the element of dereliction which he now shared with his Lord. His well-wishers in Asia Minor had all shrunk from his side. Expositors speak of Asiatic visitors to Rome who would have laid themselves open to suspicion by seeking

[1] Remark the dropped augment, an Ionic tendency.

him out; but the aorist ἀπεστράφησαν points to a definite moment when this desertion happened. We hold that this stampede took place on the occasion of the apostle's arrest, very likely in Asia Minor itself, on an accusation of the most perilous nature, association with which might involve their arrest as his accomplices. The courage of these disciples gave way under this acute test; but we must not brand their faint-heartedness as flat apostasy. In happy contrast the apostle signalizes the devotion of Onesiphorus, an Ephesian convert who had answered to his name 'Profitable' by the services he had rendered to both Timothy and Paul. A journey to Rome fell to his lot; and instead of leaving Paul in the lurch this friend in need took great pains [1] to ascertain his whereabouts and paid him repeated visits, to the apostle's no small solace. The act exposed him to serious risk of detention as a suspect, but Onesiphorus braved the danger with a stout heart and he is known to this day for his gallant staunchness, if for nothing beside.

The Roman Church has tried to make capital out of the prayer here offered on his behalf that he might find mercy in the great day, by identifying it with the practice of prayers for the dead. It is hastily assumed that the chivalrous visitor was now deceased, because his household obtains separate mention; but one reason for that may be that they were at present severed by distance—he had come to be (γενόμενος) at Rome—and another that a household and its head are inseparably linked in good wishes and prayers. To us it seems plain that the good man was alive from the very terms of this supplication, since prayers for the dead find no footing whatsoever in the Scriptures and certainly Paul was not in the habit of indulging in them. We might have expected *reward* rather than *mercy* to have been sought at the great assize of the future; but the apostle is dwelling on his benignity toward himself and recalling Mt. xxv. 36 and the beatitude: 'Blessed are the merciful, for they shall obtain mercy.' The word *ministered*, descriptive of Onesiphorus's Ephesian activities, hints at their benevolent trend. The insertion of *unto me* at Ephesus (Authorized Version) is misleading; it presumes a recent sojourn of Paul at that place which we have seen

---

[1] The reading varies between σπουδαίως and σπουδαιότερον, the more idiomatic of the two, an 'elative' comparative expressive of Onesiphorus's peculiar assiduity of quest. As this is a Pauline mannerism, and he uses the comparative distinctly in Phil. ii. 28, we prefer the second reading. Cf. II Cor. viii. 22 and βέλτιον (II Tim. i. 18).

reason to question, and the appeal to Timothy's better knowledge of his friend's doings rather points the other way. βέλτιον, *right well*, recalls the similar use of κάλλιον in Acts xxv. 10.

ii. 1, 2. EXHORTATION TO FIDELITY

ii. 1, 2. σὺ οὖν, τέκνον μου, ἐνδυναμοῦ ἐν τῇ χάριτι τῇ ἐν Χριστῷ Ἰησοῦ, καὶ ἃ ἤκουσας παρ' ἐμοῦ διὰ πολλῶν μαρτύρων, ταῦτα παράθου πιστοῖς ἀνθρώποις οἵτινες ἱκανοὶ ἔσονται καὶ ἑτέρους διδάξαι.

The apostle's solicitude for Timothy breaks out in the endearing term τέκνον, already noticed in I Tim. i. 2. ἐνδυναμοῦσθαι repeats another Pauline verb, extant in the LXX, but not found in the papyri or in profane Greek. διά with the genitive here carries the somewhat rare sense of *amid, in presence of* (Plut. *Mor.* 338, διὰ θεῶν μαρτύρων). The reference appears to signalize the occasion of the young man's ordination, but it may be, as Chrysostom holds, more general. παρατίθεσθαι (cf. παραθήκη) clearly means *to deposit, give in charge*, so used (papyri) of wills or deeds. Philodemus (*De Ira* 63) speaks of quarrels being consigned to children's children, using this verb. ἱκανός with the infinitive, meaning *competent to*, is a classical literary phrase, used by Xenophon. ἕτερος, as in popular usage, takes the place of ἄλλος much as we interchange *each other* with *one another*.

The injunction to strengthen himself in the Lord and stand fast in His grace was peculiarly timely under his lieutenant's load of vexing cares and sombre tidings. Only thus could he withstand in the evil day and, having done all, still stand. It seems to be hinted that he too might be summoned to tread the same pathway as his preceptor; so it behoves him to commit the divine verities consigned to his charge to faithful trustees able to hand on the holy doctrine to others. The torch of heavenly light must be transmitted unquenched from one generation to another, and Timothy must count himself an intermediary between apostolic and later ages. Two reflections emerge from this passage worth pondering.

(1) An era of inspired teaching and apostolic surveillance, in itself exceptional, is to be followed by an era of diffusion and consolidation of a more normal type.

(2) The Church is contemplated as a permanent institution, not to be

superseded either by a cataclysm of calamities or a Second Advent suspending its operations ere they could mature. The 'blessed hope' did not foreshorten the tract of future time, in Paul's view of it, to an interstitial span. An expanse of human history was yet to be unrolled before the conclusive *finis* put a period to its annals. Cf. II Thes. ii. 2.

ii. 3–8. ILLUSTRATIONS

ii. 3–5. συνκακοπάθησον ὡς καλὸς στρατιώτης Χριστοῦ Ἰησοῦ. οὐδεὶς στρατευόμενος ἐμπλέκεται ταῖς τοῦ βίου πραγματείαις, ἵνα τῷ στρατολογήσαντι ἀρέσῃ· ἐὰν δὲ καὶ ἀθλῇ τις, οὐ στεφανοῦται ἐὰν μὴ νομίμως ἀθλήσῃ·

Paul's exhortation waxes yet more importunate. He has shown his deputy that he has heavenly sailing-orders; his vocation has been divinely ordained, and he virtually enjoins upon him, *Spartam quam nactus es exorna.* Timothy may have longed for a less arduous post than he found Ephesus to be. But then that post had been assigned him by the Commander-in-Chief. Let him bear the strain as a gallant soldier of Jesus Christ, accoutred in armour not his own, girding up the loins of his mind for the task. Two characteristic metaphors clench this admonition. One is borrowed from the Roman soldier who has crossed the apostle's path so frequently. The spectacle of military discipline furnished a grand lesson of wholeheartedness. A soldier under arms (στρατευόμενος) does not involve himself in business affairs but confines himself to a warrior's duties.[1] (Cf. Plutarch *Aem.* xii for the sentiment.) πραγματεία forms the classical equivalent to *business* and ἐμπλέκεσθαι, the Latin *implicari* (Luther's *flechten sich in*), equally expresses in all shades of Greek *entanglement.* So in Arrian, *Epict.* iii. 22. Polybius (ii. 28) uses it of weapons getting involved in the trammels of a cloak. For a true soldier covets the praise of his superior officer or whoever summoned him to wage war. στρατολογεῖν is a somewhat rare Hellenistic term for raising a levy, found in Josephus (*Antiq.* i. 5, etc.) and Plutarch (*Caes.* 35, *Mor.* 203).

The second image, taken from the Grecian games, presents the intense earnestness of the competitors and their sedulous observance of

---

[1] *militares viros civiles curas arripere prohibemus,* says the code of Theodosius (Wetstein).

the prescribed regulations as a pattern of Christian devotion. Here it is not the perishableness or transiency of the glory gained, as in Corinthians, that is set in relief, but the strict adherence to rule. ἀθλεῖν may be rendered *contend for a prize*, but νομίμως baffles the translator, for it not only suggests 'conformably to the rules', but 'in a correct style' or something of the sort. Galen employs this very phrase οἱ νομίμως ἀθλοῦντες for *full-fledged athletes*, professionals not amateurs. So in Arrian, *Epict.* iii. 10, the idea of exclusive absorption in the pursuit, in contrast with mere dalliance with it, recurs.

ii. 6. τὸν κοπιῶντα γεωργὸν δεῖ πρῶτον τῶν καρπῶν μεταλαμβάνειν.

Both Authorized Version and some others go astray here. Their version is confuted by the order of the words and by their contextual relation; for it would be hard to show that the proposition that 'the labourer must first be partaker of the fruits' is germane to the text. Let them be translated as they stand; *the toiling husbandman must first partake of the fruits*. Then we recognize here a third appropriate illustration of wholeheartedness. It is the man who has bathed himself in sweat to secure a harvest who has the premier title to its produce. Labour expended on an object renders it our own. Personality founds itself on the imprint of personality. Untiring culture of a plot of ground, at least in nearly virgin soil, confers a right to reap its produce. Special outlay with a determinate aim deserves reward; whereas a dilatory, half-hearted pursuit of it miscarries. 'This one thing I do' should be the Christian worker's watchword. Paul bids Timothy harden himself as a valorous and unhampered soldier of his King, train as a spiritual athlete, inured to every suppling of sinew or submission to training requisite to win the palm of victory, and till his ground so as to ensure an ingathering that shall be distinctively his own handiwork.

ii. 7, 8. νόει ὃ λέγω· δώσει γάρ σοι ὁ κύριος σύνεσιν ἐν πᾶσιν. μνημόνευε Ἰησοῦν Χριστὸν ἐγηγερμένον ἐκ νεκρῶν, ἐκ σπέρματος Δαυείδ, κατὰ τὸ εὐαγγέλιόν μου.

The reading δώσει, assimilated to the δῴη of chapter i. 16, 18 in the Received Text, has superior warrant. μνημονεύειν admits of construction either with genitive or accusative object (cf. I Thes. ii. 9). The perfect ἐγηγερμένος, familiar from I Cor. xv, lays stress on the permanent result, and the phrase 'of the seed of David' re-echoes a significant expression in Romans (i. 3).

Let his correspondent ponder his obligations and Paul is sure that full illumination as to his duty will be given him. σύνεσις, meaning *perception, discernment* of the bearing of things, has been ably analysed by Lightfoot on Col. i. 9. The cardinal importance of Christ's resurrection, both in its doctrinal significance and viewed as an incentive to Christian faith and hope, none can dispute to be a Pauline speciality. He reckons it the pledge of all spiritual support, the pledge of victory to the Lord's people, the final attestation of all His claims. Of the seed of David after the flesh, He is also the Son of God girded with all might, and the evangelical history becomes an imperishable gospel in the light of the risen Redeemer. The 'exceeding greatness of His power to usward who believe' is measured by its working in His own revivification and exaltation at the right hand of the majesty on high (Eph. i. 19, 20). The Messianic heir of all things, at once our Maker and Brother, can remould our sin-crippled energies into the facsimile of His own serenity and strength.

ii. 9, 10. HIS OWN PATTERN

ii. 9, 10. ἐν ᾧ κακοπαθῶ μέχρι δεσμῶν ὡς κακοῦργος, ἀλλὰ ὁ λόγος τοῦ θεοῦ οὐ δέδεται. διὰ τοῦτο πάντα ὑπομένω διὰ τοὺς ἐκλεκτούς, ἵνα καὶ αὐτοὶ σωτηρίας τύχωσιν τῆς ἐν Χριστῷ Ἰησοῦ μετὰ δόξης αἰωνίου.

The antecedent of ἐν ᾧ is surely not the gospel but Christ. The apostle is still dwelling on the thought of His good soldier, as the repetition of the verb κακοπαθεῖν and the phrase 'in Christ' (verse 10) show. Paul suffers as a member of Christ's mystical body; hence the 'faithful saying' subjoined. κακοπαθεῖν has in recent days been construed of passive rather than active sufferings; but usage contravenes this exegesis. *Hard faring*, not afflictive conditions, is the prevalent sense in Hellenistic contexts (cf. Arrian, *Anab.* vi. 29; Plut. *Lucull.* 28; *Alex.* 40; *Num.* 3); and both Plutarch and Cebes (*Tab.* 9) contrast it with self-indulgence (ἡδυπάθεια) and Philo (ii. 282) with ῥᾳθυμία. Josephus (*Ap.* i. 19) uses the verb of 'holding out' (cf. *Antiq.* vi. 9, 1); and Philodemus (*Rhet.* ii. 205) employs it of the preparatory toils of the would-be orator and Vettius Valens (294) of the laborious task of acquiring technical knowledge. Thus Sallust enlarges on the *consueta duritia* of the Roman soldier, inured *hiemem et aestatem iuxta pati, eodem tempore inopiam et laborem tolerare*; what we call 'roughing it'. μέχρι δεσμῶν means 'to the length of bonds' (cf. Phil. ii. 8); cf. μέχρι θανάτου (Ceb. *Tab.* 26).

In the name of the gospel, or rather the gospel's Lord, the apostle was now incarcerated as a wrongdoer; but he exults in the reflection that the Word of God is not shackled like himself. This play on the verb δεῖσθαι is one of those unobtrusive tokens of Pauline authorship that carry conviction with them. All modern Bible societies bear witness to the never-ceasing evidences of the life-giving power of the Word, even in default of human interpreters. Chrysostom makes the contrast to lie between Paul's bound wrists and loosened tongue; but in this severer confinement he had little opportunity of converse with others, we may be sure. He refers either to the extended circulation of his written Epistles in common with the rest of the Scriptures, or else to the labours of the faithful brethren like Timothy, who were still at large. Therefore, because of God's elect, whom he is to be instrumental in fetching home and making heirs of everlasting bliss, he does not 'bate one jot of heart and hope, but still bears up and steers right onward'. A high and holy aspiration that, if ever there were one, and inseparably linked with a transcendent recompense of reward.

ii. 11–13. A NOTABLE UTTERANCE

ii. 11–13. πιστὸς ὁ λόγος· εἰ γὰρ συναπεθάνομεν καὶ συνζήσομεν· εἰ ὑπομένομεν καὶ συνβασιλεύσομεν· εἰ ἀρνησόμεθα κἀκεῖνος ἀρνήσεται ἡμᾶς· εἰ ἀπιστοῦμεν, ἐκεῖνος πιστὸς μένει, ἀρνήσασθαι γὰρ ἑαυτὸν οὐ δύναται.

Here we encounter the last of the five faithful sayings in the Pastorals, which we saw reason to think embodied either catechetical data or snatches of prophetical utterance current in the Church and duly ratified by the apostle. The rhythmical parallelism of this specimen seems to favour the latter suggestion. As remarked in a previous annotation on Tit. i. 16, the use of ἀρνεῖσθαι with a personal object may be classed as a New Testament idiom, born of Christian terminology now in process of growth. A visible church necessarily mints verbal coinages of its own to express fresh combinations of ideas.

At any rate the sentiment here endorsed accords fully with a leading trait of Pauline doctrine. Almost identical language had been used in Rom. vi. 8; for the union of the believer with his Lord lay very near his heart. We recall his exclamation: 'I have been crucified with Christ and now Christ liveth in me' (Gal. ii. 19 f.). Believers have died with Christ unto sin, and the last Adam is become to them a quickening spirit (I Cor. xv. 45). 'In our death Christ died; in His resurrection we live'; and because He lives, we *shall* live also. Furthermore; if called to suffer the most poignant ills, the prospect of reigning with Him lightens all terrestrial trials. *Ecclesia haeres est crucis*, wrote Luther; and the English martyr Bradford said, 'The Lord has chosen me as one in whom He will suffer'. Tribulation is the very ensign of the elect; no cross, no crown; no thorn, no throne. Note how the perseverance of the saints, covenanted though it be, is here 'attended by sergeant If'. For conversely our denial of Christ entails His denial of us (Mt. x. 33), an alternative not to be contemplated without horror. Momentary treason may (alas!) overtake even a fervid Peter; but final apostasy casts a far more darkling pall over the guilty offender.

The only stable security in a Laodicean age against the prevalence of the gates of hell consists in the divine faithfulness. The foundation of God standeth sure because He *cannot* deny Himself. His essential veracity forms the primary axis of the universe;

> If that fail,
> The pillared firmament is rottenness,
> And earth's base built on stubble.

But 'a moral impossibility inheres in the nature of a perfect Being'. Whether it be the Lord's promises or His threatenings we stumble at, they are alike certain of fulfilment. He cannot renounce Himself, nor can second thoughts revise, nor unforeseen contingencies dash, His holy counsels.

ii. 14, 15. A STERLING WORKMAN

ii. 14. ταῦτα ὑπομίμνησκε διαμαρτυρόμενος ἐνώπιον τοῦ θεοῦ μὴ λογομαχεῖν, ἐπ' οὐδὲν χρήσιμον, ἐπὶ καταστροφῇ τῶν ἀκουόντων.

ὑπομιμνήσκειν and διαμαρτύρεσθαι are both classical verbs, the latter a favourite with Luke. For the special locution λογομαχεῖν see the note on I Tim. vi. 4. Ellicott is wrong in denying that ἐπ' οὐδὲν χρήσιμον is an independent clause. If it were subordinated to μὴ λογομαχεῖν the negative should be μηδέν. Robertson holds that the οὐδέν attaches itself to the adjective (*Grammar of Greek New Testament*, p. 947); but that is very awkward, and Paul suppresses the copula frequently. The clause is best taken parenthetically, or possibly in apposition, *a thing of no use at all*. καταστροφὴ [τοῦ βίου], cf. Latin *pernicies*, is especially associated with sudden death (Menander, Polybius), but may be here taken in the wider sense of *subversion*. ἐπί here means *with the issue of*, a somewhat abnormal but Pauline usage, best represented by our idiomatic *to, to the undoing of the hearers*. Cf. καταστροφαὶ ἐθνῶν, Philodemus, *Rhet*. 255.

Once again we find the apostle inveighing against the contentious temper and quibbling tactics of the clique whom Timothy must keep in check. They deliberately turned aside from the central verities of the faith to trivialities both non-essential and unedifying, like the hair-splittings of the schoolmen. In the long run these fiddle-faddles wrought harm out of proportion to their pettiness, by warping the entire mental horizon of their pupils. We all know how the cramping influence of a craze that spends itself absorbingly over puny *minutiae* disables its devotee for nobler inquiries; the tortuous bent at length becomes inveterate.

ii. 15. σπούδασον σεαυτὸν δόκιμον παραστῆσαι τῷ θεῷ ἐργάτην ἀνεπαίσχυντον, ὀρθοτομοῦντα τὸν λόγον τῆς ἀληθείας.

We see no reason why δόκιμον should not be construed with ἐργάτην 'a sterling workman, above reproach'. The noun seems restricted to practical handicraftsmen, and that fact has some bearing on the disputed rendering of ὀρθοτομοῦντα. Calvin's notion, that it alludes to a father's division of food to his children, and Beza's, that the reference is to the Levitical sacrificial victims, are at variance with usage. Theodoret comes nearer the mark when he speaks of driving a straight furrow, tracing the metaphor to ploughing: cf. μεσοτομεῖν of reapers (Xen. *Oecon.* 18) and μέσον τέμνειν (Plat. *Laws*, 793). Others, in view of the word λιθοτόμος, discern an allusion to quarrying; cf. καινοτομεῖν. On the whole, the phrase τέμνειν ὁδόν (Virgil's *secare viam*), *to cut a road*, which is perfectly classical and receives support from the LXX ὀρθοτομεῖν ὁδούς (Pr. iii. 6, xi. 5), the only other places where this compound occurs, best meets the requirements of the case, and may be compared with ὀρθοποδεῖν (Gal. ii. 14). It enjoins on every teacher of the Word straightforward exegesis. As the subject-matter is trustworthy, let it be trustily handled.

ii. 16–18. WHAT TO SHUN

ii. 16–18. τὰς δὲ βεβήλους κενοφωνίας περιΐστασο· ἐπὶ πλεῖον γὰρ προκόψουσιν ἀσεβείας, καὶ ὁ λόγος αὐτῶν ὡς γάγγραινα νομὴν ἕξει· ὧν ἐστιν Ὑμέναιος καὶ Φίλητος, οἵτινες περὶ τὴν ἀλήθειαν ἠστόχησαν λέγοντες ἀνάστασιν ἤδη γεγονέναι, καὶ ἀνατρέπουσιν τήν τινων πίστιν.

κενοφωνία is a rare compound, met with only once in a contemporary medical writer, Dioscorides. It seems formed upon the Latin *vaniloquium*. For περιΐστασθαι see the note on Tit. iii. 9. προκόπτειν and προκοπή (frequent in Polybius) are Pauline vocables in the New Testament with a single Lucan exception. The medical figure of a gangrene, and the technical phrase νομὴν ἔχειν (Latin *latius serpere*) for its spreading tendency, suggest the beloved physician's vocabulary. So Polybius of a literal tumour writes νομὴν ποιεῖται (i. 81) and Galen employs the expression like ἐπινέμεσθαι. Of Philetus we know nothing; Hymenaeus presumably may be identified with the individual mentioned in I Tim. i. 20. For ἀστοχεῖν see I Tim. i. 6. Remark the absence of the article with ἀνάστασιν, according to the critical text; *affirming resurrection to be over*. We have had ἀνατρέπειν in a metaphorical sense already in Tit. i. 11 (see p. 99).

Let Timothy refrain from meddling with profane babblings of speculative minds which tend to worse corruptions, spreading like a cancerous growth from less to more. This specimen of morbid anatomy wears a graver aspect than those we have previously encountered. The plight of the prurient elements in the Church is plainly waxing worse, approximating to the sad picture drawn in II Peter and Jude. If heresy consist in the rejection of the kernel of Christianity, these teachers were on its verge; for their doctrine was leading to the overthrow of their disciples' faith. They have strayed from the truth into rank falsehoods. Their doctrine of the resurrection looks backward for its accomplishment. Whether they identified it with the new birth, in common with Swedenborg, or with Gnostic baptism (Irenaeus), or made the apparition of many of the saints after Christ's resurrection (Mt. xxvii. 52, 53) the sole authentic rising again, we cannot say. Probably, like multitudes of others, they stumbled at the resurrection of the body and the declarations of I Cor. xv, and vaunted the superior enlightenment of their revised creed. Baur made this statement an evidence of a second-century composition, contemporary with Marcion; but antagonism to the tenet of a resurrection of the body had grown to a head in the Corinthian church and Tertullian assures us that all philosophical students concurred in their rejection of the very notion.

ii. 19. GOD'S FOUNDATION AND ITS SEAL

ii. 19. ὁ μέντοι στερεὸς θεμέλιος τοῦ θεοῦ ἕστηκεν, ἔχων τὴν σφραγῖδα ταύτην· Ἔγνω Κύριος τοὺς ὄντας αὐτοῦ, καὶ Ἀποστήτω ἀπὸ ἀδικίας πᾶς ὁ ὀνομάζων τὸ ὄνομα Κυρίου.

The strong adversative conjunction μέντοι occurs only here in St Paul's writings; but St John employs it several times. The Authorized Version of course cannot be upheld; we must render: *notwithstanding God's solid* (or *granitic*) *basis abides* (*intact*), the temple of His redeemed shall not reel and fall. θεμέλιος here seems to have an extended sense, like our English noun *foundation*, applied to an establishment or institution, especially in view of the succeeding paragraph. Vettius Valens seven times over uses the plural θεμέλια for *buildings* or *real property*. σφραγίς, meaning *a sealing inscription*, is so used by Galen of a certified brand of eye-salve; nor can the Pauline stamp of the emblem be denied. The former inscription rehearses Nu. xvi. 5, and the latter alludes either to verse 26 of that chapter or to Is. lii. 11. We remark a Godward and a manward aspect.

It was a gloomy picture of perversity or desertion that the apostle had been outlining, and he now turns for his own and his scholar's comfort to the sustaining reflection of divine sovereignty. The Lord Jesus has Himself warned us of a season when falsehood shall be so rampant as, but for grace abounding, to seduce the very elect from their anchorage (Mt. xxiv. 24). What is their final guarantee? That the living stones are an essential part of God's spiritual building, indispensable to the completeness of the structure, and so compacted with it that they cannot be shaken out of their place. That can only be predicated of the Church invisible, the mystical body of Christ, 'the fulness of Him who filleth all in all'. The story of Korah's rebellion furnishes a parallel for later days of rebuke and blasphemy; for the true Israel, the loyal-hearted, rallied round Moses and Aaron in virtue of their genuine affiliation with the God of Israel (Nu. xvi. 5). The Lord knows His spiritual children and they know Him; that is their hallmark. And this bond of union moves them to sever themselves from unrighteousness. The proper sequel and evidence consist in a life of godliness purged from complicity with evil. Those must be unsullied by carnal-mindedness who bear the sacred vessels of the Lord.[1]

ii. 20–26. HONOUR AND DISHONOUR

ii. 20, 21. ἐν μεγάλῃ δὲ οἰκίᾳ οὐκ ἔστιν μόνον σκεύη χρυσᾶ καὶ ἀργυρᾶ ἀλλὰ καὶ ξύλινα καὶ ὀστράκινα καὶ ἃ μὲν εἰς τιμὴν ἃ δὲ εἰς ἀτιμίαν. ἐὰν οὖν τις ἐκκαθάρῃ ἑαυτὸν ἀπὸ τούτων, ἔσται σκεῦος εἰς τιμὴν ἡγιασμένον, εὔχρηστον τῷ δεσπότῃ, εἰς πᾶν ἔργον ἀγαθὸν ἡτοιμασμένον.

So far Paul has been scanning the *penetralia* of the edifice he portrays, but now his gaze fastens on its outward fabric. A visible Church was in process of erection and thitherward he turns his scrutiny. Notice the contracted forms of the adjectives in -ους, conformably to Attic usage. ἃ μέν ... ἃ δέ, a demonstrative use of the relative pronoun, as often, takes the place of τὰ μέν ... τὰ δέ. ἐκκαθαίρειν conveys the notion of 'rinsing out'. It will be remembered that Paul uses εὔχρηστος, *serviceable*, to signalize the reformed character of Onesimus in regard to

---

[1] Spitta's stately hymn, *Es kennt der Herr die Seinen*, is based on this text.

his master Philemon. The introduction of the term δεσπότης in the Pastorals has been commented on under I Tim. vi. 1. For οἰκία μεγάλη cf. Plut. *Pericl.* 16.

Notice how expansive is the apostle's conception of the Christian Church. We are frequently assured that he anticipated a proximate 'rapture of the saints'; but the very image of a durable and widespreading edifice, as well as his prophetic anticipations of developments on a large scale in its history, confutes that fancy. He tabulates worthy and unworthy phases of its external aspect, both actual and impending; and under this similitude likens the mixed elements it contains to 'vessels unto honour and dishonour' respectively. Utensils of wood and earthenware serve baser usages than those of gold and silver. Just as there were degraded members and menial Gibeonites in the congregation of Israel, and tares in the terrestrial wheat-field of the Lord's sowing, so, however desirable purity may be, and to be sought by all Scriptural means, no human discernment can infallibly winnow the precious from the vile or forestall the day of judgment in the mundane economy. 'By their fruits ye shall know them' must be the touchstone applied to professions of discipleship. Paul's exhortation here runs parallel to Peter's injunction to 'make our calling and election sure' and obtain 'an abundant entrance into the everlasting kingdom'. Let Timothy strive to be an honourable vessel in God's house and to help to fashion such, fit for every worthy use, aspiring to holiness and thinking scorn of meaner degrees of serviceability. He is not to be a Gibeonite but a prince in Israel. The figure is unquestionably Pauline, and he has already employed this very phrase in another connection (Rom. ix. 21) where he contrasts vessels of mercy with vessels of wrath. The scullery-ware has its function in a mansion as well as the rare china and plate.

ii. 22, 23. τὰς δὲ νεωτερικὰς ἐπιθυμίας φεῦγε, δίωκε δὲ δικαιοσύνην, πίστιν, ἀγάπην, εἰρήνην μετὰ τῶν ἐπικαλουμένων τὸν κύριον ἐκ καθαρᾶς καρδίας. τὰς δὲ μωρὰς καὶ ἀπαιδεύτους ζητήσεις παραιτοῦ, εἰδὼς ὅτι γεννῶσιν μάχας.

νεωτερικός, an adjective of literary Hellenistic (Polyb., Joseph.)—Vettius Valens (118) mentions νεωτερικὰ ἁμαρτήματα—may seem surprising in an admonition to Timothy at this date; but we have seen in I Tim. iv. 12 how extended was the use of νέος. ἀπαίδευτος forms another fresh adjective well known to readers of Plato in the sense of 'uncultured'. It is a LXX word, but there confined to persons. Here it signifies *senseless, inane*, 'without rhyme or reason'. For παραιτοῦ see I Tim. iv. 7. γεννᾶν, meaning *engender*, has literary precedents and is a Pauline use of the verb (Gal. iv. 24). Philodemus (*Rhet.* i. 363) speaks of ἀναίδεια as the offspring, using γεννᾶσθαι, of rhetorical study. The metaphorical sense of μάχαι, which has already crossed our path (Tit. iii. 9), appears to be restricted to the plural of the word.

With the prestige of a veteran officer, Paul urges on his lieutenant exemplary sobriety of demeanour, untinged by the volatility that we associate with youth. These are wholesome cautions, not veiled censures. There are noble virtues to be fostered, rectitude of judgment, faith, love, concord both in his own soul and in those committed to his charge who are of the true strain and cherish integrity of walk as one of their choicest treasures. To 'hold the mystery of the faith in a pure conscience' was one of the qualifications for the office of deacon in I Tim. iii. 9, and this exhortation itself re-echoes I Tim. vi. 11. But let him discountenance the sottish dialectics already reprimanded, fertile only in barren logomachies, a noun coined to express these unprofitable bickerings.

ii. 24–26. δοῦλον δὲ Κυρίου οὐ δεῖ μάχεσθαι ἀλλὰ ἤπιον εἶναι πρὸς πάντας, διδακτικόν, ἀνεξίκακον, ἐν πραΰτητι παιδεύοντα τοὺς ἀντιδιατιθεμένους, μή ποτε δώῃ αὐτοῖς ὁ θεὸς μετάνοιαν εἰς ἐπίγνωσιν ἀληθείας, καὶ ἀνανήψωσιν ἐκ τῆς τοῦ διαβόλου παγίδος ἐζωγρημένοι ὑπ' αὐτοῦ εἰς τὸ ἐκείνου θέλημα.

For διδακτικός see I Tim. iii. 2. ἀνεξίκακος is a rare adjective employed by Lucian and Vettius Valens (38), and its substantive ἀνεξικακία occurs in Plutarch and Epictetus (*Enchir.* 10). ἀντιδιατίθεσθαι forms a late complex compound, similar to the Latin *opponi* or *adversari*. The verb can hardly be paralleled except from Longinus, though the active occurs in Philo and Diodorus Siculus. Here the participle may be translated *opponents*. μή ποτε is here used in the late sense of *if perhaps*, like the Latin *num quando*. δώῃ should be the subjunctive after a primary tense, with iota subscript under η, not ω, and in order to match with ἀνανήψωσιν. This verb, meaning *regain sobriety*, belongs to literary Hellenistic, and has a figurative connotation in Philo, Josephus (*Antiq.* vi. 11), Marcus Aurelius (vi. 31). παγίς is wrongly designated a 'late form' in M. & M.; for it occurs in Aristophanes. ζωγρεῖν, in the sense of *to take alive*, we all know from the famous saying of Lk. v. 10. It is a LXX verb in its literal acceptation. ζώγρει (Plut. *Mor.* 845) was the proper cry of a soldier surrendering to the enemy. The perfect tense intimates a state of captivity.

There are seasons when controversy cannot be forborne without cowardice; but, as a rule, the business of the Lord's servant is not to challenge adverse parties, but exhibit the spirit of patience and meekness which distinguished Christ Himself so signally, of whom it had been predicted that he should not strive or debate, but instruct and enlighten. Ministerial labours presume aptitude to teach and absence of asperity in the teacher. Some render παιδεύειν 'to correct', but we think it better to understand it of indoctrination of the truth than exposure of error. The presentation of that truth may be blessed to the reclamation of dissentients. Holding unfeigned repentance to be a work of the Spirit, we need not despair of seeing sound doctrine reinstated in these backsliders. Stupefied by Satanic potions, his dupes may yet cast off their fumes and recover their sanity by the grace of God. The final clauses of the sentence have caused much difference of opinion. The parties referred to lie in the devil's clutches. He has ensnared them and holds them in thrall. The Authorized Version, following the Vulgate, views the arch-enemy as their gaoler, retaining them under his control, but the change of pronouns from αὐτοῦ to ἐκείνου should mark a change of reference, especially joined with εἰς; so that it seems necessary to translate εἰς τὸ ἐκείνου θέλημα *unto the will of God*.[1] Yet the position of the participial clause is puzzling, if that be the correct interpretation. Some of the Greek exegetes regard the captive condition spoken of to be submission to God or else God's servant, who recaptures them in pursuance of His rescuing will. But surely such a version is both arbitrary and far-fetched, even though their state of bondage should make them feel, like the prodigal son, disenchanted and not devoid of compunctious visitings, as the verb ἀνανήφειν doubtless suggests. Perhaps the career of Samson first and last affords the best commentary on this text, and may have been in the writer's thought.

[1] But there are exceptions. Cf. Xen. *Cyr.* v. 4; Plato *Protag.* 310; Luc. *Zeux.* 8.

iii. 1–9. PROPHECY OF THE LAST DAYS

iii. 1. τοῦτο δὲ γίνωσκε, ὅτι ἐν ἐσχάταις ἡμέραις ἐνστήσονται καιροὶ χαλεποί·

Notice γινώσκειν, the regular Hellenistic form of the earlier γιγνώσκειν. ἔσχαται ἡμέραι is a somewhat indefinite phrase, applicable to the entire Messianic age, but here distinctly pointing to a future epoch of history, subsequent to the apostolical era and verging on the final consummation. ἐνίστασθαι corresponds with Latin *instare, to set in.* χαλεπός might be rendered *menacing.* In the only other place of its occurrence in the New Testament (Mt. viii. 28) it describes the two demon-possessed men whom Jesus met in the country of the Gergasenes. Plutarch uses it of an 'ugly' wound (*Mor.* 131), and Vettius Valens (236) designates a certain astrological conjunction as χαλεπὸς λίαν, 'most ticklish'.

The apostle desires to make Timothy aware of the mingled yarn of hopeful and harassing contingencies he must expect to meet. Causes of joy are never lacking whilst the day of grace lasts; but on the other hand Satan is a desperate character and unsleeping in his machinations. Where he can plant a footing in the Church or the Vanity Fair engirdling it, assuredly he will do so; for nothing less than domination can content his lust for power. We are presented in the ensuing verses with a terrible catalogue of the manifold activities of this lord of misrule and fomenter of anarchy in his vassals' lives. Conscious of his doom and that his time is short for wreaking his malice on this fair earth, so richly endowed and garnished, he waxes more spiteful and aggressive and improves his weapons of destruction continually. His atomic bombs are multiplex and deadly.

iii. 2–5. ἔσονται γὰρ οἱ ἄνθρωποι φίλαυτοι, φιλάργυροι, ἀλαζόνες, ὑπερήφανοι, βλάσφημοι, γονεῦσιν ἀπειθεῖς, ἀχάριστοι, ἀνόσιοι, ἄστοργοι, ἄσπονδοι, διάβολοι, ἀκρατεῖς, ἀνήμεροι, ἀφιλάγαθοι, προδόται, προπετεῖς, τετυφωμένοι, φιλήδονοι μᾶλλον ἢ φιλόθεοι, ἔχοντες μόρφωσιν εὐσεβείας τὴν δὲ δύναμιν αὐτῆς ἠρνημένοι· καὶ τούτους ἀποτρέπου.

φίλαυτος is an Aristotelian term (*Nic. Eth.* ix. 8) for inordinate self-love, reproduced in philosophical treatises of later date (Plut., Philo).

The Revised Version inadequately renders ἀλαζών 'boastful'; but that covers only a segment of its meaning. When John writes of the ἀλαζονεία of life (I Jn. ii. 16), he is exposing its false glamour, its parade and show without substance, its false claim to be 'life indeed', in effect its *quackery*. Thus Plutarch refers to an ἰατρὸς ἀλαζών (*Mor.* 523) and Aristotle defines it as προσποίησις ἐπὶ τὸ μεῖζον (*Nic. Eth.* ii. 7). It expresses then the *bounce* of swaggering, but hollow pretensions. ἄστοργος, *unloving*, *heartless*, evidently marks a stage of depravity beyond filial disobedience. ἄσπονδος is a literary epithet descriptive of truculent hostility and may be translated *implacable*. διάβολοι means *backbiters*. ἀκρατής (opposite of ἐγκρατής) denotes *ungovernable* in passion, emotional or sensual. ἀφιλάγαθος, an ἅπαξ εἰρημένον, negatives an Aristotelian and Plutarchian compound. προπετής signalizes precipitancy of word or deed. We have already had occasion to notice τετυφωμένος under I Tim. iii. 6, vi. 4. It connotes self-importance, bumptiousness, the vapouring spirit (τῦφος) engendered by flattery (Plut. *Mor.* 59) and coupled with conceit (Polyb. iii. 81), Luther's *aufgeblasen*. When Sextus Empiricus censures οἱ δογματικοὶ τετυφωμένοι (i. 62), he really calls them (to use a colloquialism) *stuck up*. φιλήδονοι μᾶλλον ἢ φιλόθεοι may be classed among Paul's plays on words. Almost the same phraseology occurs in Philo (*De Agric.* 86). μόρφωσις means *semblance*, *configuration*, whether real or unreal (cf. Vett. Val. 248). Philo employs the phrase ἐπιμορφάζειν εὐσέβειαν (1. 340) of a simulated piety.

We have been obliged to dwell at such length on the specific wording of this passage that we must abridge our consideration of its contents. It predicts a chequered future for the Church of God, overcast by many storm-clouds and rent by many defections. The spirit of the latter-day age will prove inimical to its welfare, the world wax worldlier, so to speak. Selfish aims are set forth as the root of other evils, which do not appear to be grouped in any strict order but enumerated, after Paul's customary manner, *seriatim*. Lofty pretensions are linked with ingratitude and filial disrespect, and towering passions with treacherous practices. These vices, blended with an inordinate love of pleasure fatal to godliness, will nest themselves in the visible Church to its sore detriment, producing an outward mimicry of piety which masks a rejection of the genuine article. It is clear that iniquity as well as grace is to abound; and who can deny that the anticipation has been woefully realized? What multitudes of nominal Christians have belied their profession by unchristian practices! This black catalogue shows what a hell this globe would become, were the restraining influences of true religion banished from it. The seeds of utter corruption are latent; they only need opportunity to germinate. Therefore, in the act of prophesying of a possibly distant future, the apostle warns Timothy to turn away from such parties in Ephesus itself.

iii. 6, 7. ἐκ τούτων γάρ εἰσιν οἱ ἐνδύνοντες εἰς τὰς οἰκίας καὶ αἰχμαλωτίζοντες γυναικάρια σεσωρευμένα ἁμαρτίαις, ἀγόμενα ἐπιθυμίαις ποικίλαις, πάντοτε μανθάνοντα καὶ μηδέποτε εἰς ἐπίγνωσιν ἀληθείας ἐλθεῖν δυνάμενα.

ἐνδύειν, ἐνδύνειν is a classical vocable for insinuating entrance, furtive rather than avowed. αἰχμαλωτίζειν was a verb rejected by the Atticists as a novel formation, but found in Arrian and Diodorus, also in LXX and Josephus, and previously used by St Paul. γυναικάριον (Latin *muliercula*, Italian *donnicciuole*) is a contemptuous diminutive, occurring in Epictetus and Marcus Aurelius. σωρεύεσθαι ἁμαρτίαις seems to echo the Latin phrase *cumulari peccatis*. The metaphor is distinctly Roman. Cf. Cicero's *vitio, dedecore cumulatus*. ποικίλος signifies more than 'various' in this connection; *fickle, shifting* would come nearer the mark. The image suggests a play of colours ever changeful, because iridescent. Thus Vettius Valens (45, 47) joins ποικίλοι with ἄστατοι ταῖς γνώμαις, and Menander (Meineke, p. 97) calls τύχη a ποικίλον πρᾶγμα.

The covert propaganda of error here presented to view has always been characteristic of those prowlers who 'set springes to catch woodcocks', laying snares aimed at the seduction of the female sex in particular. They prefer covert tactics to overt, and their main appeal is made underhand to uneasy consciences rankling with a sense of guilt. The other source of fascination consists in the pabulum offered by these traffickers in religion to the craze for novelty; for the victims seize that bait with avidity and are therefore soon caught in their nets by the lure of modern enlightenment. The spell, however, will not work indefinitely; for some newer bauble rivets their gaze ere long and is sure to eclipse the old, till its charm likewise palls. Their gratification lies in the chase, not the quarry won.

iii. 8.   ὃν τρόπον δὲ Ἰαννῆς καὶ Ἰαμβρῆς ἀντέστησαν Μωυσεῖ, οὕτως καὶ οὗτοι ἀνθίστανται τῇ ἀληθείᾳ ἄνθρωποι κατεφθαρμένοι τὸν νοῦν, ἀδόκιμοι περὶ τὴν πίστιν.

ὃν τρόπον, *even as*, is a curtailed phrase for καθ' ὃν τρόπον, both forms being used by Luke in the Acts. κατεφθαρμένοι τὸν νοῦν slightly varies the corresponding expression in I Tim. vi. 5. We have noticed ἀδόκιμος under Tit. i. 16.

Expositors have commonly ascribed the mention of the Egyptian magicians' names to Jewish tradition, whilst Origen rather naïvely predicates a 'Book of Jannes and Jambres' as their source. There may, however, have been an apocryphal amalgam like the Book of Enoch current under that title. According to a doubtful reading Jannes is mentioned in conjunction with Moses in Pliny (*N.H.* xxx. 2) and Apuleius, and one of the Targums inserts these names in Ex. vii. 11. The Talmudists by an anachronism identify these necromancers with sons of Balaam. The Pythagorean philosopher Numenius also refers to them (Eusebius). These references evince a widespread tradition endorsed (may we not say?) by the Spirit of truth Himself.

These dogged gainsayers looming in the dusk of futurity are likened to the ancient antagonists of Moses and stigmatized as men of corrupt minds, renegades from 'the faith' (here again plainly objective). Their policy and interest lead them to combat the heavenly couriers with subterranean legerdemain such as they can command, up to a certain point not without success. We are reminded of the stories told of thaumaturgists like Apollonius of Tyana and his like.

iii. 9.   ἀλλ' οὐ προκόψουσιν ἐπὶ πλεῖον· ἡ γὰρ ἄνοια αὐτῶν ἔκδηλος ἔσται πᾶσιν, ὡς καὶ ἡ ἐκείνων ἐγένετο.

ἄνοια is an old-fashioned literary word quite clear of vernacular usage, only employed by St Paul here. We have observed no instance of its use later than the new comedy of Menander and Philemon. ἔκδηλος, a strengthened form of δῆλος, meaning *salient*, has classical authority. ἐγένετο is *came to be*.

There are two horizons here, one distant, one near, as so often in prophecy. To the more immediate prospect Paul now turns, lest Timothy should be too much discouraged by the sombre picture. He recalls the rapid discomfiture of the Egyptian sorcerers and foretells a similar downfall for the hoodwinkers in question. In the long run foxy cunning incurs its own nemesis.

> Truth crushed to earth shall rise again;
> The eternal years of God are hers;
> But error, wounded, writhes with pain
> And dies amid her worshippers.

iii. 10–17. EXHORTATION TO STAND FAST IN THE FAITH

iii. 10, 11. σὺ δὲ παρηκολούθησάς μου τῇ διδασκαλίᾳ, τῇ ἀγωγῇ, τῇ προθέσει, τῇ πίστει, τῇ μακροθυμίᾳ, τῇ ἀγάπῃ, τῇ ὑπομονῇ, τοῖς διωγμοῖς, τοῖς παθήμασιν οἷά μοι ἐγένετο ἐν Ἀντιοχείᾳ, ἐν Ἰκονίῳ, ἐν Λύστροις, οἵους διωγμοὺς ὑπήνεγκα· καὶ ἐκ πάντων με ἐρρύσατο ὁ κύριος.

παρακολουθεῖν was formerly understood to refer to Timothy's following in Paul's steps and suffering in consequence; but a more figurative sense is now attached to it, cognate with Luke's use of the word in his famous Preface. In this instance the papyri have afforded help to the interpreter; for they support the translation, *to be cognisant of, familiar with,* which best suits the context here (see M. & M.). Polybius and Arrian so employ the verb, and Marcus Aurelius uses the adverb παρακολουθητικῶς (vi. 42) for 'perspicaciously'. ἀγωγή may signify either *training* or *course of life,* Cicero's *actio vitae.* In Plutarch παίδων ἀγωγή means *boys' training* and he uses εὐαγωγία (*Mor.* 13) for *good breeding.* Perhaps in this passage it covers both *upbringing* and *manner of life;* for Sextus Empiricus defines it αἵρεσις βίου. πρόθεσις, meaning *chief aim,* is an Hellenistic usage, and so we may also class μακροθυμία, first met with in Menander. It is distinguished from ὑπομονή as *forbearance* is from *patient endurance* (Trench).

For his junior colleague's encouragement the toil-worn apostle rehearses some of the trials he had himself weathered unharmed. There is no self-praise in the plain insertion of such a catalogue. Conscious integrity can affirm itself without self-assumption, as all readers of II Corinthians are aware. Paul refers to his teaching as a consistent whole, to his demeanour as a constant quantity, to his determinate life-purpose, his unfeigned faith, the habitual love and patience he had exhibited, and the fierce persecutions he had braved. Because Timothy hailed from Lystra, he specifies the mishandlings that had befallen him in that region and were vivid memories to his correspondent; yet, severe as these had been, they had not crushed or slain him; for an unseen hand had safeguarded the intrepid missionary of the cross and brought him forth from them all unmaimed in soul, if not in body.

iii. 12, 13. καὶ πάντες δὲ οἱ θέλοντες εὐσεβῶς ζῆν ἐν Χριστῷ Ἰησοῦ διωχθήσονται. πονηροὶ δὲ ἄνθρωποι καὶ γόητες προκόψουσιν ἐπὶ τὸ χεῖρον, πλανῶντες καὶ πλανώμενοι.

We have had καὶ . . . δέ already in I Tim. iii. 10. As Madvig observed (*Gr. Syntax*, 229) in this formula the word inserted between acquires special emphasis. Here *all* is emphasized. In English we should say 'one and all', or 'every one'. γόης conveys the idea of imposture, wizardry of the spiritistic brand viewed on its deceptive side. Josephus calls the Theudas he portrays as a Jewish ringleader, γόης τις ἀνήρ (*Antiq.* xx. 5), in reference to the fascination he exercised over the multitude that followed him obsequiously.

A Christian curled up on the bed of sloth belies his name. He is enlisted in a holy warfare in which hard knocks will be dealt and borne. Piety and paralysis are false concords. A man does not fully discover the tyranny of this world till he casts off its yoke, and consequently incurs its enmity. Let him show his colours intrepidly and he will meet with gibes and, in some environments, foul handling. But does not Paul contradict his statement in verse 9 when he adds that seducers like the Egyptian thaumaturgists shall advance from bad to worse? That cannot be; for he repeats the very wording of that verse. Above he was writing of the spiritually awake whom these juggleries shall not beguile. But, in Cowper's line, 'those who hate truth shall be the dupe of lies'. The devil improves his inventions, like other munition-makers. In this case his instrument consists of a captivating class of errorists, fitted to beguile the unwary by charming manners or sparkling wit or wheedling sophistry. Many of them will be self-deceived, and their belief in their own falsities will gull many a hearer or reader. We see around us the obvious fulfilment of this prediction.

iii. 14, 15. σὺ δὲ μένε ἐν οἷς ἔμαθες καὶ ἐπιστώθης, εἰδὼς παρὰ τίνων ἔμαθες καὶ ὅτι ἀπὸ βρέφους ἱερὰ γράμματα οἶδας τὰ δυνάμενά σε σοφίσαι εἰς σωτηρίαν διὰ πίστεως τῆς ἐν Χριστῷ Ἰησοῦ.

ἐν οἷς is of course abbreviated for ἐν ἐκείνοις ἅ. πιστοῦσθαι must be carefully distinguished from πιστεύεσθαι. It means *to be assured, established.* Thus Marcus Aurelius (xii. 5) employs the phrase πιστούσθω σοι for 'let it be a fixed principle with thee', and Philo (*Leg. ad Gaium* 40) writes τεκμηρίοις πιστώσασθαι, 'to corroborate by proofs'. ἀπὸ βρέφους (*ab infante*) reminds us of ἀπὸ προγόνων (*supra*, i. 3) and LXX examples; the normal Greek phrase would have been ἐκ παιδός. The expression ἱερὰ γράμματα (if the τά be omitted with W. & H. the sense rests unchanged, intimating a fixed title, like our English 'Holy Scripture') does not occur elsewhere in the New Testament but is of regular usage for the Old Testament in Josephus and Philo. σοφίζειν in the active is of very rare occurrence. No parallel for it has been adduced except the LXX in Pss. xix. 8 and cv. 22.

The apostle's solicitude for Timothy breaks forth once more in an earnest exhortation to abide in the doctrines he has been taught as long as he could remember, and which his whole career has illustrated and sealed. Manifestly he had been a gracious, affectionate lad and could be appealed to as such, and moreover a diligent student of sacred lore, storing up in mind and memory the holy books. Paul could have said the same for himself, and he is plainly thinking of the nineteenth Psalm when he declares that those venerable Scriptures which he reverenced so highly can make their reader 'wise unto salvation', when Christ is seen to be their goal and scope. In Him they are lit up with heavenly radiance. Faith in the Saviour sheds a new lustre on their pages and breathes a new significance into their types and symbolisms. A torso *per se*, cemented with Him they exhibit a masterpiece of divine artistry, replete with instruction and edification. 'The Old Testament and New Testament make up the tally' (A. Barnes).

iii. 16, 17. πᾶσα γραφὴ θεόπνευστος καὶ ὠφέλιμος πρὸς διδασκαλίαν,
πρὸς ἐλεγμόν, πρὸς ἐπανόρθωσιν, πρὸς παιδείαν τὴν ἐν δικαιοσύνῃ,
ἵνα ἄρτιος ᾖ ὁ τοῦ θεοῦ ἄνθρωπος πρὸς πᾶν ἔργον ἀγαθὸν ἐξηρτισμένος.

Much controversy has raged concerning the proper rendering of the
initial portion of this verse. Latterly the opinion that θεόπνευστος is
not a predicate, but an adjunct of γραφή, has gained ground. The
decision of the matter is implicated with another question, whether
πᾶσα γραφή must be translated *every Scripture*. In view of such passages
as Acts ii. 36, Eph. ii. 21, iii. 15, Col. iv. 12 that rule seems to admit of
exceptions, especially in the case of approximations to proper names.
The objections to the adjectival interpretation which weigh with us are
the following:

(1) The tautological effect, upon this construction, of the rest of the
sentence. Surely *every God-breathed Scripture is useful*, etc., presents a
curious specimen of anticlimax.

(2) If that version be correct, θεόπνευστος should more fitly precede
γραφή.

(3) Paul has a confirmed habit of dropping the copula, particularly
in an opening clause of a sentence (cf. I Tim. i. 8, 15, etc.). We find a
close parallel to this passage in I Tim. iv. 4, where no one translates
'every good creature of God is also not one of them to be rejected'.

(4) Chrysostom understands θεόπνευστος as a predicate and πᾶσα
γραφή as referring to the ἱερὰ γράμματα of the foregoing verse.

These grounds seem to justify the old translation, so much more
forcible than that put in its place. We have noted the rarity of the term
θεόπνευστος in our Introduction (p. 20). ἐλεγμός, meaning ἔλεγξις,
is a rare LXX form, a Jewish-Greek coinage apparently. ἐπανόρθωσις,
revision, is a Hellenistic term found in legal associations in the papyri.
Here it implies a standard for the correction of error. ἄρτιος reflects
the Latin *integer, in quo nihil sit mutilum*; Calvin, *sound, entire*. Lucian
speaks of Hephaestus (Vulcan) as οὐκ ἄρτιος τὼ πόδε. There is a play
on the word in the addition of the verb ἐξαρτίζειν, *to equip*, a commercial verb rife in the papyri, less literary than ἐξαρτύειν. Plutarch
(*Mor.* 437) writes of the lofty soul as an ὄργανον ἐξηρτυμένον καὶ
εὐηχές, a well-equipped and tuneful instrument. In Marcus Aurelius
(i. 20) ἄρτιος ψυχή is an *intact soul, flawless*.

[This enthronement of the Holy Scriptures (primarily, but not exclusively, the Old Testament) in the seat of authority is so insistent and prolific of consequences that we cannot wonder that the modern spirit of licence rises in revolt against it or labours to dilute its significance. First of all we have the declaration that the sacred γραφή, the invariable meaning of the word, whether singular or plural, in the New Testament, re-echoing the ἱερὰ γράμματα of the preceding verse, *God-breathed* in quality, has the seal of divine truth stamped upon it throughout. The imprimatur of Deity countersigns these scripts, instrumentally the work of human minds, working in keeping with their native faculties, yet prompted by an unseen power. That fact sets them apart from other writings. In that capacity they should be received as replete with instruction, reproof and edification, in rightful judgment and practice, and supply a corrective for fallible criteria of good and evil.]They furnish the loyal subject of heaven with a complete *vade-mecum* so comprehensive that it forms a directory for every possible good work. Here the believer has his indispensable guide, which will never lead him astray like the products of human speculation. Well has Keble sung:

> Eye of God's word, where'er we turn
> Ever upon us! thy keen gaze
> Can all the depths of sin discern,
> Unravel every bosom's maze.
> Who that hath felt thy glance of dread
> Thrill through his heart's remotest cells,
> About his path, about his bed,
> Can doubt what Spirit in thee dwells?

iv. 1–5. A VALEDICTORY CHARGE

It behoves us here to tread softly; for we are now privileged to listen to the farewell message of the apostle to the Gentiles, with its interwoven chords of threnody and triumph. The Greatheart of the primitive Church issues his parting counsels and warnings not only to his bosom-disciple in these moving verses, but to every succeeding generation of the 'sacramental host of God's elect'. A note of deeper solemnity strikes upon our ear in this final trumpet call.

iv. 1, 2. διαμαρτύρομαι ἐνώπιον τοῦ θεοῦ καὶ Χριστοῦ Ἰησοῦ τοῦ μέλλοντος κρίνειν ζῶντας καὶ νεκροὺς καὶ τὴν ἐπιφάνειαν αὐτοῦ καὶ τὴν βασιλείαν αὐτοῦ· κήρυξον τὸν λόγον, ἐπίστηθι εὐκαίρως ἀκαίρως, ἔλεγξον ἐπιτίμησον παρακάλεσον ἐν πάσῃ μακροθυμίᾳ καὶ διδαχῇ.

διαμαρτύρεσθαι should be rendered *adjure*, for it has the weight of a legal affirmation. We have already met with this phraseology in I Tim. v. 21, though the reference to Christ's judicial office forms an additional enforcement of its solemnity. The easier reading κατὰ τὴν ἐπιφάνειαν lacks adequate corroboration, and so we must construe the appended words, *by His manifestation and His kingdom*, in connection with the opening verb as a part of the adjuration. There seems no reason, however, why it should not be translated 'I call to witness His appearing'.[1] ἐπίστηθι is commonly understood to mean *pay heed*; but it appears rather, like the Latin *insta*, to express insistent exhortation, the pressure of repetition, as in the LXX version of Je. xlvi. 14. The phrase εὐκαίρως ἀκαίρως confirms this impression. That is a kind of oxymoron more in vogue in Latin than Greek. Roman energy finds vent in such terms as *concordia discors*, *nolens volens*, *fanda nefanda*, *per aequa per iniqua*. So we find the Vulgate renders this passage *opportune*, *importune*. The aorist imperatives emphasize the obligation of prompt action. Be a sentinel ever on duty. For Timothy must deal without delay with opposition or fits of inertia, and suit his admonitions to the actual situation, but avoid all outbreaks apt to provoke resentment. Let him cherish the spirit of his Lord and maintain the dignity of His ambassador; for what higher vocation than to represent that kingdom which, when its King unveils His glory, will eclipse every other? Let the lustre of that consummation cast its coming glory over the irksomeness of some of his current tasks and conflicts, and stimulate him to unswerving fidelity. The ministration of the Word is no πάρεργον to be pursued in conjunction with other tasks, but an all-absorbing vocation for a whole manhood.

[1] Cf. LXX Judith vii. 28.

iv. 3, 4. ἔσται γὰρ καιρὸς ὅτε τῆς ὑγιαινούσης διδασκαλίας οὐκ ἀνέξονται, ἀλλὰ κατὰ τὰς ἰδίας ἐπιθυμίας ἑαυτοῖς ἐπισωρεύσουσιν διδασκάλους, κνηθόμενοι τὴν ἀκοήν, καὶ ἀπὸ μὲν τῆς ἀληθείας τὴν ἀκοὴν ἀποστρέψουσιν, ἐπὶ δὲ τοὺς μύθους ἐκτραπήσονται.

ἐπισωρεύειν, imitated apparently from Latin *accumulare*, forms a late Hellenistic compound, of which instances occur in Arrian's *Epictetus*, Plutarch (*Mor.* 830) and twice in Vettius Valens. Plutarch (*Mor.* 167) employs the phrase κνῆσις ὤτων metaphorically for *ear-tickling*, Latin *aures demulcere, scabere* (Seneca, *Ep.* ix. 4), of the effect of musical sounds, and that allusion suggests the thought that the apostle has Ezk. xxxiii. 32 in mind, where the people come to the prophet only to be entertained by a melodious discourse, regardless of any serious effect. For ἐκτρέπεσθαι cf. I Tim. i. 6.

Timothy's vigilance is yet more pressing in view of the declensions from the truth which Paul's prospective vision foresees. For a time will arrive when sound doctrine will prove distasteful and be spurned by a pampered class of hearers, whose ears itch after something more congenial to flesh and blood than the austere morality and concern about eternity of New Testament Christianity. A silkier propaganda wins their suffrage, and, as in other spheres, so here, the demand creates the supply. For silver-tongued teachers, themselves beguiled by these spells, arise to prophesy smooth things to auditors of warped receptivities. It is implied that these faddists have the choice of their instructors and choose amiss. How often has the history of churches exhibited this downward gravitation! The taste for spiritual meat has waned, and a craving for something more flattering and palatable usurped its room. Before long purveyors of the coveted *Delikatessen* loom on the scene. Then a tacit compact is struck, by which the plain dishes of the gospel bill-of-fare are surreptitiously displaced by more alluring condiments. Two stages in this process of declension are signalized: first of all, an aversion from the truth that renders its enforcement unwelcome, and secondly a liking for talk which can amuse without wounding or humbling the hearer, or for chimeras and inventions such as display, in Bacon's caustic language, 'a corrupt love of the lie itself' in preference to the 'naked and open daylight' of undiscoloured truth. Whether we reflect on the gross inanities of the Romish *Acta*

Sanctorum or the endless cobweb-spinning of destructive criticism, clutching at any solution of Biblical problems shorn of supernatural agency, we cannot but recognize how fully this prediction has been realized. At the base of the whole specious but spurious fabric Paul detects the gratification of carnal appetencies.

iv. 5. σὺ δὲ νῆφε ἐν πᾶσιν, κακοπάθησον, ἔργον ποίησον εὐαγγελιστοῦ, τὴν διακονίαν σου πληροφόρησον.

νήφειν hovers between the meaning of *sobriety* and *wakefulness*. The latter sense seems preferable here (cf. I Thes. v. 6); *Be wide-awake*. So Polybius dubs Scipio νήπτης καὶ ἀγχίνους and Vettius Valens (179, 244) employs the phrase νηπτικῶς προσέχειν of vigilant attention. The same phrase occurs in Marcus Aurelius. κακοπαθεῖν, as we have noted, conveys the notion of braced energies rather than mere holding out. πληροφορεῖν in this context signifies *to make good*, like the Latin *officium*, *munia sua*, *implere*. It occurs in the papyri of the discharge of debts (Deissmann, *Light from the Ancient East*, p. 86) and in Vettius Valens (226) of carrying out a project to the full. Timothy is exhorted to make actual the potentialities of his ministry with the utmost wholeheartedness. Cf. Acts xii. 25 for the simple phrase πληροῦν τὴν διακονίαν. We take the *evangelist* to be a title descriptive of an itinerant preacher like Philip (Acts xxi. 8), forming the intermediate link between apostolic founders of churches and ordinary pastors and teachers (Eph. iv. 11).

iv. 6–8. HIS OWN CONFIDENCE IN SPITE OF ISOLATION

iv. 6. ἐγὼ γὰρ ἤδη σπένδομαι καὶ ὁ καιρὸς τῆς ἀναλύσεώς μου ἐφέστηκεν.

σπένδομαι must be rendered as a present, not paraphrased as in the Authorized Version. Paul could easily have written, had he wished, ἕτοιμός εἰμι σπένδεσθαι. As it is, he writes, *I am being poured forth already*. Plutarch (*Mor.* 494) uses the expression σπένδεσθαι περὶ τῶν τέκνων of the animal's self-oblivion for the sake of its offspring. It is tempting to associate the term ἀνάλυσις with the loosing of a vessel from its moorings or with release from shackles; but though the allusion of unbinding may be glanced at, the word appears to signify death itself, like our term *dissolution*. The cognate verb bears this sense in sundry inscriptions and the noun itself in Philo (ii. 544) and Clement of Rome (44). Lightfoot's reference to 'breaking up camp' seems improbable (Phil. i. 23). ἐφέστηκεν, a present perfect (Latin *instat*), means 'impends'.

There is a pathos in these words that stirs the sympathy of every feeling heart. The writer's life-blood is in process of effusion, his vital energies are being drained in the Mamertine dungeon (if that tradition be true), or if not by ruthless incarceration in gloom and solitude, by the strain of trial in hostile surroundings and comparative forsakenness. The image of a libation some commentators regard as Paul's sole loan from the quarter of pagan ritual. But surely we need not seek its source in heathendom, for libations accompanied many of the Jewish sacrifices, particularly free-will offerings (Nu. xv). The apostle had employed the figure in Phil. ii. 17 to typify self-devotion without stint or reserve; and he reiterates it here in token of his consciousness that he has reached its ultimate stage and supreme expression. The earthly tabernacle is dissolving; the bars of mortality relax and the Lord's caged eagle wistfully anticipates the hour of release and the soaring flight awaiting him from the subterranean to the empyrean. It is all of divine appointment. Yet to Timothy the separation will be lacerating and, withal, a summons to faithful witness in behalf of the gospel his preceptor had taught and exemplified. Paul proceeds to take stock of his assets.

iv. 7. τὸν καλὸν ἀγῶνα ἠγώνισμαι, τὸν δρόμον τετέλεκα, τὴν πίστιν τετήρηκα.

The clarion note, *I have fought a good fight*, sounded by Tyndale, is now commonly pronounced incorrect and exchanged for the far tamer rendering of Wyclif, 'I have striven a good strife': but we doubt whether with sufficient warrant. The sense of combat predominates in the other passages in which Paul uses the term ἀγών, and it is constantly employed in Greek literature of military campaigns. Cf. Plutarch (*Cam.* 2, *Pericl.* 10) and Christ's own figure in Jn. xviii. 36. The supposition that it must conform to the athletic metaphor of the succeeding clause strikes us as exceedingly weak. In such an impassioned utterance the last thing we should look for would be tautology. Three comparisons ranged in triple file, drawn respectively from the military, athletic, and the stewardly domain, strike us as much more impressive. Is it not Paul who has taught us to speak of the Church militant? Luther's belligerent spirit led him to translate *ein guten Kampf gekämpft* with the Authorized Version; but possibly the modern German expression, *die streitende Kirche*, has influenced those familiar with it in the other direction. The vivid phrase δρόμον τελεῖν had risen to the apostle's lips at his parting with the Ephesian elders (Acts xx. 24), and is fitly recalled at the end of the course, with the goal full in view. Deissmann dwarfs the affirmation, τὴν πίστιν τετήρηκα, to a commercial level—'I have kept my engagement'. No doubt it bears that sense in the papyri, as he insists, and for that matter in Polybius also; but even if St Paul is borrowing a business formula, that is done on purpose to enhance its meaning immeasurably; for that ἡ πίστις has acquired by this time an objective sense there is plentiful evidence.

To a careless reader there may seem to be a savour of self-commendation in this assessment of his life-work; but an assertion of conscious integrity need not incur that stigma. When the glory of the achievement is steadfastly given to God, it may be timely and befitting. And whether we view Saul of Tarsus in his first or revised edition, we must own that he was born a fighter, a root-and-branch Pharisee or a Christian armed *cap-à-pie*. One thing he did, the thing enjoined him by his Commander-in-Chief, he *fought*. How his soldierly carriage rebukes our faint-hearted craving to be off duty! Paul was not only a model convert, but a model campaigner. Arduous indeed had been his warfare, life-draining his marathon-race, steadfast his fidelity to his trust. Here was a workman needing not to be ashamed. Full well had Charles Wesley caught his spirit when he wrote:

> 'I the good fight have fought.'
> O when shall I declare!
> The victory by my Saviour got
> I long with Paul to share.
> O may I triumph so,
> When all my warfare's past,
> And, dying, find my latest foe
> Under my feet at last!

That blessed word be mine
Just as the port is gained:
Kept by the power of grace divine,
I have the faith maintained.
The apostles of my Lord,
To whom it first was given,
They could not speak a greater word,
Nor all the saints in heaven.

iv. 8. λοιπὸν ἀπόκειταί μοι ὁ τῆς δικαιοσύνης στέφανος ὃν ἀποδώσει μοι ὁ κύριος ἐν ἐκείνῃ τῇ ἡμέρᾳ, ὁ δίκαιος κριτής, οὐ μόνον δὲ ἐμοὶ ἀλλὰ καὶ πᾶσιν τοῖς ἠγαπηκόσιν τὴν ἐπιφάνειαν αὐτοῦ.

λοιπόν, similar in meaning to Latin *ceterum*, French *enfin*. ἀποκεῖσθαι (cf. ἀποθήκη), *to be laid up in store*. Mark the emphatic position of ὁ δίκαιος κριτής.

This passage asserts in plainest terms the rewardableness of Christian service. To aspire to recognition appertains to human nature, even in infancy, and there is nothing intrinsically wrong in the aspiration. Christ Himself sanctioned the sentiment in the parable of the talents. The notion of disinterested virtue unalloyed with self-interest may captivate the mystic, but it ignores the principle of self-love implanted in the breast and authorized by the great commandment. The amplitude of the reward in reserve is of grace; yet it is here styled a crown of righteousness. As Calvin puts it, *Deus sua dona in nobis coronat*. It beseems divine generosity to remunerate faithful service on a royal scale, even the minor fidelities of watchmen posted in obscure corners. Labours of love, yea cups of cold water given to fellow-disciples for His name's sake, are registered on high. The award is not *propter opera*, but it is *secundum opera* (Goodwin). The magnificent reversal of Nero's verdict pending solaces the dreariness of Paul's present condition.

Those who are to gain these heavenly medals are identified with lovers of Christ's appearing. The hope of beholding their Lord in the radiance of His full glory fills them with a yearning for its unveiling. Till His enemies lie impotent under His feet, their souls cannot enjoy perfect satisfaction. He is worthy to reign with unchallenged dominion. Whatever details we assign to the Second Advent, all who believe in its assured approach regard it as the hour of their Lord's complete triumph and of the downfall of His foes. Then shall the unjust sentences of earthly tribunals or censors be rescinded by the Just Judge and slandered reputations have a glorious resurrection. In using that description of the Judge, the apostle tacitly contrasts the iniquitous condemnation of the Roman Emperor with the righteous award of his own imperial Master. To that final court of appeal, infinitely superior to Caesar's, where every false verdict shall be reversed, and every malignant accusation silenced by the King of kings, he refers his cause. We recall Sir Walter Raleigh's beautiful poem, *My Pilgrimage*, in which he turns from the tyranny of the Stuarts to lodge his plea of innocence in

> heaven's bribeless hall,
> Where no corrupted voices brawl,
> No cause deferred, no vain-spent journey,
> For there Christ is the King's Attorney.

iv. 9–15. PARTICULAR INJUNCTIONS

iv. 9–11a. σπούδασον ἐλθεῖν πρός με ταχέως. Δημᾶς γάρ με ἐγκατέλιπεν, ἀγαπήσας τὸν νῦν αἰῶνα, καὶ ἐπορεύθη εἰς Θεσσαλονίκην, Κρήσκης εἰς Γαλατίαν, Τίτος εἰς Δαλματίαν. Λουκᾶς ἐστὶν μόνος μετ᾽ ἐμοῦ.

Details like those here specified are a plain mark of authenticity, especially when some of them contravene expectation. 'Make haste to come to me' is a direction already addressed to Titus (iii. 12) on a former occasion. Now the adverb *quickly* intimates how brief a space remains for the interview so earnestly craved with Timothy. The apostle's desertion by Demas for 'saint-seducing gold' (Shakespeare) renders it more obligatory still. He had 'left him in the lurch', influenced by mercenary or selfish motives, inconsistent with thorough discipleship, but not necessarily implying downright apostasy from the faith. Paul in Philemon (24) had spoken of him as a fellow-worker. Of Crescens nothing is known, and whether Galatia here signifies the Asiatic region or Gaul remains uncertain. Plutarch and Polybius use it of the latter, which one extant inscription couples with Dalmatia. Titus has evidently completed his task in Crete, for he is now despatched to Illyria. The faithful Luke bides still with the age-worn apostle, to whom he could best minister in his painful weakness and suspense. His comradeship must have been the bright spot in the encircling gloom of his close captivity. There is a tremulous note in the *only*.

iv. 11 b–13. Μάρκον ἀναλαβὼν ἄγε μετὰ σεαυτοῦ· ἔστιν γάρ μοι εὔχρηστος εἰς διακονίαν. Τύχικον δὲ ἀπέστειλα εἰς Ἔφεσον. τὸν φελόνην ὃν ἀπέλιπον ἐν Τρῳάδι παρὰ Κάρπῳ ἐρχόμενος φέρε, καὶ τὰ βιβλία, μάλιστα τὰς μεμβράνας.

The evangelist Mark had proved a cause of dissension once upon a time, but his attendance on Paul in Col. iv. 10 shows that the breach was healed. Timothy was to take him up somewhere *en route* (cf. Acts xx. 13; Polyb. xxx. 9). Grotius deems his serviceability to Paul to have consisted in familiarity with Latin; but we think that the apostle was probably by this time acquainted with that tongue; for he borrows two Latin substantives in this very context. At an earlier date Tychicus had fulfilled an embassy in Asia in Paul's stead, and he now appears to take the supervision of the church at Ephesus lately allotted to Timothy. φελόνης (Latin *paenula*) is rendered a *cloak* by most translators in accordance with its customary meaning, found in the papyri mostly in the form φαινόλης.[1] The other suggested sense, *portfolio*, is much rarer and, though known to Chrysostom, rejected by him. Nothing whatsoever is known of Carpus, the trusted friend at Troas whom the apostle chose to be the custodian not only of his cloak but of his papers. *Membrana* is another Latinism, for which a Greek purist would have written εἰλητά or περγαμηνά. Here is proof that the apostle was addicted to reading in these later days and carried with him even on journeys material for perusal and meditation. The parchments were obviously of especial worth; and it does not seem unreasonable to identify them with copies of Holy Writ, old or new, fixed or in formation at the instance of the Holy Spirit. If any marvel at the separate mention of this long-vanished sleeveless mantle, let them bethink them of Paul's sufferings from cold, most felt in declining years, and not grudge him the solitary comfort within his reach nor fail to appreciate this peculiarly human touch in a heroic portraiture of strength perfected through weakness.

[1] The old man's cloak: *paenulis frigoris causa ut senes uterentur permisit* (Severus: quoted in Wetstein).

iv. 14, 15. Ἀλέξανδρος ὁ χαλκεὺς πολλά μοι κακὰ ἐνεδείξατο· ἀποδώσει αὐτῷ ὁ κύριος κατὰ τὰ ἔργα αὐτοῦ. ὃν καὶ σὺ φυλάσσου, λίαν γὰρ ἀντέστη τοῖς ἡμετέροις λόγοις.

The name Alexander is so common that no identification with the previously mentioned Alexanders of Acts xix. 33 or I Tim. i. 20 can be assumed. Even the surmise that this Alexander was an Ephesian may be questioned; for there is reason for concluding with Theodoret that Timothy was at this moment no longer resident in that city. The likelihood is that this worker in bronze had been instrumental in effecting Paul's re-arrest and prosecution. His malice had evidently been of an implacable cast. The man must have been a ringleader in spurring on official antagonism to Christianity; but the line of attack seems to have been political rather than theological.

The correct reading is ἀποδώσει (future indicative), not ἀποδῴη (optative), and the statement a declaration of the offender's certain judgment, not a prayer for its infliction.

iv. 16–18. PAUL'S FINAL TRIAL AND DEFENCE

iv. 16, 17. ἐν τῇ πρώτῃ μου ἀπολογίᾳ οὐδείς μοι παρεγένετο ἀλλὰ πάντες με ἐγκατέλιπον· μὴ αὐτοῖς λογισθείη. ὁ δὲ κύριός μοι παρέστη καὶ ἐνεδυνάμωσέν με, ἵνα δι᾽ ἐμοῦ τὸ κήρυγμα πληροφορηθῇ καὶ ἀκούσωσιν πάντα τὰ ἔθνη· καὶ ἐρρύσθην ἐκ στόματος λέοντος.

We have already noted the favourite verb of Paul's, ἐνδυναμοῦν. παραγίνεσθαι=to second, a classical sense of the term, needlessly questioned by M. & M. πληροφορεῖσθαι is of more difficult interpretation. As above in verse 5 we understand it of the full discharge of the apostle's divine commission as chief ambassador to the Gentile world. The reference to rescue from the lion's mouth surely contains an allusion to the deliverance of Daniel. The preposition ἐκ, followed in verse 18 by ἀπό, vivifies before our minds' eyes the scene in Babylon and Rome, the spiritual Babylon, respectively.

The supposition that St Paul here glances backward to his first imprisonment, or that he is detailing its incidents, cannot be sustained. The circumstances do not correspond; for at that period the conditions

were less hostile and more favourable by far, whereas now the lion's
mouth yawns for its victim. The very desertion of friendly parties
testifies to the extremity of Paul's danger, and the gravity of the charge
against him. He had to experience the counterpart of his Master's forsakenness; but he pleads for the defaulters as weaklings rather than
traitors. With characteristic fidelity the lonely witness for Christ had
stood his ground valiantly, and if the rest had proved recreant, his Lord
had been at his right hand, that he should not be moved. Rallying all
his remaining strength the apostle had discharged his obligation of
presenting his *apologia* to a representative Roman audience with
powerful effect. The occasion was memorable and he could thankfully
avow that he had not let it slip. As when he spoke before Agrippa, at
this *prima actio*, as it appears to have been, the impression produced
had been notable. His judges may have rated him as a fanatic, but they
had recognized, at least, that he was no sedition-monger or anarchist,
that his preoccupations were spiritual, not material. And so judgment
had been deferred, and Christ had been magnified in a higher grade of
society than had hitherto been reached by the message of salvation. To
one to whom life was Christ and Christ was life that event formed a
grand climax to his career and an appropriate vestibule to glory nigh at
hand.

iv. 18.   ῥύσεταί με ὁ κύριος ἀπὸ παντὸς ἔργου πονηροῦ καὶ σώσει εἰς
τὴν βασιλείαν αὐτοῦ τὴν ἐπουράνιον· ᾧ ἡ δόξα εἰς τοὺς αἰῶνας τῶν
αἰώνων. ἀμήν.

καί is omitted from the critical text, making this verse somewhat
abrupt. Apparently the writer is contrasting his temporary respite
from a capital sentence with his everlasting enfranchisement, now so
near at hand. The Lord will ere long withdraw him from the sphere in
which evil surges and render his safety entire by ushering him into His
heavenly kingdom 'whereinto no enemy can enter'. The change of
preposition is thus significant, implying removal from the realm of
ill-usage and inclusion in the world of bliss. The phrase 'heavenly
kingdom' may be without parallel in Paul's Epistles, but it accords
with the contextual suggestion of an earthly empire which threatened
to cut short his days. The inserted doxology breathes Paul's spirit
exactly.

It has been remarked with much truth that Paul's vigorous defence of his life before Roman tribunals lends great weight to his testimony as a martyr of Jesus Christ. Willing as he was to glorify God by life or by death, his sanity of judgment constrained him, unlike the typical fanatic, to use every legitimate means of parrying the charges brought against him and exposing their hollowness.

iv. 19–22. SALUTATIONS

iv. 19–22. ἄσπασαι Πρίσκαν καὶ Ἀκύλαν καὶ τὸν Ὀνησιφόρου οἶκον. Ἔραστος ἔμεινεν ἐν Κορίνθῳ, Τρόφιμον δὲ ἀπέλιπον ἐν Μιλήτῳ ἀσθενοῦντα. σπούδασον πρὸ χειμῶνος ἐλθεῖν. ἀσπάζεταί σε Εὔβουλος καὶ Πούδης καὶ Λίνος καὶ Κλαυδία καὶ οἱ ἀδελφοὶ πάντες. ὁ κύριος μετὰ τοῦ πνεύματός σου· ἡ χάρις μεθ' ὑμῶν.

These closing lines teem with tokens of genuineness. The names are blended of known and unknown individuals and the particulars such as no forger would have selected for remark. Paul had met Prisca (or Priscilla) and Aquila at Corinth on his second missionary journey. They accompanied him to Ephesus, where they did Christian work. They subsequently returned to Rome, but are now once more sojourning in Ephesus. The greeting to the household of Onesiphorus may indicate that its head was at a distance from home, but the conjecture that he was now dead seems to lack foundation. Whether the Erastus here mentioned can be identified with the city-treasurer of Corinth (Rom. xvi. 23) cannot be settled. The name was of common occurrence, and appears to relate here to an itinerant preacher.

We know Trophimus to have been an Ephesian and companion of Paul on his third missionary tour, who became the innocent cause of the apostle's arrest at Jerusalem. The apostle had now recently left him in an ailing plight at Miletus. Had Timothy been in that neighbourhood still, it would surely have been needless to give him this information. Note that miracles of healing were not at the command of their performers. There may be a reason in the divine counsels for a believer's sickness as well as for his health. Let Timothy make haste to voyage before winter, when sailing was reckoned impracticable, or he may not see his spiritual father again in the flesh. Time presses; if he dallies, he is likely to be too late. The end is obviously at hand.

It is comforting to learn that there were faithful hearts, even at this painful juncture, in the church at Rome, though nothing is really known of them but their names. Eubulus, Claudia, Linus and Pudens engage notice as parties with whom Timothy was acquainted. The mention in two poems of Martial of a married Roman couple, the wife being British, named Pudens and Claudia, has produced a theory that they were the selfsame persons here specified. But Martial did not come to Rome until A.D. 66 and most of his epigrams belong to the next generation. His Claudia moreover is a young woman freshly wedded. All we can affirm is that these were Roman names. There are more clues to the identity of Linus, whom Irenaeus views as the first bishop of the Roman church, and to whom the *Apostolic Constitutions* (a late authority) assign Claudia as mother.

The benediction re-echoes those of Gal. vi. 18 and Phm. 25. The plural pronoun which concludes the Epistle shows that the letter was not designed for Timothy alone but had a general application.

The late subscription (cf. Authorized Version) is devoid of authority; but it bears testimony to the patristic tradition of Paul's second Roman imprisonment.

LIST OF ABBREVIATIONS

Appian, *B.C.* Appian's *Bellum Civile*.
Aristoph. *Lys.* Aristophanes's *Lysistrata*.
Aristot. Aristotle.
Aristot. *Nic. Eth.* Aristotle's *Nicomachean Ethics*.
Aristot. *Pol.* Aristotle's *Politics*.
Arrian, *Anab.* Arrian's *Anabasis*.
Arrian, *Epict.* Arrian's *Epictetus*.
Aug. *Enchir.* Augustine's *Enchiridion*.

Ceb. *Tab.* Cebes, *Tabula*.
Cic. Cicero.
Cic. *Acad.* Cicero's *Academics*.
Cic. *Att.* Cicero's *Letters to Atticus*.
Cic. *De Fin.* Cicero's *De Finibus*.
Cic. *De Off.* Cicero's *De Officiis*.
Cic. *Fam.* Cicero's *Letters to his Friends* (*Ad Familiares*).
Cic. *Nat. Deor.* Cicero's *Natura Deorum*.
Cic. *Phil.* Cicero's *Philippics*.
Clem. Clement of Rome.
Clem. *Ep. ad Corinth.* Clement's *Epistle to the Corinthians*.

Demosthenes, *Olynth.* Demosthenes's *Olynthiacs*.
Dion. Hal. Dionysius of Halicarnassus.

Epict. Epictetus.
Epict. *Enchir.* Epictetus's *Enchiridion*.
Eur. *El.* Euripides's *Electra*.
Eur. *Hec.* Euripides's *Hecuba*.
Eur. *Iph. in Aul.* Euripides's *Iphigenia in Aulide*.
Eur. *Iph. in Taur.* Euripides's *Iphigenia in Taurica*.
Eur. *Or.* Euripides's *Orestes*.
Eur. *Phoen.* Euripides's *Phoenissae*.
Eur. *Suppl.* Euripides's *Supplices*.

Field, *Ot. Norv.* *Otium Norvicense* (Francis Field).
Fr. *Fragment.*

Hesiod, *Theog.* Hesiod's *Theogony.*
Homer, *Il.* Homer's *Iliad.*

I.C.C. International Critical Commentary.
Ignatius, *ad Trall.* Ignatius's *Letter to the Trallians.*
Isoc. *Evag.* Isocrates's *Evagoras.*

Joseph. Josephus.
Joseph. *Antiq.* Josephus's *Antiquities.*
Joseph. *Ap.* Josephus's *Treatise against Apion.*
Joseph. *B.J.* Josephus's *Bellum Judaicum.*
Justin, *Apol.* Justin Martyr's *Apology.*

L. & S. Liddell and Scott's *Greek Lexicon.*
Lucian, *Calumn.* Lucian's *On Calumny.*
Lucian, *Deor. Concil.* Lucian's *Council of the Gods.*
Lucian, *Dial. Deor.* Lucian's *Dialogue of the Gods.*
Lucian, *Ep.* Lucian's *Epigrams.*
Lucian, *Hermot.* Lucian's *Hermotimus.*
Lucian, *Jup. Confut.* Lucian's *Jupiter Confuted.*
Lucian, *Paras.* Lucian's *The Parasite.*
Lucian, *Philops.* Lucian's *Philopseudes.*
Lucian, *Pisc.* Lucian's *Piscator.*
Lucian, *V.H.* Lucian's *Vera Historia.*
Lucian, *Zeux.* Lucian's *Zeuxis.*
LXX, Septuagint.

Milton, *P.L.* Milton's *Paradise Lost.*
M. & M. Moulton and Milligan's *Vocabulary of the Greek Testament.*

Philo, *Alleg. Interp.* Philo's *Allegorical Interpretation of Genesis ii and iii.*
Philo, *De Agric.* Philo's, *On Agriculture.*

Philo, *Leg. ad Gaium.* Philo's *Embassy to Gaius.*
Philodemus, *Oecon.* Philodemus's *On Economy.*
Philodemus, *Rhet.* Philodemus's *On Rhetoric.*
Philostratus, *Apoll.* Philostratus's *Life of Apollonius.*
Pind. *Pyth.* Pindar's *Pythian Odes.*
Plat. *Crat.* Plato's *Cratylus.*
Plat. *Euthyd.* Plato's *Euthydemus.*
Plat. *Gorg.* Plato's *Gorgias.*
Plat. *Menex.* Plato's *Menexedemus.*
Plat. *Parm.* Plato's *Parmenides.*
Plat. *Protag.* Plato's *Protagoras.*
Plat. *Rep.* Plato's *Republic.*
Plat. *Symp.* Plato's *Symposium.*
Plat. *Theaet.* Plato's *Theaetetus.*
Plat. *Theag.* Plato's *Theages.*
Plin. *N.H.* Pliny the Elder's *Natural History.*
Plut. *Aem.* Plutarch's *Life of Aemilius Paullus.*
Plut. *Ages.* Plutarch's *Life of Agesilaus.*
Plut. *Alex.* Plutarch's *Life of Alexander.*
Plut. *Ant.* Plutarch's *Life of Antony.*
Plut. *Arat.* Plutarch's *Life of Aratus.*
Plut. *Brut.* Plutarch's *Life of Brutus.*
Plut. *Caes.* Plutarch's *Life of Caesar.*
Plut. *Cam.* Plutarch's *Life of Camillus.*
Plut. *Cic.* Plutarch's *Life of Cicero.*
Plut. *Crass.* Plutarch's *Life of Crassus.*
Plut. *Demetr.* Plutarch's *Life of Demetrius.*
Plut. *Galb.* Plutarch's *Life of Galba.*
Plut. *Lucull.* Plutarch's *Life of Lucullus.*
Plut. *M. Ant.* Plutarch's *Life of Mark Antony.*
Plut. *Marcell.* Plutarch's *Life of Marcellus.*
Plut. *Mor.* Plutarch's *Moral Essays.*
Plut. *Nic.* Plutarch's *Life of Nicias.*
Plut. *Num.* Plutarch's *Life of Numa.*
Plut. *Pericl.* Plutarch's *Life of Pericles.*
Plut. *Pomp.* Plutarch's *Life of Pompey.*
Plut. *Poplic.* Plutarch's *Life of Poplicola (Publicola).*

Plut. *Sert.* Plutarch's *Life of Sertorius.*
Plut. *Sull.* Plutarch's *Life of Sulla.*
Plut. *Sympos.* Plutarch's *Symposium.*
Polyb. Polybius.

Quintilian, *Inst.* (*Orat.*) Quintilian's *Institutes* (*of Oratory*).

Sen. *Ep.* (*Mor.*). Seneca's (*Moral*) *Epistles.*
Sextus Empiricus, *Pyrrh.* Sextus Empiricus's *Pyrrhonic Outlines.*
Soph. *Aj.* Sophocles's *Ajax.*
Soph. *El.* Sophocles's *Electra.*
Soph. *Oed. in Col.* Sophocles's *Oedipus in Colonus.*
Soph. *Trach.* Sophocles's *Trachinian Women.*

T.R. Textus Receptus.

W. &. H. Westcott and Hort, *The New Testament in Greek.*

Xen. *Cyr.* Xenophon's *Cyropaedia.*
Xen. *Hier.* Xenophon's *Hieron.*
Xen. *Lac. Pol.* Xenophon's *Lacedaemonian Polity.*
Xen. *Mem.* Xenophon's *Memorabilia of Socrates.*
Xen. *Oecon.* Xenophon's *On Economy.*

SHORT BIBLIOGRAPHY

H. ALFORD. *The Greek Testament* (Cambridge, 1877).

F. C. BAUR. *Die sogenannten Pastoralbriefe des Apostels Paulus* (Stuttgart, 1835).

J. A. BENGEL. *Gnomon Novi Testamenti* (Tübingen, 1742).

F. BLASS. *Grammar of New Testament Greek* (Eng. tr., London, 1911).

J. CALVIN. *Commentaries on the Epistles to Timothy and Titus* (Eng. tr., Edinburgh, 1856).

A. DEISSMANN. *Light from the Ancient East* (Eng. tr., London, 1927).

W. M. L. DE WETTE. *Kurze Erklärung der Briefe an Titus, Timotheus* (Leipzig, 1844).

B. S. EASTON. *The Pastoral Epistles* (London, 1948).

C. J. ELLICOTT. *Commentary on the Pastoral Epistles* (London, 1864).

P. FAIRBAIRN. *The Pastoral Epistles* (Edinburgh, 1874).

R. FALCONER. *The Pastoral Epistles* (Oxford, 1937).

F. FIELD. *Otium Norvicense*, III (Cambridge, 1899).

A. HARNACK. *Chronologie der altchristlichen Literatur*, I (Leipzig, 1897).

P. N. HARRISON. *The Problem of the Pastoral Epistles* (Oxford, 1921).

H. J. HOLTZMANN. *Die Pastoralbriefe* (Leipzig, 1880).

F. J. A. HORT. *Judaistic Christianity* (London, 1894).

F. J. A. HORT. *The Christian Ecclesia* (London, 1897).

J. D. JAMES. *The Genuineness and Authorship of the Pastoral Epistles* (London, 1906).

H. G. LIDDELL and R. SCOTT. *A Greek-English Lexicon*, 9th (revised) edition (Oxford, 1940).

J. B. LIGHTFOOT. *Biblical Essays* (London, 1893).

J. B. LIGHTFOOT. *Dissertations on the Apostolic Age* (London, 1892).

W. LOCK. *The Pastoral Epistles* (International Critical Commentary, Edinburgh, 1924).

T. F. MIDDLETON. *The Doctrine of the Greek Article* (ed. H. J. Rose, London, 1841).

J. MOFFATT. *Introduction to the Literature of the New Testament* (Edinburgh, 1920).

J. H. MOULTON. *Grammar of New Testament Greek*. Vol. I: *Prolegomena* (Edinburgh, 1906).

J. H. MOULTON and G. MILLIGAN. *The Vocabulary of the Greek Testament* (Edinburgh, 1930).

R. ST. J. PARRY. *The Pastoral Epistles* (Cambridge, 1920).

A. S. PEAKE. *A Critical Introduction to the New Testament* (London, 1909).

W. M. RAMSAY. *The Church in the Roman Empire* (London, 1897).

W. M. RAMSAY. *Historical Commentary on the Epistles to Timothy*, in *The Expositor* VII. vii (1909), pp. 481 ff.; viii (1909), pp. 1 ff., 167 ff., 264 ff., 339 ff., 399 ff., 557 ff.; ix (1910), pp. 172 ff., 319 ff., 433 ff.; VIII. i (1911), pp. 262 ff., 356 ff.

SHORT BIBLIOGRAPHY

A. T. ROBERTSON. *A Grammar of the Greek New Testament in the Light of Historical Research* (London, 1919).

E. F. SCOTT. *The Pastoral Epistles* (London, 1936).

R. D. SHAW. *The Pauline Epistles* (Edinburgh, 1903–4).

C. SPICQ. *Saint Paul: Les Épîtres Pastorales* (Paris, 1947).

R. C. TRENCH. *Synonyms of the New Testament* (London, 1894).

B. F. WESTCOTT and F. J. A. HORT. *The New Testament in Greek* (London, 1881).

J. J. WETSTEIN. *Novum Testamentum Graecum* (Amsterdam, 1751–2).

N. J. D. WHITE. *The First and Second Epistles to Timothy and the Epistle to Titus* (Expositor's Greek Testament, London, 1910).

K. WIESELER. *Chronologie des apostolischen Zeitalters* (Göttingen, 1848).

G. B. WINER. *Grammar of New Testament Greek* (Eng. tr., ed. W. F. Moulton, Edinburgh, 1882).

T. ZAHN. *Introduction to the New Testament*, II (Eng. tr., Edinburgh, 1909).

INDEX OF CLASSICAL AND
PATRISTIC AUTHORS

INDEX OF MODERN AUTHORS